N

T

Series Editor
F. F. Ridley

HANSARD SOCIETY SERIES IN POLITICS AND GOVERNMENT

Edited by
F. F. Ridley

The Hansard Society Series in Politics and Government brings to the wider public the debates and analyses of important issues first discussed in the pages of its journal, *Parliamentary Affairs*

Women in Politics

Edited by
Joni Lovenduski and Pippa Norris

Series Editor
F. F. Ridley

OXFORD UNIVERSITY PRESS
in association with
THE HANSARD SOCIETY FOR
PARLIAMENTARY GOVERNMENT

Oxford University Press, Walton Street, Oxford OX2 6DP
Oxford New York
Athens Auckland Bangkok Bombay
Calcutta Cape Town Dar es Salaam Delhi
Florence Hong Kong Istanbul Karachi
Kuala Lumpur Madras Madrid Melbourne
Mexico City Nairobi Paris Singapore
Taipei Tokyo Toronto
and associated companies in
Berlin Ibadan

Oxford is a trade mark of Oxford University Press

Published in the United States
by Oxford University Press Inc., New York

First published in Parliamentary Affairs, 1996
New as paperback, 1996

A catalogue for this book is available from the British Library

Library of Congress Cataloging in Publication Data
(Data available)

ISBN 0-19-922275-4

Printed in Great Britain
by Headley Brothers Limited, The Invicta Press,
Ashford, Kent and London

CONTENTS

CONTRIBUTORS TO THIS VOLUME

Stefania Abrar is a researcher in the Department of Government, London School of Economics

Alice Brown is Head of the Politics Department, University of Edinburgh

Paul Byrne is Senior Lecturer in Politics in the Department of European Studies, Loughborough University

Evelyn Collins is Chief Equality Officer at the Equal Opportunities Commission for Northern Ireland but is writing in a personal capacity.

Ian Forbes is Senior Lecturer in the Department of Politics, University of Southampton

Joni Lovenduski is Professor of Politics, University of Southampton

Fiona Mackay is researcher at the International Social Sciences Institute, University of Edinburgh

Helen Margetts is Lecturer in the Department of Politics and Sociology, Birkbeck College, London

Elizabeth Meehan is Professor of Politics, The Queens University, Belfast

Susan Millns is Lecturer in Law, University of Liverpool

Pippa Norris is Associate Director of the Joan Shorenstein Center on the Press, Politics and Policies, Kennedy School, Harvard University, USA

Sarah Perrigo is Lecturer in Politics in the Department of Peace Studies, University of Bradford

Vicky Randall is Senior Lecturer in the Department of Government, University of Essex

Karen Ross is Research Officer at the Cheltenham and Gloucester College of Higher Education

Clare Short MP is Labour's Shadow Secretary of State for Transport and was Shadow Minister for Women at the time of writing

Judith Squires is Lecturer in the Politics Department, University of Bristol

Annabelle Sreberny-Mohammadi is Professor and Director of the Centre for Mass Communication Research at the University of Leicester

Rick Wilford is Lecturer in the Politics Department, The Queens University, Belfast

Preface

In a way, current issues for this series select themselves. Quangos, Sleaze, now Women. Women as actors in British politics and British politics as it affects women. But the choice of topics is not as simple as that. Getting a team of writers together depends on finding good editors with an overview of the subject and the right contacts. We have succeeded remarkably well in this book thanks to Joni Lovenduski and Pippa Norris, two names well known in political science and women's studies. They have drawn on the established Women and Politics groups of the Political Studies Association as well as others.

Of course, this is not a 'balanced' collection in the way, for example, that the Quango volume was, with arguments for and against. There are no anti chapters, nor will readers expect them. Indeed, it would be difficult to get such contributions at academic rather than popular-journalist standard. While the theme is coherent, there is, however, a varied approach within it, amounting at times to differences of line in regard to the issues involved. That said, a common approach is proper since advocacy is a purpose of the book, as well as analysis. The disinterested reader is not often to be found in women's studies—not all that often, indeed, in other fields of political science.

There are omissions, no doubt. We have two contributions on the Labour Party (one by Clare Short, Shadow Minister for Women when she wrote it) but none on the Conservative Party—not deliberate but editorial problems in findings an appropriate Conservative in time. We cover Scotland and Northern Ireland but not Wales—for no reasons of bias either. On the other hand, contributions do cover a wide field, not just the central aspects of British government and politics that are the staple diet of politics students but a range of policies covering the most important issues that concern the women's movement. A glance at the chapter headings will confirm the wide spread of topics and the links between them.

Current issues are inevitably caught in currents of change. By the time this book appears on reading lists, by the time it is read in libraries or bought in bookshops, a change in government may have occurred—and other changes may follow (one hopes so, at least). But the problems analysed here and the behaviour described are not going to change so quickly. The discussion that follows will thus remain relevant.

Series editors generally refer to the politically interested public as potential readers of their books, their hopeful tones hiding a degree of scepticism about that market. There is no case for such doubt here. The contributions to this volume are relevant to students and activists alike. The reason, perhaps, is that in this field the two groups are less distinct than in most areas of study. Women's studies students are often committed, involved in one way or another, and non-academic women activists seem more likely than other activists to read relevant work as part of further self-education. That link, indeed, is a strength of the women's movement.

Finally, it is particularly appropriate that this book appears in the Hansard Society Series. In 1990, the Hansard Society published the warmly welcomed report of its Commission on Women at the Top which identified many barriers to women's progress. An updating study, looking at how many of those barriers still remain, has been produced.

F. F. Ridley

Sex, Gender and British Politics

BY JONI LOVENDUSKI

WHEN British feminists struggled for the suffrage at the end of the last century they thought that the women's vote would bring their concerns to the political agenda, would elect more women representatives and change the nature of politics. In the 1960s and 1970s activists in a new wave of feminism, the 'Women's Liberation Movement', were sceptical of traditional political institutions, reasoning that the constitutional changes won by the suffragists had brought little tangible advantage for women. By the 1990s the tide had turned again and Feminist activists were organised in political institutions including the political parties, trade unions, employer and professional organisations, the civil service, and in local and national government. Feminists organised their own pressure groups on some important policy areas (for example the Women's Reproductive Rights Campaign) and sought to influence groups already active on others (for example the Association of Radical Midwives). A great variety of demands were pressed, but in each arena an explicit claim for an increased presence of women in decision-making was made. Perhaps the most notable responses to such claims were made in the Labour Party which is now uneasily committed to a policy of quotas for women candidates. Behind the recurrent demand for women's presence amongst decision-makers was an under-standing, sometimes publicly argued, sometimes simply assumed that women had interests which were best represented by women. That understanding has been fiercely contested by feminists, their sympathis-ers and their opponents in a continuing and sometimes acrimonious debate.

Here we set out the political context of that debate, describing important differences of power and advantage between men and women in contemporary Britain. First, some of the concepts feminist have developed to analyse differences between men and women are defined, then, in the main discussion, they are used to evaluate the status of women in British politics.

Feminism, sex and gender

Since the 1970s the women's studies movement has been preoccupied with scholarly examination of the differences of power and advantage between women and men. The investigation has proceeded in distinct stages and may be likened to peeling away the layers of an onion. As each layer is peeled away, another is revealed. In the same way that the onion essentially consists of its layers, so do the layers of relations between women and men constitute contemporary society.

The layers of revelation are reflected in the changing vocabulary of feminist analyses of social life. In any account of such exercises, feminism is the first word to define. Definitions of feminism vary according to the circumstances and outlook of those who make the definition. This is complicated by the fact that many who support equality for women and belong to women's organisations are reluctant to be called feminists because there is a social stigma and/or political penalty attached to the word. Such constraints pose problems of definition, making for analysts who wish to identify feminists in a particular setting. A useful, if somewhat arbitrary definition of feminism is 'those ideologies, activities and policies whose goal it is to remove discrimination against women and to break down male domination of society'.[1]

The terms sex and gender also present definitional difficulties. There is no single agreed definition of gender, or of sex for that matter, which may be offered here. Often gender is used interchangeably with sex, but in feminist scholarship the term is more loaded and complex. To understand the various meanings of gender it is helpful to explore how the use of the term has shifted as feminist scholarship has developed. In the early days of feminist political science attention was focused on identifying, correcting and deconstructing previous androcentric and often misogynistic research on politics. The immediate tangible result was an improved empirical basis of knowledge about women. Initially there was a concern to ensure women's political activities were recorded and the biases against women exposed. At that stage no distinctions were made between sex and gender. Before long however, some feminist scholars were insisting on a distinction between sex, defined as a biological marker, and gender, defined as the social consequences of sexual identity. To simplify, the terms women and men refer to biological females and males, whilst the term gender is used to denote the way relations between the sexes are produced and institutionalised. The shift to the use of the term gender became more widespread as ways in which it was implicated in seemingly neutral political arrangements and practices were revealed. Inevitably, the evolving vocabulary has caused confusion. Gender is now used as a synonym for women, for biological sex, as a noun, as a verb, the gerund 'gendering' makes frequent appearances as does the adverb 'gendered'. Recognising that confusion some theorists now use such awkward terms as 'gender relations analysis' or 'theories of gender bias' or 'processes of gendering' to signify that they are theorising rather than simply describing (as though this would not otherwise be apparent). Needless to say, there is little agreement about which of the many available terms is most useful. Such confusion is emblematic of the interdisciplinary nature of the field of women's studies, its rapid growth and its multiple address to theorists, activists and practitioners. In what follows the terms sex, women and men will designate biological sex, and gender will refer to the social construction of biological sex.

Gender and British politics

Despite the surrounding confusion, it is possible to use these concepts to illuminate the position of women in British politics. The understanding of British politics offered here is straightforward. British politics consists of institutions and processes set in a changing social context and informed by ideas and conventions about the appropriate goals and tasks of government. Institutions are the organisations, including government institutions, in which political decisions are made. Processes are the formal and informal procedures and practices that are followed in decision-making. Policies are the outputs and outcomes of those processes. In Britain the prevailing ideas about government are drawn from traditions of liberal democratic practice which may be more or less radical in their current interpretation. During the twentieth century competing interpretations of democratic ideas have included liberal, socialist and conservative understandings of the good society. Feminist ideas now compete to influence such understandings. Ideas about the appropriate goals and arrangement of politics offer criteria of fairness according to which institutions, processes and policies may be assessed. Criteria of fairness insist on equality between the sexes. Disagreement occurs over both definitions of equality and the appropriate means to achieve it.

Feminist critics of British politics agree that its organisations and structures institutionalise the predominance of particular masculinities, thereby empowering and/or advantaging certain men over almost all women and some men. Such biases are both causes and effects of women's political under-representation, a likely consequence of which is that policy makers are less attuned than they would otherwise be to women's interests. Moreover, the continued male predominance of politics allows a particular and exclusive kind of masculinity to dominate the culture of political organisations. To evaluate such claims it is necessary to elaborate the sex and gender biases of political institutions and to map in detail their component parts. Here we may draw on the concept of gender balance that is being developed for the Gender and New Urban Governance Project.[2] This typology distinguishes between positional, policy and organisational sex and gender balances. Organisations may be either balanced or biased in respect of sex and/or gender. Biases may be either masculine or feminine. Positional balance is more to do with sex than gender. It refers to the numbers of men and women in organisations as a whole and, within those organisations, to their presence in decision-making positions. Policy gender balance includes dimensions of both sex and gender, occurring when public policy even-handedly reflects the changing needs of both women and men. Organisational gender balance is mainly about gender and is present when positional and policy balance are institutionalised.

Positional balance is present where neither sex dominates an institution numerically. Bias may be horizontal, whereby one sex holds the majority of positions in an organisation, or vertical whereby one sex holds the majority of decision-making positions. There are many examples of positional gender bias. Various authors have demonstrated women's absence from the heart of government and from the leadership of participatory organisations such as parties, unions and business organisations.[3] Good systematic evidence has been produced of male predominance in key organisations at local, regional and national levels in most democratic states.[4]

Policy gender balance alerts us to the way seemingly 'neutral' policies are often not neutral but gender blind and, ignoring gender differences, tend to favour men. The dominance of men in decision-making positions in core issue areas has a gendered effect on policy making and implementation. Thus male policy gender bias has at least three manifestations: women may be disadvantaged by a policy; policy initiatives to redress inequalities experienced by women may be poorly funded or lack prestige; and such issues may be marginal to, or absent from, the policy agenda. Examples of each abound. Throughout the world the paid and unpaid work of women is undervalued. Male institutional advantage enables men to resist government policies for employment and pay equality between men and women. Policy and positional bias may combine in ways that are dysfunctional to agreed policy. An example of the way male predominance may lead to distorted policy implementation is to be found in the police. Male dominated police forces charged with the control of domestic violence and the policing of other forms of sexual violence are inhibited from implementing the policies even where good will and willingness are present. This is because survivors of male sexual violence tend not to trust any men. In addition, the attitudes of bonded male groups to sexual relationships and activities inhibit their ability to perceive and treat the crimes. Other examples are male local trades union representatives charged with the negotiation of maternity leave or child care arrangements. Without considerable direction and training, and despite national union policies, such issues seem inappropriate activities to trade unionists steeped in traditional organisational cultures of fraternal loyalties and male pursuits. Analogous arguments may be made about all male sex equality committees in government.

By contrast, male organisational bias implies that male biases are integral to the organisation, shaping its rules, values, norms, structures and policies. In such organisations positional gender biases are well established in a culture of masculinity which makes it difficult for most women and some men to pursue and often to perceive their gender interests. Jeff Hearn, who has written at length about the establishment and evolution of the relationship between bureaucratisation and masculinity offers many examples. He distinguishes between various masculinities and locates the hegemony of the narrow range of acceptable (heterosexual) masculinities in the development and spread of public organisations. Such developments both empowered certain men and sustained their power by increasing the quantity of sites on which male power could operate. The development of public organisations was predicated on the existence of male power over women, and some other men, in private life and in private organisations such as the family. Hearn argues persuasively that increases in the importance and scale of public organisations institutionalised predominant forms of male power. Though it would be wrong to see bureaucracies as somehow fundamentally male, historically the relationship between bureaucracy and masculinity has been intimate and sustained. 'While it may be unwarranted to see bureaucratic ways and means as "essentially male", the connections between bureaucracies and masculinities are socially and historically intense.'[5] Hearn examines the effects of the expansion of public organisations on dominant masculinities; he does not consider what happens if public organisations get smaller, less important, less public.

Other evidence of male organisational gender bias is more familiar. Men in organisations have been good at setting rules of the game which ensure that the qualifications of men are better valued, lead more reliably to power and rewards. Often mentioned are the historical association of state formation with physical strength, violence and war and the importance of the citizen soldier to the formation of the modern state. The state arms men, but most states do not arm women. Diplomatic, colonial and military policy in most states is formed around an unquestioning concept of masculinity that places a premium on toughness and force.

The state is of course the crucial public organisation or set of organisations for discussions such as this. State attempts to control sexuality and intervention in the sexual division of labour are widespread and apparent. The characteristic separation of state and society parallels a gendered division of labour in which much of the contribution of women has historically been invisible to the public gaze. The situation of the line between public and private life has in practice concealed the political implications of the power that men have over women. Political practices involving demagoguery, ruthlessness and aggression require qualities which are culturally accepted in men but not women. Some feminists argue that a top-down approach to policy making and a clear distinction between policy making and policy implementation are examples of masculine biases in the policy process.[6] They argue that failure to value iterative models of policy development is characteristic of common masculine forms of 'leadership' and management, alien to the communication and working styles of the majority of women.

The discourse of politics in liberal democratic systems is also implicated in the masculine biases of the state. The very definitions of politics
are commonly built around notions of democratic processes that do not
encompass struggles over power and advantage in domestic life and
resist explicit addresses to problems about the location of the boundaries between public and private life. The myths and rhetoric that pervade
Labour Party discourse are a good example of how a masculine ethos is
an important part of the mobilisation of gender bias. Organisational
gender biases may operate at a number of different levels and may serve
to prevent women from acquiring and expressing a public identity.
Research on British candidate selection indicates that women often
perceive the roles of MPs to be largely based on typically male life
styles, hence do not regard themselves to be eligible.[7] These findings are
mirrored by research on recruitment and promotion in the senior civil
service, in the ranks of the civil service, in local authority employment,
in trade unions, retail firms and the financial services.[8] The most
desirable 'qualifications' for desirable jobs are normally held by middle-
class, white men.

Positional bias

Applied to British political institutions and processes, the typology of
gender balance illuminates a pattern of male gender biases in which
male images and particular forms of masculinity dominate political life.
Positional gender bias is particularly apparent in the House of Commons. The low proportions of women in the House of Commons
contrasts sharply with the presence of women in other Liberal Democratic legislatures. Amongst European Union countries in 1994, only
France, Greece and Portugal had lower percentages of women deputies.

1: Women Candidates in British General Elections, 1945–1992

	Con.	Lab.	Lib.	PC/SNP	% of candidates
1945	14	41	20	1	4.9
1950	29	42	45	0	6.7
1951	25	41	11	0	5.7
1955	33	43	14	1	6.6
1959	28	36	16	0	5.5
1964	24	33	24	1	4.9
1966	21	30	20	0	4.4
1970	26	29	23	10	5.2
1974 (F)	33	40	40	10	6.2
1974 (O)	30	50	49	9	7.0
1979	31	52	52	7	7.4
1983	40	78	76	16	10.4
1987	46	92	105	15	12.9
1992	63	138	143	22	18.3

Positional gender biases in the House of Commons are translated into
a low women's presence in the Cabinet and government, although, at
this level, pressure on the Prime Minister to appoint women may work

in favour of those few women who become MPs. However, this varies both by party and by Prime Minister. Mrs Thatcher never appointed another woman MP to her Cabinet. John Major suffered considerable embarrassment when he failed to appoint any women to his first cabinet, an oversight he corrected after the 1992 general election. The leader of the Opposition is subject to Labour party rules governing the composition of the elected Shadow Cabinet each MP is required to vote for four women.

Positional biases are less apparent in the membership of the political parties. In 1992 women made up 49% of the Conservative Party's members and 40% of Labour's, but 45% of those recruited to Labour since Tony Blair's election as leader. Women are less likely than men to number amongst party activists and decision-makers, however. Labour Party research in 1994 found that women were 22% of constituency chairs, 6% of trade union liaison officers, yet these are offices which are constitutionally subject to 50% quotas. In the Conservative Party women are about as likely as men to be party activists but less likely to be candidates.[9] Table 1 shows that women were 18% of candidates for the main political parties in 1992.

2: Women Elected in British General Elections, 1945–1992 (Northern Ireland excluded)

	Con.	Lab.	Lib.	Others	Total	% of MPs
1945	1	21	1	1	23	3.8
1950	6	14	1	0	21	3.4
1951	6	11	0	0	17	2.7
1955	10	14	0	0	24	3.8
1959	12	13	0	0	25	4.0
1964	11	18	0	0	29	4.6
1966	7	19	0	0	26	4.1
1970	15	10	0	1	26	4.1
1974 (F)	9	13	0	1	23	3.6
1974 (O)	7	18	0	2	27	4.3
1979	8	11	0	0	19	3.0
1983	13	10	0	0	23	3.5
1987	17	21	2	1	41	6.3
1992	20	37	2	1	60	9.2

The success rates of women candidates actually decreased between 1945 and 1992. Repeated studies of sex and voting indicate that such patterns are not the result of voting in general elections, but of party nomination practices. A good presence of women candidates feminises party images but does not lose votes, an insight that has undoubtedly increased the interest of party leaders in nominating more women. Successive Conservative governments have pledged to increase the proportions of women appointed to public bodies. In 1994 they were 28% of such appointees, up from 23% in 1986. Throughout the executive branch of government slow progress has been made in increasing the proportions of women decision-makers.

It is worth noting that the current low percentages of women in

British political elites are peaks, figures achieved only after years of efforts to bring about more equitable representation. The figures are the surface of a deep rooted pattern of exclusion of women from public life. They indicate a considerable amount of both vertical and horizontal positional male gender bias. They are reflected in other decision-making hierarchies including the judiciary, the police, the civil service, the professions and in the leadership of both sides of British industry. Although some important advances have been made since the 1970s, a pattern of male advantage in the British elite has yet to be broken.

Policy gender bias

Gender biases in policy are an important factor in levels of women's political representation. Policies requiring quotas of women in key positions are part of the arsenal of many political parties, including the Labour Party. It is less common for governments to legislate such quotas but other government policies have direct effects on women's political power. This is perhaps most apparent in policy about their economic status.

The Department of Employment and Education includes a 'Ministry for Women' and Labour offers a separate Ministry for Women, the location of which is currently promised to be in the Cabinet Office. Two agencies have responsibility for sex equality issues—the Equal Opportunities Commission and the Women's National Commission. Both of these are accountable to the Secretary of State for Education and Employment . Neither agency has secure status. The work of the Women's National Commission is not well known, it was moved from the Cabinet Office to the Department of Employment in 1992, when oversight of the EOC was transferred there. Both were moved again in 1995. A Ministerial Group on Women's Issues was established by Mrs Thatcher, but she failed to attend its meetings and ministers only reluctantly accepted the brief. It was re-established as a Cabinet Sub-Committee on Women's Issues in 1992 with 17 to 18 members, ministers in key departments.

In Britain, women's economic position is normally significantly worse than men's, a situation which reinforces women's political disadvantages by denying most of them the resources that are usually necessary for political participation and influence. Many democratic theorists would argue that positional biases are significant only in so far as they lead to failure to reflect the interests of the excluded groups. Such contentions raise difficult questions about what those interests are and tactical questions about the rate at which failures should be corrected. The circumstances of British women differ greatly and not all women regard their interests to be a matter of their sex—class, race, nationality, age and ability all affect the way women interpret their circumstances. Efforts to identify a unitary 'women's' interest soon discover a multitude of diverse and competing identities and needs. Family circumstances are very important, tying the interests of individuals to those of their partners and children. Some (but not all) women who live with children and partners favour policies designed to maximise family income. A history of better paid men's jobs ensures that in most such families the protection of paid work for male 'breadwinners' takes precedence over other employment policy preferences. Many such preferences seem irrational in that they reflect a world which no longer exists. Changes in patterns of men's and women's employment have combined with changes in family structures to bring dramatic changes in the financial situation of men and women and their families. This means that the interests of women as individuals may well conflict with their interests as members of class, race or family groups. Nevertheless, equal pay and equal opportunities at work continue to be an important element of the women's policy agenda. This was underlined in the summer of 1995 when the Equal Opportunities Commission, the Equal Opportunities Commission of Northern Ireland and the Women's National Commission, in consultation with numerous women's organisations, launched their National Agenda for Action in Pursuit of Equality. Employment issues are a large part of that agenda which lists political, social, economic and health concerns that are specific to women in a comprehensive set of demands for policies to bring about sex equality.

Despite its complexity, the employment status of women offers a sensitive indicator of policy bias. The pattern of inequality is striking and is an established feature of British employment statistics. Economic activity rates in Britain vary by sex, race and age. In spring 1994, 95% of white men and 85% of black men aged 25–44 were economically active. 75% of white women and 71% of black women were active.[10] Women's economic activity rates have increased substantially since 1970. In the 25 to 34-year age group the rate rose from 60 to 77% and is projected to rise to 85% by 2006. Over the same period rates for men declined in every age group. Men's rates are likely to continue to decline. On current official projections women will be 46% of the work force in 2006 compared to 44% in 1993 and 37% in 1971.

Employment is highly stratified by sex. Nearly one in five employed men, but only one of ten women work as managers or administrators. One in five men, but only one of thirty women work in craft or related occupations. Women are three-quarters of workers in clerical or secretarial jobs. Employment sectors are also patterned by sex. Since 1971 there has been a shift away from employment in manufacturing for both sexes but male predominance continued. By 1994, 28% of men and 12% of women were employed in manufacturing. A further sex difference occurs between full-time and part-time work. About 47% of economically active women but only 7% of men worked part-time in 1994.

The complex relationship between women's family and employment status has considerable effects on the outcomes of sex equality policy.

To be effective, a policy of sex equality in employment must be able to address the causes of inequality both in the labour market and in the household. Changes in women's working patterns appear to have done little to alter the division of domestic labour. Women still do more than twice the amount of housework and child care than equivalent men. In 1992 the average woman in full-time employment spent 46 hours per week on cooking, shopping, housework, child care and related tasks, compared to 26 hours spent by full-time employed men.[11] Such imbalances underpin policy and organisational biases.

The core employment issues for sex equality strategists are pay, status and conditions. It is difficult, as Labour discovered in 1992, to gain support for policies that might equalise men's and women's earnings through the tax system as employment and family circumstances interact with significant effects on household income. Many feminists favour a national minimum wage as a means of achieving pay parity. Their concentration in part-time work is part of the explanation of the low pay, poor training, pension and promotion prospects for women. Lower hourly pay for part-time workers is part of the explanation for women's average earnings remaining at about two-thirds those of men. The hourly pay of part-time women workers is 59% of that of full-time men, the similar figure for full-time women is 79%. The possibility of generational change is apparent in the pay data which indicate that the earnings of younger women without children are about 90% of average earnings of men the same age. This may of course be a life cycle effect, to be lost as many of these women reduce their hours at work to take up child-rearing activities. Even so, improvement for full-time working women is an accomplishment worth noting. The Report of the Commission on Social Justice pointed out that changes in men's and women's employment are combining to produce a new problem—a widening gap between work-rich families with one and one-half or two jobs and work-poor families with no job at all. By 1992, 60% employed men had partners who were also in employment, but almost 80% of unemployed men had unemployed partners. Women married to employed men were almost three times as likely to have jobs as women married to men without jobs.[12]

'Family' income is expressed in official statistics as 'real weekly earning after income tax, national insurance contributions, child benefit and family credit'. Official statistics indicate that 'real terms' increases occurred at all levels between 1971 and 1993, but increases generally were much less for the less well-off. The Commission for Social Justice pointed out that once indirect taxes are included in the calculation, the poorest 10% became worse off between 1979 and 1994. Moreover, the official statistics of increases received by many of the groups concealed considerable poverty. The weekly income in the lowest decile for a single woman with two children claiming family credit was £172 in 1994, for a married man with two children the similar figure was

£174. In Britain, as elsewhere, both women and men live in poverty, but poverty tends to be feminised; single parents and the aged are amongst the overwhelmingly female groups most likely to experience poverty.

This thumbnail sketch of women's economic status gives an indication both of the disadvantaged economic status of British women and of the wide ambit necessary for effective policy on sex equality in employment. Moreover, the indicators shed considerable light on women's under-representation in political decision-making. All three forms of policy bias are present. Many employment policies are disadvantageous to women, for example provisions that workers should work a certain number of hours per week before earning entitlement to pension rights or employment protection. Moreover, sex equality policies have low status, they are marginal to the policy agenda. Britain has employment equality legislation in the form of the variously amended Equal Pay Act of 1970 and the Sex Discrimination Act of 1975 and the five equality directives of the European Communities. These UK laws are widely recognised to be inadequate (see Meehan and Forbes in this volume) and overdue for modernisation. The separation of policies directed at pay, employment and child care has produced effects that are disadvantageous to many women. In Britain the mother of two cuts her potential lifetime earnings in half as a direct result of having children, the highest such income loss in the European Union.

An indication of the low status of sex equality policy is the continued location of the headquarters of the Equal Opportunities Commission in Manchester, away from the heart of government and is underlined by the 1992 appointment of a part-time Commission chair. A striking indicator of the marginality of sex equality issues to the national policy agenda is that there has been only one parliamentary debate on equal opportunities policies since the legislation was first passed more than twenty years ago. Another example is the introduction of Compulsory Competitive Tendering (CCT) for local authorities without government requirements for sex equality provision. As a result, local authorities (who are the largest employers of women workers) made provision for sex equality in CCT in accordance with whatever (if any) sex equality policies they happened to have.

Organisational bias

The identification of organisational gender biases requires specific research on institutional practices and cultures and into women's and men's' behaviour in different organisational settings. Good examples of such work are Sophie Watson's writing on the 'chap' culture of the senior civil service[13] Susan Halford's accounts of Local Government Women's Committees.[14] The masculine ethos of the Labour Party offers a telling example of such bias. Labours dominant ethos has been well documented. Labour's traditional politics depended upon the opportun-

ity 'to inhabit a culture that brings together the umbrella of masculine identity, of male fraternity: work, working class allegiance, trade union membership and Labour Party affiliation.[15] It is increasingly apparent that many women do not feel comfortable in this culture, that they may not prefer the ties between the union movement and Labour. When feminists began to join the Labour Party at the end of the 1970s they found a well-established, elaborately ritualised and formalised politics. To be effective, individuals needed to learn the rules of the game and to be able to use them. The culture was a barrier to all new members and it proved particularly unpleasant for women who often had little other experience of organised politics. The exclusionary culture also constrained long established women party members. Party women's organisations were moribund, the Women's Conference was a ritual occasion, women played little part in branch activities or party conferences which were overwhelmingly male. According to Sarah Perrigo, Labour's attitudes to and accommodation of women scarcely changed between the 1920s and the end of the 1970s.[16] Party women's organisations lacked power and could not easily be used to press issues of interest to women. Change, when it came, was slow and intermittent. Traditional attitudes are most prevalent in Labour's old heartlands, in the declining manufacturing and mining areas, the places where the safe seats are. Many of the battles over introducing the controversial party policy of all-women short-lists in half of all winnable seats took place in these constituencies. The policy of compulsory quotas was introduced precisely because other means to increase the nomination of women candidates failed. As one MP who was asked about the chances of Labour nominating more women candidates for winnable seats commented in 1992 'in a region like this there is a very substantial prejudice against women because it's a traditionally very heavy industry area and many people take the view that women have a place and it ain't' at the meetings that men attend'. This is a view endorsed by a woman candidate who described her experiences at the 1992 annual conference:
'You come from London and you think things are beginning to improve, and then you go to national conference and you sit next to people who say "I'm here because I'm the women's delegate". And I say, "there's no such thing as the women's delegate—you've got 400 additional members so you've come as an additional delegate". And the man has got the votes, and sits with his mates in the union block and never consults her about how they are going to vote. And on Wednesday, she says to me, "I've got to go home today", and I say "Why?". And she says "Well I can't afford to stay any longer". I say "You're entitled to expenses". She said, "Oh no, he got all the expenses". The "real" delegate she kept calling him.' [17]

Labour's masculine image has been a target for feminists who have succeeded in establishing a policy of quotas throughout the party. Party conferences in 1993 and 1994 brought many women to the platform, and party offices at branch and constituency level are slowly being filled by women. Although such changes are a direct result of feminist mobilisation in the party, they were made possible by the opportunities created by a modernisation process in which radical change is on Labour's agenda.

Despite their low number of women MPs, the Conservatives have not historically reflected the kinds of masculine images and ethos that plague Labour. Images of the annual conferences have long been notoriously feminine, party organisation in the constituencies relies on women; and the Conservatives have been able to rely on substantial electoral support from them. No one knows exactly why the Conservatives are so successful at attracting women's votes, but many believe that party images have something to do with it. Clare Short believes that women are the Conservatives' 'secret weapon', that they make a point of listening to women's demands and construct appeals accordingly. Nevertheless, Conservative men have been reluctant to relinquish power. The party has been unable to raise its complement of women MPs. The row over Labour's quotas in the summer of 1995 helped obscure the fact that by mid-1995 not one Conservative woman inheritor had been chosen for a seat where a Tory retired: the six women chosen as candidates by then were in Labour seats. High-flying aspirant women candidates were rejected by constituency associations.[18]

In both major parties, but particularly among the Conservatives, pressure on the supply of candidates operates because of the demanding nature of political selection. The British Candidate Study concluded that supply-side explanations may account for a substantial amount of the social bias of Parliament. Here the differences in women's and men's access to resources discussed above are particularly telling. Constraints on resources such as time, money and political experience, and motivational factors such as drive and ambition, play a large part in determining who applies to go to Westminster. The narrow path leading to a political career is usually risky, gruelling and unglamorous, requiring stamina, optimism and dedication as well as considerable resources. These are less available to women than men. Parliamentary careers are facilitated by the resources which certain middle-class occupations offer: flexible working hours, useful political skills, social status and political contacts are all enhanced by what have been termed brokerage occupations. The argument is simple but the insight is important. To run for Parliament an individual must have financial security, public networks, social status, policy experience, technical and social skills. Those who have brokerage jobs—barristers, lecturers, trade union officials, journalists, political researchers—work in fields which are complementary to politics. Their skills translate between public and private life. The idea of brokerage employment helps to illuminate class, ethnic and gender disparities between the composition of Parliament and that of the electorate and shows, how important the terms of women's labour

market participation are to their opportunities to gain political influence. Women and members of ethnic minorities are often concentrated
in low-paying occupations or in small family businesses. Such jobs,
combined with family responsibilities, mean long hours which do not
fit in with the demands of political activism. Important too is the
interplay between gender, class and race. Analysts seeking to explore
the components of the masculinity of public life must address both
middle-class dominance and attitudes and working-class culture and
attitudes. Such interdisciplinary research is at an early stage in Britain.

The Gender and New Urban Governance research offers other
examples of organisational gender biases. Interviews with senior women
officials show that resistance to sex equality is part of the culture of
local authorities, of the normal operating practices of local government
organisations. During the 1980s some British local authorities introduced radical sex equality policies and developed wide-ranging plans to
achieve organisational gender balance. The combined effects of running
down local democracy and internal male resistance limited the effects
of such policies, many of which were quietly dropped in the early
1990s. Particularly in Conservative councils, senior officers are hostile
to equality issues and some are overtly hostile to women's rights. A
culture in which women employees are regarded as problems, and Equal
Opportunities is seen as threatening, impedes processes to secure
women's rights in such a way that the most successful women are
'macho' types who mimic male management styles and cannot be seen
to be pro-women for fear of being undermined by senior male managers.
The following extracts from interviews with women officials give a
sense of the organisational culture in one authority:
'It's that sort of niggling attitude you still get but it makes a difference
to how you are perceived, So you have got to be more that 100%
absolutely professional in what you are doing. I guess some of them on
the way up cannot be seen to be too female . . . '

'One man said I was a lesbian because I asked him not to call me
love.'
Political support for sex equality is lacking.
'We do not talk about women's issues. We talk about issues. The idea
of positive discrimination is as alien to most of us as is discrimination,
so we do not have a women's committee or talk about women's issues
as such.'
'I do not feel as a local authority it is my job to change society and to
change the role of women.'

Being associated with Sex Equality initiatives is damaging to credibility in the organisation. Chairwomen insist on being called chairman and
will not answer to chair. Men and some women collude to maintain the
male organisational gender bias. This is greatly resented by some women
who experience discrimination at work and are annoyed by the way sex
equality policy is contained in the authority:

'If it is a good idea, why doesn't the council introduce it as a project and try and encourage it in all departments ... Women are doing something about it, but why should it have to come from us? Why shouldn't the council say that we ought to be doing this, that and the other. It's like, there is a problem here, but you sort it out, not us. But the problem is with the organisation not with the women.'

Conclusions

Concepts of positional, policy and organisational gender bias facilitate the exploration of the political disadvantages experienced by British women and go some way to explaining them. Explication of different forms of sex and gender bias makes it possible to trace the connections between the presence of women in politics, the policies they advocate and the institutions they seek to inhabit. Ultimately, they leave unanswered the perennial question for feminist politics—does it make a difference to have women politicians and officials? Will the disadvantages experienced by so many women be changed by increasing the representation of women in institutions designed by men? Will state institutions change women before women change state institutions? These questions will frame the agendas of research on women and politics into the next century.

Two patterns emerge. On the one hand there is evidence of change, a slow improvement in women's presence in politics, of the establishment of some sex equality policies. Positional gender biases are slowly altering. On the other hand, policy and organisational gender biases appear to be under no immediate threat. Only occasional sensitivities to the gendered implications of public policy are evident; cultural change in organisations is rare. This presents the classic dichotomy of perception between a glass that is half full and half empty. The determined optimist enthuses over the half full glass, points to legislative achievements, the changes in the Labour Party and the problems of the Conservatives, the rise in women appointed to public bodies, as portents of far reaching change. The pessimist focuses on the half empty glass and draws attention to the fact that persistent inequalities are embedded in British political institutions and processes. Nearly eighty years after the women's suffrage was won, the political system continues to be dominated by men, to favour men and to institutionalise and reproduce inequalities between the sexes. Such biases are, of course, present in other democracies. Yet in positional terms Britain compares badly with most otherwise comparable countries. In policy terms it compares particularly badly with those countries where proportions of women representatives are high.

Policy and organisational gender biases in the executive have been addressed by recent governments which have followed international trends of establishing executive agencies to deal with women's issues. Progress has been limited however. Both government and opposition have women's briefs but in neither case do women's agencies have high status. Today, women seek political power in institutions that are changing rapidly. The changes may offer opportunities for women as old organisational certainties are abandoned. But the decline of public institutions may inspire fierce battles over a decreasing number of positions of public power. As Helen Margetts argues in this volume, changes in public management withhold at least as much as they offer. In such a situation the feminist challenge to political institutions is crucial. Feminists in political organisations make claims on behalf of women and, despite resistances of all kinds, have led to some institutionalisation of their concerns. Thus small gains may, in times of rapid change, have been major setbacks. This suggests that the expenditure of feminist energies on influencing and changing political institutions is worthwhile and should continue.

1   D. Dahlerup, *The New Women's Movement, Feminism and Political Power In Europe and the USA* 1986), p. 6.
2   Directed by Joni Lovenduski, Helen Margetts and Patrick Dunleavy.
3   J. Lovenduski, *Women and European Politics* Wheatsheaf, 1986); V. Randall *Women and Politics* 1987).
4   European Commission, *Women and Decision-Making*
5   J. Hearn, *Men in the Public Eye* 1992).
6   M. Savage and A. Witz (eds), *Gender and Bureaucracy*
7   P. Norris and J. Lovenduski, *Political Recruitment: Gender, Race and Class in the British Parliament* University Press, 1995).
8   See Sophie Watson 'Producing the Right Sort of Chap: The Senior Civil Service as an Exclusionary Culture' *Policy and Politics*, 1994/3; B. Bagihole, *Women, Work and Equal Opportunity* Press, 1994). C. Cockburn (1991) *In the Way of Women* 1991).
9   P. Norris and J. Lovenduski, *Political Recruitment*, op.cit.
10 Unless otherwise indicated, data are from *Social Trends* 25, (1995).
11 'Mothers, Human Capital And Child Care in Britain', *National Institute Economic Review*
12 Commission on Social Justice, *Social Justice, Strategies for National Renewal* Books, 1994), p. 38.
13 S. Watson, loc.cit.
14 S. Halford, 'Women's Initiatives in Local Government', *Policy and Politics*, 1988/4; 'Feminist Change in Patriarchal Organisations' in Savage and Witz op.cit.
15 C. Cockburn *Women, Trade Unions and Political Parties* Research Series, 1987).
16 S. Perrigo 'Gender Struggles in the British Labour Party', *Party Politics*, 1995/3.
17 British Candidate Study, 1992.
18 *Sunday Telegraph* 6.8.95.

Women and the Labour Party

BY CLARE SHORT

SINCE 1987, a quiet revolution has been taking place in the Labour Party. It is inspired by the need for Labour to win more women's votes, the need to regenerate the party and to improve women's representation in public life. The consequences have not yet been felt either in the big increase it will bring in women's representation in the House of Commons, or in the possible change it may lead to in women's voting. If these changes help Labour to be seen as a more women-friendly party, they could change voting behaviour in a way which could significantly affect the balance of power between the two major parties in Britain.

Women in Britain vote Conservative disproportionately. If women had voted Labour in equal numbers to men in postwar Britain, Labour would have been in power continuously from 1945 to 1979. If women had swung to Labour in equal numbers with men in 1992, Labour would have won the election. In fact, in 1992, older, low-income women swung away from Labour when men of the same age and income level moved heavily towards Labour. A major part of the explanation of the Conservative domination of postwar Britain is their success with women voters. Given Labour's record as the party that created the welfare state, introduced family allowance, then child benefit, passed the Equal Pay and Sex Discrimination Acts and introduced SERPS which massively improved women's pension entitlement, Labour's failure with women voters is surprising. It is true that women have tended to vote more conservatively than men elsewhere but the bias in Britain is larger and more deeply embedded. [1] Labour's failure to win women's votes has been one of its major postwar political failures and the Tory party's electoral success with women a major part of the explanation of its political success.

Since 1987, Labour has begun to understand the consequences of its electoral failure with women. Following the 1987 defeat, a highly influential study was undertaken by Labour's Shadow Communication Agency which demonstrated how the Labour Party was seen by women as the most masculine of all parties and how women supported values Labour believed to be its own but did now hear Labour articulating these values.

These findings were presented to the Shadow Cabinet and National Executive Committee. [2] They had a strong influence on the Kinnock leadership which consciously began to set about making the Labour

Party more women-friendly. Increased numbers of women MPs were appointed to junior frontbench positions; and in 1989 a proposal that originated from the Tribune group of MPs to introduce a quota of three votes in Shadow Cabinet elections which must be cast for women, found favour with the leadership and was supported by the Parliamentary Party. The Shadow Cabinet was increased from 15 to 18 in number to accommodate the change but it immediately led to an increase in women's representation at the highest level in the party.

This move from leadership level to try to make the Labour Party more women-friendly came at a time when Socialist International Women—the women's section of the worldwide alliance of social democratic parties—were strongly recommending the use of quotas within its member parties to increase women's representation. The Socialist International Women's recommendation was inspired by the success of the Scandinavian parties in using quotas to transform the balance of representation which has led to them achieving virtually equal numbers of men and women in parliament and government.

There was strong support amongst crucial union votes for these changes because the trade union movement had been through a process of self-examination and change as a result of the changes that took place in the Labour market during the 1980s. Following the election of the first Thatcher government in 1979, Britain entered a major recession, destroying as many as two million jobs which were largely in manufacturing industries and which were overwhelmingly male and unionised. The new jobs of the Lawson boom of the late 1980s were concentrated in the service sector, were largely low paid and part-time, and were overwhelmingly taken by women. The new workers were in sectors that were not traditionally well unionised, and general unions like the Transport and General Workers Union (T&G) and the General, Municipal and Boilermakers Union (GMB) which had lost many members in the early 1980s recession were anxious to recruit these new workers. They therefore engaged in special research and recruitment campaigns and programmes of internal reforms in order to make themselves more women-friendly. At the same time, public sector unions like NUPE, whose membership was 80% women but whose officers and executive were predominantly male, were engaging in a similar programme of reform as the women members of the union demanded change. Thus the trade union influence in the Labour Part was strongly in favour of positive action to make the party more representative and more women friendly.

The women's organisation in the party had been pushing for a number of years for reform to improve women's representation, but until very late in the day the organisational demands were for an increase in the power of the women's organisation within the party rather than the Scandinavian style quotas. The Women's Action Committee was the dominant voice for change at this time. Its style was confrontational and the reforms it demanded were that the women's conference should elect the five women members of the national executive, that the women's conference should be able to introduce five resolutions to the national conference, and that the women's conference general powers be strengthened. The quota programme inspired by Socialist International Women overtook these demands and was clearly more radical in its likely effect. The Women's Action Committee moved to support the call for quotas when it was put forward.

Thus, once the demand for a move to quotas was made, it passed the Conference very easily before there had been a full debate within the party. Reform was speeded forward by the General Secretary of the Labour Party, Larry Whitty, a strategic political thinker who understood that the party had to make itself more women-friendly in order to modernise and advance. Vicky Phillips was the Women's Officer who, inspired by the lessons from SIW, strongly supported the move to quotas. Thus in 1989 a resolution was passed at Conference with overwhelming support which committed the party to introduce a quota of 40% for elections at every level and to achieve 50% representation of women in the Parliamentary Party in ten years or after three elections. Following this, rule changes were introduced to require the party at every level to ensure that 40% of its officers were women. These changes affected the party everywhere. Suddenly every local branch and constituency had to find 40% women officers. In many areas this was strongly and easily supported. In other backward areas — often safe Labour seats — the rule was not honoured, but this left open the process of local argument followed by enforcement from above which meant that all elements of the party became part or the process of change.

One of the most successful processes of reform were the rule changes applied to the National Executive Committee (NEC). It was agreed that the quota should be introduced under a rolling programme. Thus both the trade union and constituency section of the NEC is gradually being transformed: with the already existing five women members elected under the old rules, the balance of the national executive is now 12 women and 18 men and will change again after the 1995 Conference. From 1990 onwards the General Secretary also ensured that all policy-making bodies of the party and all committees were made up of 40% women. Thus with little fuss or argument the senior committees of the Labour Party were made up of almost equal numbers of men and women. The senior committees around the leader's office were not similarly improved because appointments were more informal and party rules did not apply. But these changes led to an important and unremarked change in the ethos and balance of power of the party.

There was one notable part of the 1989 resolution that was not taken forward. This was the commitment that 50% of the Parliamentary Labour Party (PLP) should be women with ten years or three elections. The party did undertake a consultation in 1990 on how this was to be achieved. There was general support within the party for the principle, but overwhelmingly opposition to any action from the centre to enforce change. Thus the NEC felt unable to enforce action. It did adopt a rule change to require that where a women was nominated for selection, she must be short-listed. It also set up a 'W' list of women candidates. But progress was slow and following the 1992 election Labour moved from 21 to 37 women MPs. This is, of course, a considerable increase but left women as still only 14% of the PLP, and whilst 20 Labour MPs retired 18 of them were replaced by men. So the new women were elected in the most marginal seats.

It is notable that changes in party rules to require 40% representation of women at every level was accepted fairly quietly. It was the implementation of the commitment to increase the number of women in Parliament that caused most trouble and was the noisiest part of the quiet revolution. Following the 1992 election defeat, Neil Kinnock resigned and John Smith became leader of the Labour Party. Few had realised before his election how deeply he was committed to the advancement of women. As soon as he became leader, he set about promoting women throughout the party.

Following the 1992 general election, it was clearly important to move quickly to changes in the methods of selecting candidates for Parliament if improvements were to be made for the 1997 election. The responsibility fell to me as the chair of the Women's Committee. I therefore convened informal meetings with senior women to discuss possible procedures. We were aware that in countries which elected their parliaments through list systems, progress had been made by requiring a fixed percentage of the list to be women candidates. In the British system this was not possible. The only realistic alternative was to group seats regionally and require that half the vacant seats selected from an all-women short-list. This was the only way to be fair to popular male candidates who had fought previously, protect local choice and secure a guaranteed advance in women's representation. The women's conference had voted on a number of occasions that there should be all-women short-lists in the seats of all retiring MPs until the PLP was 50% women. One of the reasons for this was that women MPs are largely grouped in marginal seats. This option was voted down repeatedly by Annual Conference and therefore a compromise had to be found. The option of all-women short-lists in half the winnable seats and half the safe seats where MPs were retiring was the obvious compromise. The then chair of the Organisation Committee, Gordon Colling, supported this option as the only way the NEC could implement the principle of increased representation of women agreed in 1989.

John Smith decided to attend the meeting of the NEC Women's Committee that debated the options. The debate was influenced by the fact that there had been no increase in women selected to fight winnable seats in the forthcoming European elections. (As it happened, we increased our representation of women in the European Parliament because our vote was so good and we won many marginal seats that we had not expected to take.) Following this meeting, the leader of the party committed himself to implementing this proposal at the 1993 Conference; it was overwhelmingly carried. It is notable that the rule change which implemented this proposal was linked to the rule change that moved Labour from selecting local candidates through an electoral college made up of up to 40% trade union votes to a straight forward one member one vote (OMOV) ballot. This is considered to be an historic part of Labour's recent process of modernisation. It was passed only because the Manufacturing, Scientific and Finance Union (MSF) so strongly supported an increase of women's representation that it abstained rather than cast its votes against OMOV to which it was opposed. The MSF vote was crucial to the outcome, thus Labour's commitment to increase women's representation has had historic consequences in more than one direction.

The commitment to increase the number of women candidates for Parliament has been undoubtedly the most difficult part of this programme of change. The change of leader in 1994 made the implementation more difficult as Tony Blair was less firmly convinced of the policy than John Smith. There has been a campaign of opposition organised within the party with some MPs—of the traditional 'old Labour' fixing variety—orchestrating the opposition. There have been some women in support, most notably Ann Carlton—a previous political adviser to John Silkin who published frequent newspaper articles to attempt to damage and undermine the party's policy. In some areas of the country, local male aspirants have encouraged opposition and dissent. Despite all of this and the hysterical opposition of the *Daily Mail* newspaper, the majority of the Labour Party stood firmly behind the policy. The challenge mounted at the 1994 Conference was massively defeated. By autumn 1995, Labour had already selected 37 new women who are likely to win their seats and is thus already close to a guarantee of 80 to 90 in the next Parliament. With more selections yet to take place, this could increase, but 20–25% of the next PLP is already guaranteed to be women.

There is one possible problem. A Labour party member called Peter Jepson has taken legal action before an Industrial Tribunal to claim sex discrimination because he was not allowed to stand for selection in two seats. Obviously the party took legal advice before adopting the policy and an early challenge to the Equal Opportunities Commission led them to take legal advice which found Labour's policy in compliance with the law. The basic case is that although the Sex Discrimination Act exempts political parties from its requirements, it requires no discrimination between men and women in awarding a professional qualification. Our opponents argue that selection as a parliamentary candidate leads to the possibility of becoming an MP, which is a profession, therefore they say all-women short-lists area a breach of the law. Previous court actions on selections have found that the electorate rather than the selectorate create MPs, therefore we expect the challenge to be defeated but the action is yet to be heard.

It is notable that just at this time the Conservative Party, which currently has 20 women MPs of its 327 total, is likely to see a decline in the number and proportion of women, recently estimated by *The Times* to be likely to reduce to 12. This is partly because women MPs in both parties are concentrated in more marginal seats and therefore an electoral setback reduces their number. The second reason is that the expected electoral setback is causing senior men to seek safer seats and thus squeezing out newcomers or women MPs who might consider relocating. The general stance of the Tory party is to publicly criticise Labour's positive action programme but we are told that great efforts have been made to increase the proportion of women on the centrally approved panel. If this indirect method of improving women's representation proves to be as big a failure as currently seems likely, it will help to vindicate Labour's positive action programme. Evidence from other countries also suggests that when one party makes a breakthrough on women's representation, the others feel obliged to follow. It is probable therefore that the 1996/7 election will be a watershed for the representation of women in the British House of Commons.

Our commitment to increase women's representation in local government remained the one gap in the progress of the quota. In 1994 the party circulated a consultation paper, and as I write is planning to take proposals to the 1995 Conference to secure increased representation of women from the existing 23% of Labour councillors. We also plan to ensure that women take positions as group officers and chairs of committees on local councils at least in proportion to their growing numbers in each group.

Another major strand in Labour's reform programme is its commitment to establish a Ministry for Women. Labour has been committed since 1986 to establish such a ministry and Labour's Shadow Minister for Women (then Jo Richardson) undertook considerable work on the detail. In fact, during the consultation between opposition and civil service in the six months before the 1992 election, Jo Richardson met with Sir Robin Butler, Head of the Civil Service, to discuss how the machinery would be established. It was agreed that a sex equality branch would be set up in the Department of Employment, transferring relevant responsibilities from the Home Office and Cabinet Office, and that a Cabinet sub-committee should be established. When Gillian Shephard became Secretary of State for Employment in 1992 this machinery was set up within the Department of Employment.

Mo Mowlem was appointment Labour's Shadow Minister for Women in 1992 and at that time there was talk of dropping the commitment to a Ministry for Women. The debate was not held openly but, like most of the modernisers' project, was canvassed through the media. The suggestion was that a Women's Ministry, like Women's Committees in local government, had become part of Labour's 'loony left' image and needed to be dropped. When John Smith appointed me Shadow Minister for Women, he asked me to review our commitment to a Women's Ministry and report back to him. Sadly, he died before this could be done. I was myself convinced that a left-right tokenistic battle about a Women's Ministry would help no one. I was anxious to move the debate forward. We therefore issued a consultation document in early 1995 which described existing government machinery and lessons from other countries and asked for the views of the party and women's organisations on the alternative ways forward. Again, as I write, a policy document is about to be considered before seeking endorsement at the 1995 Conference. Our recommendation is a Minister for Women in the Cabinet Office who may or may not take on the existing responsibilities which lie in the Cabinet Office and are largely for the civil service. We also propose to incorporate in the structures the method of working which Labour has developed in opposition. This would mean a reformed Women's National Commission, in cooperation with the Equal Opportunities Commission, conducting an annual consultation on priorities for advancement to women's equality. The Minister for Women would respond to the programme in an annual debate in the House of Commons. There would also be a monthly question time which would bring the women's agenda onto the floor of the House of Commons, and the possibility of establishing a select committee would be considered. These proposals are intended to create lean and efficient machinery which will bring a strategic influence to bear at the heart of the government policy. Lessons from abroad suggest that the Women's Ministry can be a tokenistic dumping ground or strategically influential. We hope that our proposals have built on the lessons from overseas.

The prospect of the 40% quota bringing about a transformation in the culture and style of the Labour Party at local level is the least developed part of the programme of reform. The NEC has been convinced since 1992 that more effort must be made to regenerate the party at local level in order to make it more representative, as well as more able to convey Labour's message to the electorate and the people's views to the Labour leadership. There were some amongst Labour's modernisers who seemed more anxious to weaken the base of the party and move to a leadership-led balloting party with little real local existence. However, various electoral studies showed clearly that where the party was strong and active locally, it was likely to win a swing as great as 5% more than the average, [3] and this, together with the preference of many members of the National Executive for strong local roots, led to a firm commitment to regeneration.

My own view is that it is at local level that the Conservative Party succeeds in creating its women-friendly face and that Labour's local face is massively more male, bureaucratic and off-putting. This would help to explain how the Conservative Party has a smaller number of women MPs, has opposed social reforms that have benefited women, and yet retains the women's vote. Locally it is often run by middle-aged women who are efficient, able and articulate. It also uses social events much more successfully than the Labour Party to bond with local people. Thus at local level throughout the country older women, who are of the generation whose greatest pride is their achievements in bringing up a happy and successful family, see many women like themselves in positions of seniority and influence. In contrast, the Labour Party is run to a rule book, with a pyramid of meetings dominated by activists with plenty of time to attend meetings and argue over points of procedure. I greatly value the democratic core of Labour's constitution which provides for local members to send resolutions to Annual Conference or at any time to the National Executive so that the centre has to listen to local members. But the need to protect these democratic rights does not require a culture of local organisation which is intensely bureaucratic, argumentative and time-consuming. This is a problem faced by social democratic parties and trade unions throughout the world.

There is growing appreciation of the need to change the style and culture of local party organisation. My own hope was that Labour's commitment to a 40% quota of officers at every level would force the party to become more women-friendly and thus more human-friendly. Based on this thinking, the party held an enormously successful Women's Training Conference in Southport in 1994 which was intended to provide women members with access to knowledge, skills and confidence to begin the process of transformation locally. But there has been little further progress in this area of work. I remain hopeful that it will prove possible to recruit and train more women members to take up the places allocated by the quota and at the same time to challenge the bureaucratic style and ethos of local organisation.

The changes described above amount to a very considerable pro-gramme of reform. If they succeed in changing the image of the Labour Party with older, women voters, they could transform the party-political balance of power in twenty-first century Britain. It is notable how little commentary there has been on the significance of these changes. Beyond the *Daily Mail* sneering at the process of selecting more women political candidates and the *Sunday Times* attempting to paint the Ministry for Women commitment as a loony policy that Blair would drop, few political commentators have noticed any of this. It remains to be seen how influential it might be.

Most institutions change significantly in their culture and style as women are promoted in significant number. We should therefore expect the culture and style of the Labour Party to change significantly. It is also likely that the presence of such a large number of women in the House of Commons will lead to major change.

Clearly, this whole programme of change has been driven by the need to improve the quality and representativeness of political institutions. It is right and necessary that women should be represented in the leadership of political parties and in the parliaments of the world in order that the talent and view of the people should be properly represented. The case for this change stands whatever its electoral impact. Nonetheless, it will be very interesting to watch the voting behaviour of women over the next ten to fifteen years. It seems likely that the reforms will have relatively little impact on the 1996/7 election. But after a full Parliament with one party representing women in much larger numbers than the other and with the internal reforms bedding-in in local government and local party organisation, it is possible that the transformation of Labour's image may help to change women's voting behaviour.

1   P. Norris, Mobilising the Women's Vote: The Gender Generation Gap in Voting Behaviour, *Parliamentary Affairs*, 1996/2.
2   This later formed the basis of a pamphlet: P. Hewitt and D. Mattinson, *Women's Votes: The Key to Winning* (Fabian, 1989).
3   P. Seyd and P. Whiteley, Labour's Grass Roots, Clarendon Press, 1992.

Women and Politics in Scotland

BY ALICE BROWN

THE ROLE of women in Scottish politics has been a relatively neglected
area of academic enquiry. The 1980s and 1990s have, however,
witnessed a growing interest, which has in turn led to a number of
research projects and publications. As a result, work is now available
on the history of women's involvement in politics, on the role of women
in local government, on the women's movement and on the involvement
of women in the constitutional debate; a comparative study of the
participation of women in politics in Scotland and the Republic of
Ireland has also been conducted.[1]

While women involved in politics in Scotland share similar experiences and concerns with those in other parts of the United Kingdom
and elsewhere, it can be argued that the politics of Scotland have
impacted in a particular way on their political participation. More
specifically, the challenge to the current constitutional arrangements
and the campaigns for a Scottish parliament have provided a political
opportunity for women to articulate their own demands. The movement
for constitutional change has included policies for electoral reform, for
the 'democratisation' of the parliamentary process, and for more
openness and accountability in decision-making. Women have added
their voice to these campaigns and have incorporated their claim for
equal representation as an integral part of the proposals for radical
change in the government of Scotland.

The mobilisation of women in Scotland behind the critical mass of
opinion in favour of constitutional reform has been significant. It
provides an example of a form of coalition and agenda-building politics
which has proved one of the most successful strategies for women's
advancement. Other examples can be found in the gains made in the
mid-1960s in the United States which can be explained partially as a
result of the political legacy of the civil rights movement; in the
European Union where women were able to take advantage of attempts
to harmonise labour costs and put forward their own claim for equal
pay; and in Britain, where the modernisation process taking place
within the Labour Party allowed women to push for a greater say in the
running of the party and for the policy of all-women short-lists in half
of the vacant, winnable, parliamentary seats. Similarly, the strategies
adopted by political activists in Scotland can be analysed within the
theoretical frameworks of the activities of political movements and the
role of specific political opportunity structures.

Here we outline the involvement of women in contemporary Scottish politics and their networking both within and outside the formal structures of political power. Evidence is drawn from interviews carried out with activists in the political parties, the trade unions and local government, and with women involved in the wider women's movement in Scotland. It is argued that, although women in Scotland are poorly represented in top posts in key political institutions, they are actively engaged in the political life of the country. Reflecting the experience of women in other countries and cultures, political activists in Scotland have seized the chance to advance their demands as part of a broad coalition and pressure for change.

Women's political representation in Scotland

It has been possible for women in Scotland, as in other parts of the UK, to stand for election to the House of Commons since 1918, the same year as women over the age of 30 were first given the right to vote. Since that time, just 24 have represented Scottish constituencies at Westminster. The pattern has been one of fluctuation around a low level and, unlike other European countries, the level of representation has not risen significantly in the postwar period. At the general election in 1992, five women MPs were elected from a total of 72 Scottish MPs, the same number as were elected at the 1959 and 1964 general elections. The election of two more women at by-elections in Scotland in 1994 (Labour) and 1995 (SNP) brought the number to a record level of 7.

1: Women MPs at the General Election and Following By-Elections

	1992		1995	
	UK	Scotland	UK	Scotland
Conservative	20	0	20	0
Labour	37	3	39	4
Liberal Democrats	2	1	2	1
SNP	1	1	2	2
Total	60	5	63	7
	(9.2%)	(6.9%)	(9.7%)	(9.7%)

At local government level, the representation of women is higher. Under the old two-tier system of local government, around 22% of councillors elected at the District elections in 1992 were women and some 17% at the Regional elections in 1994. In the first elections for the new unitary authorities in Scotland, held in April 1995, just over one in five of the new councillors were women. The results of the elections for the shadow councils were a disappointment for women activists who had campaigned for more equal representation, especially as the next local elections will not take place until 1999. Finally, the representation of Scottish women MEPs at the European level dropped from 2 to 1 in 1994, against the trend in all other European countries except Portugal.

2: Elections for Shadow Unitary Authorities in 1995

	% Women Candidates	% Women Elected
Conservative	26	27
Labour	27	24
Liberal Democrats	33	29
SNP	24	20
Ind./Other	18	13
Total	26	22

Growing awareness of the relatively low level of women's representation in Scotland, and knowledge of the experience of improved
representation in other west European countries, has led to claims for
gender balance with positive action to effect change. Such demands run
in parallel to claims in other spheres in Scottish society for greater
equality and autonomy. Women are under-represented in all areas of
decision-making, including business, the trade unions, the judiciary, the
media and public bodies; and they are disadvantaged in terms of their
labour market position, levels of income, poverty, housing and health.[2]
Strategies by women in the political parties for equal representation
should be interpreted within wider economic, social and political
changes in Scotland and the UK, but also as part of a broader movement
by women in Europe and beyond for a greater say in decision-making
bodies and for an equal share of resources. However, the prospects of
constitutional change and the establishment of a parliament in Scotland,
have provided a specific set of political opportunities for women in
Scotland. Similar debates are taking place in Wales.[3]

Political pressure to improve representation has not been confined to
women within the political parties; it is apparent in the trade union
movement and local government, and significantly within the various
women's groups and organisations in Scotland. Writing in 1990, Esther
Breitenbach argued that 'the current political situation in Scotland
provides an opportunity for a resurgent feminism to organise anew and
to act more effectively on political institutions and ideologies'. Evidence
of this resurgence can be found in the creation of a new women's
organisation, *Engender*, and the publication of a new feminist magazine,
Harpies and Quines, in 1992; the achievements of feminists within local
government in initiatives such as the Zero Tolerance Campaign; and
the coming together of women from different feminist perspectives
around the issue of women's representation. Feminists in Scotland have
demonstrated their willingness to engage with wider political developments, the state and other formal political power structures in order to
make their claim in Scotland.

Why so few Scottish women MPs?

The low number of women recruited to the House of Commons and
other levels of government raises an obvious question and that is why

has representation in Scotland and other parts of the UK remained so low? No simple answer to this question can be provided. Explanations are, in part, linked to the more general reasons cited for the poor representation of women in legislatures throughout the world. At the UK level, the most comprehensive summary of the potential reasons can be found in the survey of candidates for the 1992 general election carried out by Pippa Norris and Joni Lovenduski who analyse the influences on participation and recruitment at three different levels. The first level, or 'systematic factors', relate to the broad context in which recruitment of political candidates will take place in a country, and will include the legal system, electoral system, party system and structure of opportunities. The second context involves 'political party factors', such as party organisation, rules and ideology. The third influence will be 'individual recruitment factors' which will include factors determining the supply of candidates, (for example the resources and motivation of aspirants) and the demand factors (such as the attitudes and practices of 'gatekeepers').[4]

Interviews with ten women activists in each of the main political parties in Scotland in 1994 revealed that they perceived that the reasons for poor participation are interrelated in a complex way and operate on all three levels identified by Norris and Lovenduski. At the 'systematic' level, the women interviewed highlighted the particular practical difficulties imposed by the location of Parliament in London, and the unsocial hours of parliamentary meetings. Added to this, the first-past-the-post electoral system was believed by some to disadvantage women, as is the adversarial nature of the party system and the dominance of the two main parties, Conservative and Labour. The career structure for elected office, with recruitment in the main from the party, local government or trade unions, was considered to work to the advantage of men within the parties.

Barriers to involvement in politics were also identified at the 'political party' level. Party rules and organisation, the timing of meetings, ways of conducting political business, and method of political appointments within the party were not viewed as conducive to the equal participation of women. Some, particularly those in the Scottish Liberal Democrats and the SNP, felt their party was doing more to actively involve women. In contrast, women in the Scottish Labour Party were most critical of the rate of change within their party, while in the Conservative Party they were inclined to the view that able women would succeed in spite of the obstacles which they face.

Both supply and demand factors were specified as influencing 'individual recruitment'. Women's role in the family was considered to be a key factor limiting the supply or participation of women in Scottish political life. Even where the reality of women's lives is that they combine paid work with family responsibilities, or indeed do not have a family of their own, those interviewed felt that traditional attitudes

towards women as home-makers and men as decision-makers continue
to influence the expectations of both women and men. Responsibility
for the family came first, and before political ambition, for most of the
women in the different parties, some interviewees arguing more positively that after women had raised their children they brought an added
understanding to politics and had more to offer. However, there was an
acknowledgement amongst some women that family responsibility was
a relatively 'easy' explanation for the low representation of women
which avoided analysing potentially more contentious reasons such as
discrimination against them. If women in modern Scotland are expected
to combine a full-time paid job with looking after a family, then the
question remains as to why specifically a parliamentary career is
relatively closed to them.

Contrary to the findings of Norris and Lovenduski that the lack of
resources were a key determinant, few women in the Scottish study
volunteered finance as a serious barrier for women (the financial
assistance offered through 'Emily's list' in the Labour Party was not
taken up in Scotland). This does not necessarily mean that resources are
not important, rather that other barriers were seen as more pressing: for
example, lack of confidence including inexperience in public speaking,
or fear of making a fool of themselves, were cited as important factors
which prevented women from putting themselves forward. In arguing
that men are 'more likely to put themselves forward', a number of
women noted the importance of being asked to consider themselves as
candidates.

The individual factors relating to the supply of women available for
political positions were therefore accompanied by an identification of
demand side factors and party variables which interviewees believed
also played a role in deciding the level of women's political participation. A number of those who had stood for office had been encouraged
to do so by a male colleague. Indeed, somewhat ironically, some,
particularly those in the Conservative Party, identified other women in
their parties as more biased against promoting and selecting women
candidates. However, women within the Scottish Labour Party were
much more likely to explain exclusion from selection to safe seats in
terms of the reluctance of men in the party to give up power.

With regard to demand factors and the actual selection process,
responses from the Scottish activists varied across party. Women in the
Scottish Liberal Democrats and SNP did not identify any specific
problems for women at the selection stage, although they saw it as more
of a problem in the Conservative Party in Scotland and particularly for
women in the Scottish Labour Party. They considered that men and
women in the Conservative Party were more inclined to hold traditional
views on the role of women in society and that the Scottish Labour
Party was very male and trade union dominated. Some women in the
Conservative Party agreed that women often faced problems at the

selection stage in their party because of the attitudes of both male and female selectors. Although at a national level the policy of the party has changed, they considered that women were disadvantaged because of power over selection still rests in the hands of the local party.

Women in the Scottish Labour Party believed there were great difficulties for women in being selected, partially as a result of Labour's dominance in Scottish politics. As the party with 49 of the 72 parliamentary seats in Scotland following the 1992 election, Labour holds a considerable degree of power. In the first-past-the-post electoral system, incumbency is also an important factor. When Labour seats do become available, then the competition for them is fierce. The party now has a policy that there should be all-women short-lists in half of the vacant winnable seats in Scotland. (Some women activists in the Scottish Labour Party proposed that there should be all-women lists in all vacant seats in Scotland because of the slow rate of seats becoming available, but this was rejected by the party Conference.) Given the slow rate of turnover, it will be some time before women in the party gain equality as Westminster parliamentarians.[5]

The Labour women interviewed gave specific examples where they or other experienced women candidates had not been short-listed for the selection interview, or had been disadvantaged at the selection meeting. For them it was clearly an issue of power and the refusal of many men to share power with women in the party. There is a strong sense of injustice that often very able and high profile women, who have worked in the party for twenty or more years and have considerable experience, are not being selected for parliamentary seats. Thus, although men in the Labour Party employ the rhetoric of women's equality, it was felt that these principles were not always practised within the party.

An important influence which operated at all three levels was the political culture in Scotland and, more specifically, in the House of Commons. The predominantly male culture in which politics is conducted was cited across the party divide as a key inhibiting factor for women. Some made the link between women's apparent lack of confidence and their reluctance to participate in what many described as the macho, adversarial style of politics which they consider dominates parties and the Parliament in Britain. Thus the whole political culture and way in which politics is conducted is perceived as a disincentive to women's participation and a more subtle way of excluding them from the political process. The women who do reach high office are those who are most able to fit in with the male culture which predominates. (Studies, mainly in Scandinavia suggest that culture is unlikely to change until there is a critical mass of women, 30% or more.)

Women activists in Scotland, therefore, referred to factors operating at the systematic, political party and individual recruitment level. The many and varied explanations demonstrate that participants perceive a complex interplay between the three dimensions, and also between the supply of and demand for potential candidates. Although the views of these in the survey do not provide concrete evidence of the actual existence of barriers to women's political participation, such views are important and can prevent women, both directly and indirectly, from taking part in conventional politics. If women believe they will be discriminated against at the selection stage, or will be treated as inferior because of their sex, or if they are simply not encouraged to see themselves as potential candidates, it is not surprising that they are less inclined to put themselves forward.

Many of the views expressed were shared by women across the party divide. However, there were also differences between the four main political parties. These differences are significant and affect the proposals for change advocated by the women involved, and the policies which they believe are necessary to improve women's representation. The contrast in approach can be illustrated through examining the involvement of women in the constitutional debate in Scotland.

Campaigns for a Scottish parliament with gender equality

Electoral support for the Conservative Party in Scotland has declined rapidly from the 1950s, and fell further under the administrations of Margaret Thatcher and John Major. In the 1950s, it stood at just over 50%. By the 1992 general election it had dropped to under 26%. At the elections for the new shadow local authorities in 1995 it reached an unprecedented low of 11%.[6] In the 1987 general election, when the Conservatives won only 10 of the 72 parliamentary seats, strength was added to the argument that the Conservative government did not have a mandate to rule in Scotland. It was contended by the government's opponents that Scotland was suffering from a democratic deficit. The campaign for a Scottish parliament gathered force within the opposition political parties and through such organisations at the Campaign for a Scottish Assembly (later to become the Campaign for a Scottish Parliament). Some women activists held that they were experiencing a 'double democratic deficit', first on the grounds that they supported political parties which favoured an independent or devolved Scottish parliament, and second because as women they were grossly under-represented as MPs.

Following publication of the document, *A Claim of Right for Scotland*, by the Campaign for a Scottish Assembly in 1988 and the establishment of the Scottish Constitutional Convention in 1989, working groups were established by the latter to prepare options for the future devolved government of Scotland. Membership of the Convention included representatives from the Scottish Labour Party, the Scottish Liberal Democrats, the Scottish Trades Union Congress, the Campaign for a Scottish Parliament, and others from local government, the churches, small political parties and civic organisations including the Scottish Convention of Women. The Scottish National Party decided not to join because it advocates an independent Scottish parliament within Europe, and the Conservative Party declared its total opposition to constitutional change. One of the groups set up by the Convention was the Women's Issues Group, chaired by the Labour MP, Maria Fyfe. The agreement to have a group looking specifically at women's representation in a Scottish parliament was a significant step forward. It was made possible because of pressure from women representing political parties, the trade union movement, and women's groups, together with the support of some men within the Convention.[7]

It was at this early stage that other women activists in Scotland entered the debate and formed the Woman's Claim of Right Group. This comprised women from different political parties, but predominantly the Scottish Green Party, in addition to women who were not formally involved in party politics. They came together mainly in protest at the small number of women, some 10%, who had been nominated for membership of the newly established Scottish Constitutional Convention: 'Once again, major proposals and decisions affecting the life and well-being of Scottish people would be made with women being significantly under-represented.' The group monitored the work of the Convention and submitted a separate document to the Women's Issues Group, later publishing a book of the same title.[8]

The Women's Issues Group invited submissions from women in Scotland, and the question of representation within a new Scottish parliament was discussed amongst women in political parties, trade unions, local government, women's organisations, community groups and the voluntary sector. Reaction to the constitutional debate in the 1980s can be contrasted to involvement in the 1970s. Both Esther Breitenbach and Catriona Levy discuss the role of women in the devolution debate in the 1970s and the division between them on the issue.[9] While some took an active part in the campaigns for a Scottish Assembly, others felt that such a body could be more reactionary in its attitudes and policies towards women than the Westminster Parliament. Catriona Levy quotes the feminist journal, *MsPrint*: 'On the whole the women's movement ignored the referendum or saw it as irrelevant.' An attempt by the Scottish Convention of Women to raise the issue of women's representation by distributing a questionnaire to the political parties met with little success.

By the late 1980s the political situation had changed in Scotland. Women activists across the party divide and outside party politics became increasingly aware that women's representation was extremely low and that it compared unfavourably with most other European countries. They began to ask why. The possibility of a new Scottish parliament which was to be run on a radically different basis from the Westminster Parliament added impetus to demands for change and provided a common focus for political action. In contrast to the 1970s, there was broad agreement that such a parliament could act as a progressive force for women and the campaign to ensure more equal representation gathered steam. The reasons for this change of strategy are discussed in more detail elsewhere[10] and relate to the impact of Thatcherism on women in Scotland; the increase in political involvement of women in the political parties, local government and trade unions in the 1980s and 1990s; their growing frustration with the British political system, the Westminster style of government and the slowness of change; a dislike for the adversarial nature of party politics and the political behaviour of MPs; and the realisation that as women they had to be involved in shaping the plans for the new parliament for their perspectives to be taken into account.

The aim of gender balance and fair representation of others traditionally excluded from elected office thus became intertwined with plans to build a more democratic new parliament. In its first report, *Towards Scotland's Parliament*, in 1990 the Scottish Constitutional Convention committed itself to the principle of equal representation. It set up two new groups to undertake more detailed work on the *Procedures and Preparations for Scottish Parliament* and the *Electoral System for Scottish Parliament*. The group examining the electoral system had to take into account the need for gender balance and fair representation of ethnic minority groups. Although there was general agreement that something had to be done to ensure that the Scottish parliament did not repeat the Westminster pattern, there was no consensus on the policies needed to ensure gender balance. In particular, the two main parties within the Convention divided along ideological lines, the Scottish Labour Party favouring positive discrimination, which the Scottish Liberal Democrats opposed. The Scottish Labour Party adopted a proposal for 'active intervention', first put forward by the Scottish TUC's Women's Committee, that there should be a statutory imposition on the political parties to select a man and a woman for each of Scotland's 72 constituencies—the 50:50 option. For their part, the Liberal Democrats were totally opposed to any form of statutory restriction on the freedom of parties to select and voters to elect their members of parliament. Instead they proposed electoral change on the basis of 'STV-plus', arguing that under a list system and with other 'promotional' policies the representation of women would improve.[11]

While women were involved directly in the Constitutional Convention as representatives from the political parties or other organisations, they were also actively engaged in the debate within Scottish civil society and in organising women's conferences and other events.[12] Their aim was to widen the debate to include women in parties not involved in the Convention and from outside the formal political structures with the objective of maintaining pressure on the main parties. There was a broad consensus within and outside the parties that women should be more equally represented within a new Scottish parliament. The increased involvement of women was also reflected in the setting up of a new research and campaign organisation, *Engender*.

In the run-up to the general election in 1992, the need for the parties within the Convention to reach a compromise position became more urgent if they were to present a united opposition to the government. Just before the election, the Convention was able to announce an agreed scheme: an Additional Member System for elections, an obligation on parties to select an equal number of men and women candidates, and the use of the additional list of the Additional Member System to achieve gender balance if this was not achieved through the constituency elections. This settlement did not mean full endorsement of the '50:50' option proposed by the Scottish Labour Party, nor acceptance of the 'Single Transferable Vote-plus' electoral system advocated by the Scottish Liberal Democrats. Nevertheless, it represented a significant compromise by the parties involved and a leap forward in guaranteeing more equal representation for women within a future Scottish parliament. These plans received an enormous setback when the Conservative Party were re-elected in 1992, although in Scotland with just 11 MPs.

Following the Conservatives return to office, some commentators anticipated that the demands for constitutional change would be shelved, and with it the campaign for equal representation, at least until the run-up to the next general election. However, as the parties which supported either a devolved or an independent parliament for Scotland obtained 75% of the vote, it was unlikely that the pressure for constitutional change would immediately evaporate.

After the election, campaign groups were formed to keep demands for a Scottish parliament on the political agenda, including Common Cause, Scotland United and Democracy for Scotland. Continued commitment to the campaign for democratic renewal was illustrated in the well-attended Democracy demonstration organised to coincide with the European Summit held in Edinburgh in December 1992. Despite some initial difficulties, the Scottish Constitutional Convention also continued in existence, and established a Scottish Constitutional Commission in 1993 to examine the issues left unresolved before to the 1992 election. In 1993 the Coalition for Scottish Democracy was also formed, bringing together many political activists in the different pressure groups and political parties. It put forward the case for a Scottish Senate to allow civic organisations a positive input into the debate about the future governance of Scotland and was successful in setting up a Scottish Civic Assembly. The first meeting of the Assembly took place in March 1995; reflecting the broader campaign for gender equality, it operated a 50:50 gender representation policy in inviting a wide range of non-party organisations to attend.

The women's movement maintained its pressure on the political parties and trade unions for equal representation and formed the Women's Coordination Group drawn from the main women's groups. Its objectives were to coordinate campaigns and political action, and to lobby the Scottish Office and the parties in Scotland on the issue of women's representation. It organised discussions and conferences on strategies for improving representation both within party structures and in a future Scottish parliament, and it published reports from women in Scotland to the UN Conference in Beijing in 1995 and the European Union's Fourth Action Programme.

The Scottish Constitutional Commission delivered its report to the Scottish Constitutional Convention at the end of 1994. The Commission's task was to make recommendations on an electoral system with gender balance provisions, and consider the constitutional implications at UK level and for local government of the establishment of a Scottish Parliament. Its report recommended a Scottish parliament of 112 members elected by the Additional Member System, of which 72 constituency members would be elected on a first-past-the-post basis using the existing Westminster parliamentary constituencies, and an additional 40 on a proportional basis from party lists using the eight European Parliament constituencies. In order to achieve greater gender balance, it proposed that parties should be asked to achieve a target of 40%-plus representation of women in the parliament within the first five years, taking into account both the constituency and list seats. It advocated the removal of social, economic and other barriers to women's political participation through measures such as: changing parliamentary working hours and meeting times, facilities for caring, and attendance and carer allowances; changing the adversarial style and ethos of parliamentary behaviour; encouraging participation of women in parliamentary committees. The establishment of a Public Appointments Commission to ensure the full participation of women and others in public bodies was recommended in addition to a Parliamentary Equal Opportunities Commission.

In making these recommendations, the Commission rejected the adoption of a statutory scheme for the equal representation of women, but it acknowledged that a 'dual ballot' system which gave political parties the opportunity to put forward an equal number of female and male candidates on a 50:50 basis was 'the most straightforward way of ensuring equal representation of men and women in the Scottish parliament'. It also noted that in the event of voluntary targets not being reached in the five year period, the Parliamentary Equal Opportunities Commission should re-examine statutory means of ensuring gender balance and fair representation of minorities. In making this recommendation the Commission referred to the UN Charter on the Rights of Women which makes provision for 'temporary special measures' to redress the inequality experienced by women.

The Commission's report was strongly criticised by activists who had campaigned long and hard for a firm and statutory commitment to gender equality for the first Scottish parliament. But it also did not attract endorsement from those supporting a more voluntarist approach. The report had one, perhaps unintended, consequence and that was in bringing women together to put forward an alternative scheme of their own. Talks between women within the two parties and the Women's Coordination Group took place to find an alternative solution to that of the Scottish Constitutional Commission. All involved agreed that it was vital to begin with equal representation because it is much more difficult to reform a political institution once it is well established and parliamentary seats are already occupied. They drew up an Electoral Contract for consideration by the executives and conferences of the Labour and Liberal parties. On the understanding that the Contract would pertain only to the first Scottish parliamentary elections, the parties were asked to endorse the principle that there should be an equal number of men and women members in that parliament. This aim is to be achieved by fielding of an equal number of male and female candidates, the fair distribution of female candidates in winnable seats, and the use of the Additional Member System.[13] It was agreed that the detailed mechanisms for ensuring the selection of an equal number of women in winnable seats, and their distribution between the constituency and list seats, should be left to the discretion of each party.

The consensus reached between Labour and Liberal Democrat women activists reflects the importance they attached to the opportunities which a Scottish parliament could offer. The strategic importance of the new parliament was also reflected in interviews with the women activists both inside and outside the parties. Their vision of a parliament which is located in Scotland, has equal numbers of men and women, a more proportional electoral system, meeting times compatible with family life, payment of carer allowances, and which is more accountable to Scottish society, has acted as a strong mobilising force in campaigns. Women across the party divide and non-party women strongly believed that more women in parliament will make a substantial difference to political life in Scotland. Women would bring their specific life experiences and expertise to the job, and would alter the style of political debate. Often used phrases were 'women are more consensual', 'women are less confrontational and better at getting things done', 'women have a much more open and sharing approach', or 'with more women the whole political ethos would change'. There was also a broad consensus that the policies of a new Scottish parliament would be different with the equal participation of women. The Child Support Act was quoted as legislation which would not have passed through Parliament in its original form if more women had been involved in the drafting. Others cited the influence women would have on education, health and housing policies, in addition to economic and taxation decisions. There was a widely held belief that current policies tend to be seen as 'gender neutral' and thus fail to reflect the specific impact they could have on women's lives. In summary, there was general agreement that politics and political decisions are the poorer for the absence of women.

The view that women have an important contribution to make to political life is not confined to political activists. In an opinion poll survey carried out by ICM for *The Scotsman* in 1994, there was strong support for the proposition that more women should be involved in politics. Of those questioned, 85% agreed that there were not enough women participating in politics, and 76% thought that political parties should make special efforts to involve more women. A majority of 72% believed that governments would make better decisions if more women were in politics, and 75% disagreed with the statement that men are better at politics than women.

It is interesting to note that in their desire for a Scottish parliament with equal representation, the potential problems for women associated with direct involvement in formal political structures appear to have been put in the background by women activists and have ceased to be crucial to the debate. Instead, the key objective has been to put the issue of women's access to political power high on the political agenda in Scotland on the assumption that significantly more women within the parliament will make a difference. The success of women activists in Scotland in achieving their objective has met with some reactions, particularly from some men who consider that their political careers will suffer as a result of women-only short-lists for Westminster and 50:50 gender balance in a Scottish parliament. One male Labour activist is reported as saying that the 'parade of quota queens' would shut-out a whole generation of male politicians. Echoing the fears expressed by men when women campaigned for the right to vote at the beginning of the century, some male activists would appear to fear that more women politicians will 'upset' the political balance and bring instability to the current (predominantly male) structures of power.

Conclusion

It has been demonstrated above that Scottish women are under-represented at the political elite level but are active in politics across different political parties, institutions, organisations and groups. In this respect the women's movement in Scotland is alive and well. In their study of contemporary feminist politics and the influence of the women's movement in Britain, Joni Lovenduski and Vicky Randall put forward the view that the feminist movement had declined, that activists were fewer and that old networks had broken down.[14] However, they observed that Scotland was different and did not fit this pattern as they noted evidence of a resurgence from 1987 onwards. This resurgence can be linked to campaigns for constitutional reform. While in the past, the women's movement in Scotland has very much paralleled the develop-ment of the women's movement in Britain as a whole, as Esther Breitenbach has argued, a distinctive Scottish identity has become more pronounced over time and women have formed new alliances and networks.[15] This can be explained partly as a result of a growing perception of a distinctive Scottish identity more generally and because of the context of the politics of Scotland. In addition, women's involvement in the relatively small political and policy community in Scotland has helped to facilitate the networking between women in different spheres.

Women activists in Scotland have taken part in the broad coalition for constitutional change and have added their voice to the debate. In adopting this strategy, they have been successful in pushing the issue of equal representation high up the political agenda. In Scotland, the real possibility of establishing a completely new parliament has offered a historic political opportunity for the advancement of women, and one in which activists have mobilised in order to ensure gender balance. Recognising the difficulties of reforming an institution once it is established, they have campaigned for equal representation from day one of the parliament. Their concern to begin with a fundamentally different model from Westminster is reflected in their willingness to put aside party, ideological and policy differences in drawing up plans for the first parliament. The consensus is also based on the belief that a Scottish parliament with gender equality will be foster a more representative, accessible, accountable and democratic form of government which will work to the benefit of Scottish society.

The Scottish case illustrates what has been referred to as the 'Third Wave of Feminism',[16] and the way in which women from different political arenas and sections of the women's movement have campaigned together to improve women's representation. They have been successful in combining their knowledge of political institutions and their experiences of autonomous working in other groups and organisations. Working together, they have developed a mutual respect for the contribution and role of different women, and through their activities they have challenged the traditional view that politics is confined to party politics. It can also be argued that they have mounted a challenge to the traditional political culture which has existed in Scotland and which has been hostile to the involvement of women in the formal arenas of power. Through their campaigns, Scottish women have demonstrated a vision of a different kind of politics and have succeeded in laying the foundations for a Scottish parliament with gender equality.

1   E. Breitenbach, 'Sisters are Doing it for Themselves': the Women's Movement in Scotland', in A. Brown and R. Parry (eds), *The Scottish Government Yearbook 1990*, (The Unit for the Study of Government in Scotland, University of Edinburgh). E. Breitenbach, 'Out of Sight, Out of Mind? The History of Women in Scottish Politics', *Scottish Affairs*, Winter 1993. E. Breitenbach, *Quality Through Equality: Good Practice in Equal Opportunities in Scottish Local Authorities,* (EOC, Glasgow, 1995). A. Brown, 'Building a New House' in Y.Ali, C. Ellis and C.Jackson (eds), *A Third Wave of Feminism? Women and Democratic Renewa,* (Penguin, 1995). A. Brown, 'Women and Scottish Politics' in A. Brown, D. McCrone and L. Paterson, *Politics and Society in Scotland,* (Macmillan, 1996). A. Brown and Y. Galligan, 'Changing the Political Agenda for Women in the Republic of Ireland and in Scotland', *West European Politics*, 1993/2. A. Brown and Y. Galligan, 'Why So Few Seats in the House for Irish and Scottish Women?: Women's Views from the Periphery of Europe', paper at PSAI Conference, 1995. S. Henderson and A. Mackay, *Grit and Diamonds: Women in Scotland Making History 1980–1990*

(Strathmullion Ltd and the Cauldron Collective, Edinburgh, 1990). E. Kelly, 'The Future of Women in Scottish Local Government', *Scottish Affairs,* Autumn 1992. E. Kelly, *Sweeties from the Boys' Poke? An Examination of Women's Committees in Scottish Local Government* (MSc thesis, 1995). S. Lieberman, 'Women's Committees in Scotland', in A. Brown and D. McCrone (eds),*The Scottish Government Yearbook 1989,* (Unit for the Study of Government in Scotland). C. Levy, 'Counting Women In' in A. Brown (ed), *Women in Scottish Politics,* Unit for the Study of Government in Scotland, 1991. C. Levy, 'A Woman's Place? The Future Scottish Parliament' in L. Paterson and D. McCrone (eds),*The Scottish Government Yearbook 1992* (Unit for the Study of Government in Scotland).Woman's Claim of Right Group (eds), *A Woman's Claim of Right in Scotland* (Polygon, 1991).

2 See the Gender Audits for 1993, 1994 and 1995 published by Engender, Edinburgh.
3 See J. Osmond (ed), *A Parliament for Wales* (Gomer, 1994), especially ch. 8.
4 See P. Norris and J. Lovenduski, *Political Recruitment: Gender, Race and Class in the British Parliament,* (Cambridge University Press, 1995). For 'supply' and 'demand' factors see also V. Randall, *Women and Politics* (Macmillan, 1987).
5 For the effect of turnover rates see P. Norris, 'Slow Progress for Women MPs', *Parliamentary Brief,* Nov./Dec. 1993. For the Labour Party's policy on quotas see J. Lovenduski, 'Will Quotas Make Labour More Woman-Friendly?', *Renewal,* 1994/1.
6 For the general election result in Scotland see, J. Mitchell, 'The 1992 Election in Scotland in Context', and L. Paterson, A. Brown and D. McCrone, 'Constitutional Crisis: The Causes and Consequences of the 1992 Scottish General Election Result', both *Parliamentary Affairs,* 1992, 4.
7 See A. Brown in Ali, Ellis and Jackson, *A Third Wave of Feminism?,* 'Plans for a Scottish Parliament: Did Women Make a Difference?' (Waverley Paper, Department of Politics, University of Edinburgh, 1995).
8 Woman's Claim of Right Group, op.cit.
9 E. Breitenbach, 'Sisters are Doing it for Themselves', loc.cit and C. Levy, 'A Woman's Place', loc.cit.
10 See discussion in Brown, McCrone and Paterson, 1996, op.cit.
11 See model outlined in Brown and Galligan, 1993, op.cit.
12 See A Brown, 'Plans for a Scottish Parliament: Have Women Made a Difference?', Paper at Gender and Power Workshop, ECPR (University of Limerick, 1992).
13 For the Electoral Contract see A. Brown, 'The Scotswoman's Parliament', in *Parliamentary Brief,* April 1995.
14 See J. Lovenduski and V. Randall, *Contemporary Feminist Politics* (Oxford University Press, 1993).
15 See E. Breitenbach, 'Sisters are Doing it for Themselves', loc.cit.
16 See Ali, Ellis and Jackson op.cit.

This article draws in part on A. Brown, D. McCrone and L. Paterson, *Politics and Society in Scotland* (Macmillan, 1996).

Women and Politics in Northern Ireland

BY RICK WILFORD

DESPITE periodic efforts to forge a common front, the women's movement in Northern Ireland has foundered over the mutually reinforcing cleavages of nationality and religion that structure its political alignments.[1] Yet the cessation of violence following the cease-fires of 1994 has raised the possibility of a more stable polity within which 'normal' politics can develop. Among other things, this altered, if fragile, situation creates the opportunity for strategic coalitions of women to emerge campaigning on issues previously marginalised by 'high' policy, even forging a wider unity among women.

Recent research suggests that such a widened opportunity is welcome.[2] There is, for example, a demand for increased political representation by women and a belief that if elected in sufficient numbers, they can make a difference to politics in the province: a view shared by the region's women councillors.[3] Moreover, there is a widespread perception among women of all religious and political persuasions that the political parties in Northern Ireland have failed them, as well as broad support among women (and men) for a liberal feminist agenda. This, however, falls short of the endorsement of a pro-choice position on the abortion issue: on matters of body/sexual politics, women in Northern Ireland generally embrace more conservative attitudes than their cohorts in the more secular climate of Britain.[4]

Findings from the study of women's political participation in Northern Ireland indicate that while gender gaps do exist, women are more like men than they are different, at least in terms of their rates of participation. This is consistent with the 'revisionist' theory of political participation outlined by Pippa Norris.[5] There is evidence, however, that their modes and arenas of political activity are somewhat different. In that respect, there is support for the 'radical' theory of participation, also outlined by her, which suggests that women are active in relatively unstructured, fragmented and transitory groups normally neglected by mainstream studies of political participation. Before discussing such findings, a brief survey of the historical and cultural context of Northern Ireland will serve to situate women in its public realm.

The context of history and culture

Since its inception, Northern Ireland has been a divided society within which politics has resembled a proxy war which has infused the terms of political debate with martial, thus, 'manly', virtues, epitomised in the republican camp by the 'ballot and bullet' strategy and on the loyalist side in the slogan 'not an inch, no surrender'. The salience of competing national aspirations has inhibited other distinctions of identity, lending a zero-sum character to its politics, 'if *they* win, *we* lose'. Whether nationalist, republican, loyalist or unionist, women in general, and feminists in particular, have discovered that debate about citizenship has revolved around national identity, leaving little scope for consideration of its gendered dimensions.

The political instability and inter-communal violence of Northern Ireland do not provide an auspicious context for women's entry to the realms of politics. While they have never achieved parity of representation in any political system, deeply divided societies appear particularly uncongenial. Mooted or actual linkages between paramilitary organisations and political parties, coupled with the readiness to sanction force, tend to consolidate the male dominance of public spaces in such societies. Though not providing a sufficient explanation, such conditions do contribute to the conspicuous absence of women from elected office.

Armed patriarchy in Northern Ireland has to some extent been attenuated by the active involvement of women in paramilitary organisations, especially within the republican movement, but this has not resolved the historically unhappy marriage between feminism and Irish nationalism. While the formal claim to socialist credentials espoused by Irish republicanism creates the ideological space for a commitment to gender equality, not all women in the republican movement are persuaded that this is taken seriously. Similarly, the status of women within the unionist tradition has been an historically subordinate one. Its conservatism, expressed most obviously in its determination to maintain the constitutional status quo, has spilled over into gender relations: the province's unionist parties have paid scant attention to women's issues, while loyalist paramilitarism has remained an almost exclusively male activity.

The martial character of politics in Northern Ireland, together with the influence exerted by differing cultural and religious traditions, generate gender differences in political interest and participation, and also different levels of interest and participation among women. These were precisely the conclusions in Inglehart's comparative study of women in eight west European nations.[6] She found that the cultural legacy of the 'hierarchical', 'authoritarian' and 'anti-feminist' Catholic Church and/or a national history of militarism served to depress levels of political interest among women, while the absence of military tradition and/or the stress on equality found in Protestantism was associated with higher levels of interest.

Such findings have more than a passing relevance for Northern Ireland. A militarised national history, a 'paramilitarised' present and the presence of a large Catholic minority (almost 40%), offer a test of

Inglehart's hypotheses: women in the province should generally exhibit lower levels of interest in politics than men; those who profess faith in an ostensibly egalitarian Protestantism should be more interested and active than Catholic women. These propositions are not supported by the results of the study of women's political participation, however.

Despite the active involvement of women in the struggle for Irish independence, feminists were particularly ill-served by the nationalist movement. The roots of the unhappy marriage between feminism and nationalism and, latterly, republicanism, were laid well before partition. Encouraged by the apparent promise of the Easter Rising of 1916 to deliver equality for all, feminists quickly recognised that Irish national-ism was inhospitable to their demands.[7] The Irish Constitution of 1937 celebrated De Valera's vision of a Catholic, predominantly rural, state in which women were expected to pursue their wifely and maternal duties within the home.

The legacy of that experience endures. While both the Provisional IRA and Sinn Fein accorded full equality to the women in their ranks during the early 1970s, feminists within the contemporary republican movement are by no means confident that their agenda is an integral element of its wider project. One contributor to a recent publication from Sinn Fein's Women's Department, reflecting on the mobilisation of women during the hunger strikes of 1980 and 1981, notes that the 'sense of purpose, of solidarity and common cause' that they generated was swiftly dispersed, and that while women in the republican move-ment 'always fought alongside our brothers without preconditions, men's support for women's demands has always been conditional'.[8]

A Sinn Fein councillor comments that 'equality within our republican communities is still something that politically active women have to achieve'. Acknowledging end to partition as key priority, at the same time she insists that 'gender-based inequality must also be fought against now; we must recognise that the struggle for women's liberation is an integral part of that overall struggle against oppression'. The unreflec-tive faith of an earlier nationalist leader (and the first woman to be elected to the Westminster Parliament), Countess Markievicz — 'fix your minds on the idea of Ireland free, with her women enjoying the full rights of citizenship in their own nation' — is not shared by contempor-ary feminist republicans: having 'borne the brunt of Britain's war in Ireland', they are not prepared to wait on their 'brothers' and risk the fate of their predecessors.

The historic secondary status of women in the nationalist and republican movements is mirrored within the unionist/loyalist tradition. Confronted by the prospect of home rule, in 1912 the Irish Unionists demonstrated their willingness to engage in rebellion by devising the Ulster Covenant whose signatories committed themselves to defend the union by force: women were only permitted to sign a Women's Declaration which obliged them to support the 'uncompromising opposition of the men of Ulster'. This helpmate role was reflected in the newly-formed Ulster Women's Unionist Council, whose primary objective was the maintenance of the Union between Great Britain and Ireland to which 'all other questions in which individual members may be specially interested shall be subordinated'. Included among these was female suffrage.

Though eventually enfranchised, the lesson for women was that their rights were secondary to the imperatives of territorial politics, despite the fact that many were prepared to, and some did, fight either for the retention of the union or the creation of an independent Ireland. While women in Northern Ireland were spared the formally subordinate status imposed by the Irish Constitution of 1937, they too have faced formidable obstacles preventing their full enjoyment of equal citizenship. They were confronted by a bar to married women in the public service that persisted until the late 1960s, while their participation in the work force has not only been subject to the wearingly familiar patterns of occupational segregation but their rates of economic activity have been historically low and still lag approximately 10% behind the UK. Additionally, the double-burden carried by women is shown by the unequal division of domestic labour, influenced in part by the fact that Northern Ireland has the lowest level of publicly funded childcare provision in the UK.

The unresolved national question; the readiness to resort to violence; the doctrinal and institutional patriarchy of the Catholic Church; the resilience of a traditional model of gender relations among ministers and ordinands within the two largest non-Catholic denominations (the Church of Ireland and the Presbyterian Church); together with the inclemency of both nationalist and unionist movements to feminism— all have combined to create a formidable set of hurdles in the path of women seeking entry to the public realm. This is amply borne out in relation to elected office.

Elected and appointed office

The creation of Northern Ireland in 1920 established a new political regime with its own 52-seat Parliament. Between 1921 and 1969 there were twelve general elections to Stormont, attracting a total of 1,008 candidacies, of which 37 were female. Together with a further six at by-elections, over the course of almost half a century there was a total of 43 female candidacies shared among twenty women, nine of whom were elected (six Unionists, of whom Dame Dehra Parker, returned six times, was the only woman to serve as a minister). Never constituting more than 6% of candidates, no more than four women were returned to any one of the dozen Parliaments. At the final election in 1969 the proportion of female candidates dwindled to 2%, matching the paltry level achieved at the first held almost fifty years before. Male monopoly was thus all the more apparent when sectarian tension and conflict escalated, as was the case at both the Parliament's birth and its eventual demise.

Following the imposition of direct rule in 1972, the British governments made three attempts to create region-wide institutions intended to promote the principle of power-sharing between the two communities. Each of these failed institutions, the Assembly of 1973–74, the Constitutional Convention of 1975–76 and the Assembly of 1982–86, had 78 members elected by STV, and each mustered only four women members.

The situation described above is only marginally bettered at local authority level. In the wake of direct rule, the discredited local government system was subjected to wholesale reform, leaving the councils with a residue of minor and uncontroversial functions. STV elections to the 26 District Councils, first contested in 1973, are held every four years. Since 1977, when reliable candidate data first became available, the total number of women contesting local elections has shown a modest upward trend.

1: NI Local Government Elections

	Seats	Total Candidates	Women Candidates		Women Elected	
1977	526	1002	95	9.5%	38	7.2%
1981	526	982	107	10.9%	42	8.0%
1985	566	994	109	11.0%	55	9.7%
1989	566	905	128	14.1%	64	11.3%
1993	582	933	132	14.1%	70	12.0%

The increased representation by women in local government can not be explained in terms of the adoption of 'women-friendly' selection procedures. According to the 1989 intake of women councillors, the residual role of local government has deterred men from seeking candidacy, a perception confirmed by the decline in party competition at local elections from 1.9 to 1.6 candidates per seat between 1977 and 1993. The parties have, the councillors believe, turned to women merely to complete their slates.

This dismal picture of local and regional representation is surpassed at the national level. At the seven general elections of the interwar period, there were no women candidates for Northern Ireland's twelve Westminster seats, while at the 14 postwar elections only 42 women have stood, one-third in 1992 (the number of seats was increased to 17 in 1983). Just three have been elected: two Ulster Unionists, Patricia Ford and Patricia McLaughlin (1953–1955 and 1955–1964 respectively) and Bernadette Devlin (1969–1974). Until 1994, when there were five candidates, Bernadette Devlin (McAliskey) was, in 1979, the only woman to have run for one of the province's three European seats.

The bleakness of this record is redeemed to some extent by the exercise of patronage. An American study suggests that appointment as a method of selection for public office tends to favour women, partly because it has become increasingly difficult for those dispensing patronage to rationalise their exclusion and partly for the social benefit gained from gender balance in public appointments. It also suggests that women are better represented in appointed positions because these are 'usually less politically important than elected positions'.[9] However, this proposition applies less well in Northern Ireland.

The demotion of local authorities required the creation of a wide array of nominated bodies to administer services they had formerly provided. Expressly designed to be free of sectarianism and to ensure the efficient administration of public housing, education, health and the personal social services, besides monitoring the implementation of legislation to combat sex and religious discrimination, these bodies are invested with great symbolic, as well as practical, significance. Their membership is determined by the Northern Ireland Office, whose successive ministerial teams have used their powers of patronage to the benefit of women. Between 1991 and 1995, for instance, the proportion of women serving on the province's 128 nominated bodies increased from 25% to 32%. Appointment, rather than election, has proved a surer route to numerical representation.

Political participation

Women have not, of course, had to rely on appointed office to make their presence felt; they have also proved adept at movement politics, whether as deliberate or accidental activists. Before the renewal of sectarian violence in the late 1960s, for example, women were prominent in the formation of the Campaign for Social Justice in 1964; the Northern Ireland Civil Rights Association established in 1967; and People's Democracy, the radical, student-led group formed in 1968. Since the outbreak of 'the troubles', they have also been active in organisations that constitute a response to the pathologies of Northern Ireland. They were, for instance, instrumental in launching the campaign for denominationally integrated schools and in establishing groups opposed to the rough 'justice' ('punishment' beatings and shootings) meted out by both republican and loyalist paramilitaries.

The most pronounced, if fleeting, impact made by women en masse was associated with the Women's Peace Movement—subsequently the Peace People—which emerged in 1976. Prompted by the deaths of three children in a troubles-related incident, one of its founders struck the note that became the movement's leitmotif: 'I believe it is time for the women to have a go and see what the women of both sides, working together, can do.'[10] The campaign swiftly attracted international recognition, culminating in 1977 with the award of the Nobel Peace Prize to its co-founders. Here it seemed was the effective answer to 'the troubles', one, moreover, which prized an association of women with nonviolence. Within three years, however, the movement was in disarray. Accused by republicans of being pro-British because of its refusal to condemn the violence of the security forces, riven by internal disputes over policy and the focus of widespread criticism over the allocation of the Nobel Prize money, its support ebbed away. The unhappy circumstances of its decline are, though, perhaps less significant than the gender stereotype it appeared to perpetuate. The close identity of women with the Peace People fed an image of them as peace-makers. Yet, while the link between women and non-violence implies moral strength, it can also be interpreted as a measure of powerlessness.

Less dramatic than the emergence of the Peace People is the quiet growth of a wide range of voluntary bodies organised by and for women.[11] In plugging the gaps of an inadequate welfare regime, many have an instrumental purpose — rape crisis centres, legal advice centres, refuges, mother and toddler groups, for instance. But they also serve expressive and communitarian functions. The survey of women's political participation in Northern Ireland shows that women are significantly more likely than men to be actively involved in a wide range of charitable, communal, voluntary and church-related organisations that 'can be seen as political since ... they address policy issues of public concern',[12] even if in an indirect way. That they are engaged in such half-hidden arenas does tend to buttress the assumptions of the radical theory of political participation, not least that women participate differently from, rather than less than men. While men are more likely than women to engage both in conventional forms of political activity (party or pressure group membership, employment-related organisations, contacting behaviour) and in unconventional forms (petitioning, letter writing, various forms of protests, boycotts), such differences are not statistically significant. Gender in Northern Ireland is not a reliable predictor of political participation: neither is one's religious affiliation. The more politically active or interested are the highly educated, those with a high occupational status and those in their middle years, irrespective of sex, religious beliefs or stated national identity.

The definition of political participation employed in the study was an expansive one, encompassing activities in both the domestic and the public realms, thereby incorporating direct and indirect attempts to influence policy makers. The inclusion of the domestic realm created the opportunity to explore its interactions with the public realm. The family emerged, especially among women, as a primary and, in the context of Northern Ireland, safe venue for the discussion of politics. Another family-based index of political participation concerned the socialisation of children, especially in relation to the promotion of civic (or uncivic) virtues. Women appear as moral arbiters, particularly in terms of the transmission of religious beliefs and attitudes concerning sexual equality and behaviour: men appear to vacate these areas, concentrating instead on imparting their preferred partisan identity to their children.

In exploring the family, whether in relation to the discussion of politics, the division of domestic labour, the management of household finances, the socialisation of children or the reciprocal influence of spouses on each other's beliefs and political activities, it is evident that 'like attracts like'. The most politically active, whether women or men, are commonly the partners of equally participative individuals. This mutual support lends another dimension to the aphorism that the personal is political, as does the finding that children in the household can act as a spur rather than an impediment to participation by women, especially concerning activities connected to their secular and religious education.

'Communitarianism'

Qualitative data from the study also shows that women's greater involvement in voluntary, charitable and church-related groups is motivated primarily by the search for personal fulfilment and the desire to be socially useful. The latter is consistent with the argument that 'where people are highly integrated into the local community and where they identify strongly with it, participation would be greater'.[13] Underlying this motive are feelings of interdependence, neighbourliness and an awareness of shared needs believed to be characteristic of small, tightly-knit societies.

Northern Ireland is a small society within which political identities remain sharply drawn. While mutual suspicion has tended to accentuate difference, among highly participative women there is an acknowledgement of a nascent community of women's interests. Even 'diehards' find little difficulty in asserting the existence of a 'sisterhood' within the province, albeit one that chimes with notions of female essentialism and resonates with traditional assumptions about gendered family roles. As a respondent puts it: 'Women are far more tolerant and it's inbred — it must have something to do with our chromosomes or something. Bringing up children has a lot to do with it because you've got to listen to their tantrums and take both sides.' Another self-defined 'dyed-in-the-wool' unionist also subscribes to a belief in a shared identity: 'There is a sisterhood here, just by being a woman even. Women don't ask other women who they are and where they're from, they mix better: men don't.' This appears consistent with Hedlund's dualistic portrayal of women's culture as an 'invisible sphere suppressed in the world of men' but which 'carries a potential for change and liberation that effects the entire society'.[14] There is a negative dimension, implied by the image of a keening mother Ireland shouldering the miseries inflicted by men, and a more positive aspect: unencumbered by sectarianism, women are believed to possess a clearer vision of a 'solution', focused both by their oppression and the experience of motherhood. Each respondent embodied the dovetailing of self and other-directedness that is characteristic of many women in Northern Ireland who are highly active in more broadly defined, less formal, public realms.

Such motives among activist women suggest they are able to negotiate, if not slough off completely, the divisions of a segmented society. While male activists tend to engage in intra-communal activities, activist women are more likely to voice a woman-centred grasp of the concept of community. The finding that women activists tend to occupy a civic space poised between the formal realms of politics and the domestic arena might be interpreted as a means of rationalising their absence from elected office: necessity proving, as it were, the mother of political invention. This, though, would be to devalue the positive orientations many bring to the more submerged arenas of political participation. Equally, this marginal terrain may seem, in the Northern Ireland context, to be safer ground upon which to become engaged in the public realm. But though activist women tend to regard female identity as conferring the advantage of relative physical safety, they do not believe it provides a badge of immunity either for themselves or their families.

Women and party offices

Nor are women deterred by any perceived risks of a more formal involvement in politics, even though most have experienced 'the troubles' at first hand. Almost two-thirds of all women respondents wish to see more women in Parliament and on local councils (compared to half of men). There is also widespread evidence of disillusion with the parties. Asked which of the parties best serve the interests of women, almost two-thirds of women answered none (an opinion shared by a little under half the men), while just under two-thirds of women (and half of men) agreed that the region's parties do not give women the opportunity to enter politics. Such findings direct attention to party strategies concerning the selection of candidates and the extent of office-holding by women within the parties.

2: **Female Party Membership (1995)**

Alliance Party	50%
Ulster Unionist	42%
Social Democratic and Labour	47%
Sinn Fein	33%

Note: The DUP failed to respond to requests for information.

With the exception of the Alliance Party (APNI), which has a spokesperson on women's issues, each of the major parties from which information was obtained has a dedicated 'women's section'. The oldest of these is the Ulster Unionist Party's (UUP) Ulster Women's Unionist Council established in 1911. This is organised on a constituency basis and delegates members to the party's 900-member Council. The key policy-making body, however, is the 120-strong Executive Committee (elected by members of the constituency associations), with 18 women. In total, there are 120 constituency offices, 27 currently held by women, including two constituency association chairmen (sic.). All of the UUP's 14 full-time party office holders are male.

The APNI is one of two that has been chaired by a woman (the other is the SDLP). Currently four women sit on its 12-member Executive. Six of its 23 local associations (based on District electoral areas) are chaired by women; ten treasurers and ten secretaries are also women. Like the UUP, the Alliance Party makes no provision for positive discrimination on behalf of women. Unlike the UUP, however, which restricts itself to a strategy of exhortation, it does embrace positive action in the form of training seminars for potential candidates.

The SDLP has six full-time party officers, one of whom (the party's administrator) is a woman. There are six women on its 15-member Executive, including the chair of its newly reorganised Women's Group which provides training and development courses for women interested in standing for election to public or party office. This positive action strategy has recently been complemented by the introduction of a quota system for party offices. At a special delegate conference in June 1995, it was agreed to guarantee 40% of places on the Executive to women and to reserve at least two places for women councillors on a new General Council responsible for developing party policy.

Until the SDLP's recent change, Sinn Fein was the only party to employ a gender quota for the election of its National Executive and other committees. Currently, there are nine women on its 24 member Executive. Two of Sinn Fein's five-member team presently negotiating with the Northern Ireland Office are women, including the party's General Secretary, Lucilita Bhreatnach, as are two of its five delegates/alternates to the Dublin-based Forum for Peace and Reconciliation. Internally, the party is organised into nine departments, six of which have female directors. It is currently examining the possibility of gender quotas in candidate selection.

Policy issues

While differing over provision for internal representation by women, in policy terms the parties tend to converge around a more or less developed 'gender recognition strategy' by focusing upon the particular obstacles impeding women's equality.[15] However, the attention devoted to gender issues by the parties shows considerable variation.

The SDLP has not produced a policy document on women since 1976, while its manifestos for the 1992 Westminster and the 1994 European Parliament elections offered few concrete proposals for the achievement of equal rights. Its Euro-manifesto couched its appeal to women in a brief statement which reiterated the commitment to pursue equal rights adopted by the Parliamentary Group of the Party of European Socialists to which it belongs. This agenda includes the strict application of the principle of equal pay for equal work, equal treatment within the social security system, equality of opportunity in education, training and employment, and the availability of childcare to all those who need it.

The province's largest party, the UUP, has published even less. Its

Policy Statement on Women's Issues produced for the 1992 general election, less than two pages long, affirmed support for existing legislation against sex discrimination and endorsed the principle of equal pay for equal work and the statutory provision of pregnancy and maternity rights consistent with the Treaty of Rome. In addition, it proposed the extension of tax concessions to encourage childcare facilities in the workplace and endorsed improved educational access designed to 'encourage girls to achieve in areas which have traditionally been male-dominated'. Such proposals were entirely consistent with its belief in 'a society of equal opportunity' and its explicit rejection of positive discrimination.

The Democratic Unionist Party (DUP) included a short (86-word) statement on women's issues in its 1992 manifesto, acknowledging that 'women are a majority and should no longer be treated as a minority'. To that end, and alone of the parties, it called for the creation of a 'Ministry for Women' whose remit would include the promotion of equal pay and pensions, improved maternity rights, a parental leave scheme and expanded childcare provision facilitated by tax relief. More a series of slogans than a set of policy proposals, equal prominence in its manifesto was given to the 'fight for family and moral values' which was focused on its (failed) campaign to prevent the opening of a Brook Advisory Centre in Belfast on the grounds that it would undermine parental authority and family values.

3: 'Which Party in Northern Ireland Best Represents the Interests of Women?'

	Own	Other	None
UUP	27.2%	13.5%	59.3%
DUP	21.5%	19.1%	59.4%
APNI	36.9%	8.6%	54.5%
SDLP	32.9%	14.9%	52.2%
Sinn Fein	10.5%	31.2%	58.3%

The party with the most expansive set of policies for women is Sinn Fein. Its proposals, contained in 'Women in Ireland', are addressed to both parts of the island and are sustained by a concern to empower women in the public and private realms and by its belief that 'gender and social class are the two most important determinants of a person's life-chances'. The discourse of the policy document is woman-centred although it inclines to a maternalist perspective: 'Present economic and social structures are built around the life cycles of men. Women's life-cycles are different; changes will have to reflect the needs of women as mothers, within the family, as well as their right to participate fully in all the economic, social and political aspects of society.' It proposes a statutory minimum wage, equal pay for work of equal value, the abolition of mandatory retirement ages, the extension of maternity leave on full pay, the provision of free comprehensive childcare, and the introduction of positive action programmes 'to enable women to get

access to education and retraining, especially in non-traditional occupations'. Consistent with its wider project, it assets that the rights of
women to full equality will only be secured with the ending of partition
and the creation of a 32-County Socialist Republic.

The APNI's policy paper, 'Women's Issues', is steeped in an equal
rights philosophy fully consistent with its membership of the Federation
of European Liberal, Democratic and Reform Parties. Endorsing equality of opportunity for men and women at all levels of society, like the
other parties it proposes the expansion of nursery and childcare
provision and supports equal pay for equal work. It, too, sets it face
against positive discrimination measures on behalf of women, preferring
to endorse a variety of positive action measures intended to encourage
women to compete for training and employment opportunities.

Conclusion

The shared sensitivity among the parties to the constraints impeding
women's enjoyment of equal rights, notably those associated with
parenthood, is consistent with the gender recognition strategy identified
by Chamberlayne in relation to social policy.[16] While none of the parties
ignore the specificity of women's position by adopting a gender neutral
approach, there is little to indicate their awareness of a gender recon-
struction strategy which stresses the need to change men's roles. The
clear tilt of the parties towards gender recognition is, however, tempered
by lingering evidence of a more conservative gender reinforcement
approach. The common emphasis on maternity rights, the Alliance
Party's stress on value and respect for those who work in the home, the
UUP's emphasis on the family unit, the DUP's trenchant defence of
family values, together with more than a hint of mother-centredness in
Sinn Fein's proposals, are each symptomatic of a more traditional, pro-
family view of women's roles.

The survey of women's political participation within the province
also disclosed high levels of support for a gender recognition strategy,
indicating a broad congruence between female voters and their preferred
parties. This, however, raises an apparent anomaly. If there is symmetry
between the stated policy preferences of the parties and popular
attitudes concerning women's rights, why does a significant majority of
women believe that no party adequately represents their interests?

The affinity between the parties and the various blocs of women
voters concerning the endorsement of gender recognition policies suggests that the failings of the parties are seen to reside elsewhere, notably
in relation to the constitutional issue. In particular, the participation
study demonstrates that it is the unwillingness of male politicians to
reach a political settlement that creates a sense of unrepresentation.
This does not mean that women believe themselves to be less, or men
more, principled on this priority issue, rather that the 'ruthlessness' and
'ambition' of male politicians frustrates compromise. The disposition to

seek consensus is regarded by both sexes within the general population to be characteristic of female, not male, politicians.

There is also evidence indicating the existence of a shared agenda among women in the province, the neglect of which contributes to disillusion with the parties. Women of all political persuasions and none were critical of the tendency of male politicians to ignore everyday problems, commonly citing education, the health service, childcare, unemployment and the care of the elderly as issues that languished below the high politics of the constitutional question.

The frequency with which politically active women are clustered into voluntary bodies involved with health, education and welfare matters tends to confirm the salience of such issues for them. On the one hand, this could be construed as the exercise of self-interest: women are seeking to ameliorate the inadequacies of the welfare regime for primarily instrumental reasons. On the other hand, it may be rationalised as an instance of faut de mieux: tucked into the folds of 'the troubles', women participate in such organisations because they have nowhere else to go. Both interpretations diminish the motives that underpin such activities. The reward of self-fulfilment, allied to the desire to be socially useful, is consistent with Hedlund's delineation of the positive aspects of women's culture: an emphasis on connectedness, on care for others, and a behavioural style that is cooperative and unaggressive, suggesting that women are not wholly powerless but rather enact distinctive values that are independent of the male world and not merely compensatory to it.[17]

The mobilisation of such values seems especially appropriate at a moment when Northern Ireland may be inching towards an established peace and perhaps even a political settlement. This is not to imply that women, unlike men, have the future in their bones, nor that they are more likely to regard the past as a foreign country. The prospect, for instance, that like women in Scotland (see Brown in this volume) they can combine to ensure parity of representation in a new regional assembly is, if not entirely idle, rather more remote: the weight of history still bears heavily on the present among both women and men. There are, however, increasing signs that parity of esteem for women is being actively pursued by new organisations seeking to ensure that they are included fully in any talks designed to secure a political settlement.

Whether or not more women would make a positive difference remains untested. Yet, the popular belief that women politicians are inclined towards compromise, the frequency with which communitarianism informs women's motives for political participation, and the desire for more women in public office offer a challenging vision. But, as Joni Lovenduski reminds us, attempts to increase their presence in elected office will continue to rest largely on the efforts of women themselves.[18] And while there is a growing demand by women's groups for inclusion in the peace process, the very fragility of the cease-fire, together with the record of the parties, suggest that for the foreseeable future male dominance will prevail in the province's public realms.

The study of women's political participation cited in the text was conducted by the author, R. L. Miller, F. Donoghue and Y. Bell between 1991 and 1993. The quantitative data is based on a sample of 1402 women and 384 men, the qualitative data on interviews with sub-sets of the politically active and inactive. The concurrent study of women councillors was conducted by the same team.

1   See E. Evason, *Against the Grain* (Attic Press, 1991); M. McWilliams, 'Women in Northern Ireland: An Overview' in E. Hughes (ed), *Culture and Politics in Northern Ireland* (Open University Press, 1991); M. Ward, *A Difficult, Dangerous Honesty* (Belfast Women's Book Collective, 1987); C. Loughran, 'Armagh and Feminist Strategy' in T. Lovell (ed) *British Feminist Thought* (Basil Blackwell, 1990).
2   R. Miller, R. Wilford and F. Donoghue, *Women and Political Participation in Northern Ireland* (Avebury, 1996).
3   R. Wilford et al, 'In Their Own Voices: Women Councillors in Northern Ireland', *Public Administration*, Autumn 1993.
4   P. Montgomery and C. Davies, 'A Woman's Place in Northern Ireland' in P. Stringer and G. Robinson (eds), *Social Attitudes in Northern Ireland* (Blackstaff Press, 1991).
5   P. Norris, 'Gender Differences in Political Participation in Britain: Traditional, Radical and Revisionist Models', *Government and Opposition*, Winter 1991.
6   M. Inglehart, 'Political Interest in West European Women: An Historical and Empirical Comparative Analysis', *Comparative Political Studies*, October 1981.
7   M. Ward, *Unmanageable Revolutionaries: Women and Irish Nationalism*(Pluto Press, 1983); M. Ward, *In Our Own Voices* (Attic Press, 1995).
8   Sinn Fein Women's Department, *Women in Struggle: 25 Years of Resistance* (Sinn Fein, 1994).
9   R. Darcy, S. Welch and J. Clark, *Women, Elections and Representation* (University of Nebraska Press, 2e,1994).
10 Mairead Corrigan, quoted in P. Bew and G. Gillespie, *Northern Ireland: A Chronology of the Troubles, 1968–1993* (Gill and Macmillan, 1994).
11 R. Taillon, *Directory of Women's Organisations in Northern Ireland* (Women's Support Network, 1992), listing 197 organisations throughout the province.
12 P. Norris, loc.cit.
13 G. Parry, G. Moyser and N. Day, *Political Participation and Democracy in Britain* (Cambridge University Press, 1992).
14 G. Hedlund, 'Women's Interests in Local Politics' in K. B. Jones and A. G. Jonasdottir (eds), *The Political Interests of Gender* (Sage, 1988), p. 13.
15 P. Chamberlayne, 'Women and the State: Changes in Roles and Rights in France, West Germany, Italy and Britain, 1970–1990' in J. Lewis (ed), *Women and Social Policies in Europe* (Edward Elgar, 1993).
16 Chamberlayne, loc.cit., pp. 172–5.
17 Hedlund, loc.cit., p. 13.
18 'Introduction' in J. Lovenduski and P. Norris (eds), *Gender and Party Politics* (Sage, 1993).

The Politics of the Women's Movement

BY PAUL BYRNE

WOMEN have had a significant role to play in British politics through-out this century, but that significance has fluctuated. Whilst there have been times when women's rights, opportunities and status have been politically salient, there have also been lengthy periods when such issues were not on the agenda of those with influence in the political system. It can be argued that women have only figured as a significant political issue in British politics either when politicians have perceived a particu-lar need for women's active involvement in economic and social life (as, for example, during the second world war) or when women have forced their concerns onto the agenda. In the latter instance, it is generally accepted that there have been waves of political mobilisation by women—the first wave being the suffragette movement which peaked between 1900 and 1914, and the second wave espousing the ideology of feminism[1] from the late sixties to the present.

As the other contributions in this volume make clear, there have been significant legislative changes over the last three decades—for example abortion reform, equal pay, employment protection, the creation of the Equal Opportunities Commission and the Sex Discrimination Act. Over the last decade both Labour and the Liberal Democrats have made commitments which (if realised) will make far-reaching changes to the presence and impact of women in parliamentary politics. As important, the issues raised by feminist analysis and prescriptions have entered into virtually all aspects of political, economic and social life. This is not to say that everyone has accepted arguments advanced by feminism, but it is hard to imagine circumstances in which anyone is not aware of at least some of the basic issues raised. In short, there has been substantial cultural as well as political change.

Establishing causality is a notoriously difficult undertaking, but from a conventional pluralist viewpoint it is tempting to assume there must be some kind of direct causal relationship at work here. On the one hand we have a dramatic upturn since the 1960s in the scope and variety of collective action on the part of women, and on the other we have significant political and cultural changes. Yet the relationship is ambiguous. In broad terms, the 1970s was an era in which women created the loosely linked network of activities and ideas that became known as the women's liberation movement. As we shall see, however, this devoted most of its energies to activities inside the movement rather than outside lobbying; and in any case some of the most significant legislative milestones actually preceded the time when it was at its most vibrant. During the 1980s and into the nineties, the commonly accepted picture is one of this movement disintegrating and fragmenting, and yet this is the time when women have made a real impact upon the mainstream politics of political parties, trade unions and local authorities. This is not to imply that there is no relationship between women's collective action and societal change, but it does suggest that the form this collective action has taken requires an analytical perspective other than that provided by conventional pressure group theory.

Such a perspective is provided by the concept of social movements, and it is generally accepted that this is the most useful approach not only for the rise of second-wave feminism across the developed world, but also for apparently similar mobilisations like the peace and environmental movements. One can discern significantly different perspectives within the overall conceptualisation of social movements—an American and a European perspective—and this gives rise to different assessments of the success or failure of the women's movement, and its future prospects. Both perspectives need to be integrated with conventional pressure group theory if we are to reach the best possible understanding of this contemporary phenomenon.

The concept of a social movement has been used rather indiscriminately over the last thirty years, applied to anything from localised protests over single issues within a particular country to ideological standpoints which have had global impact. A movement does not have the clear boundaries of a party or group, and social covers all aspects of behaviour from the public and collective to the private and personal. Here we are taking the term to mean a new social movement (post-1960s, as distinct from late nineteenth/early twentieth century movements), with its defining features to be grounded in ideological, organisational and tactical characteristics. Ideological, in that social movements are challengers which seek to change the agenda of the system within which they work. They advance ideas which, to be realised, would require fundamental and widespread change in policies and in values—change which may be partially achieved through government action and legislation but can not be wholly achieved in this way. They raise issues which question the dominant values that constitute the political culture of their society, and hence have a 'political' and a 'cultural' dimension. They aim to change people's attitudes and behaviour on a personal as well as public level. Thus, for example, environmental movements campaign not only on specific issues amenable to state action (pollution, renewable energy resources) but also question the basic values of developed industrial society which assume the innate desirability of economic growth and technological progress. The women's movement encompasses both those who equate feminism with equal opportunities and parity of representation in established institutions, and those who believe its central concern to be the struggle against patriarchy (in its public and private manifestations) and the recognition of difference rather than just equality in contemporary society.

Organisational: although social movements may have groups within them that are formally structured—movements as a whole are not formally organised. As Diani has argued from a European perspective, social movements are networks of interaction between different actors which may either include formal organisations or not, depending on shifting circumstances.[2] The key concept is networks of interaction; movements come about when people get together and, through interaction that may be on a one-to-one basis, within a group or between groups, come to share the same values and outlooks. Networks are the basis on which movements are built, and they perform different kinds of functions—as means of teaching people about the values of the movement and reinforcing solidarity, as well as the more obvious functions of exchanging information and organising activities.

Tactical: if there is one characteristic which sets movements apart from other forms of political action, it lies in what they do. All movements engage in at least some action outside of the institutional or legal channels of political access. We can not talk of completely clear-cut boundaries here; parties and conventional interest groups will occasionally engage in campaigns or even (at least in the case of interest groups) protest actions. On the whole, however, their energies are concentrated upon the established channels of access and influence— Parliament, local government, the civil service. Social movements casts their nets much more widely. They also will seek to influence the political elites through lobbying and persuasion, but this only ever represents a part of their efforts, often quite a minor part. Their prime target is the population as whole, and their actions are often unfocused, in that they are more akin to 'bearing witness' in public about their particular values or beliefs than aimed at influencing certain decision-makers over particular policies.

In short, the concept of a social movement allows us to capture the important characteristics of the particular kind of collective action that is the women's movement. It directs our attention not only to the more visible and formally organised dimension of action, ranging from participation in major political parties to protest and demonstrations, but also to the informal and much less visible—the development of new perspectives on self and society which impact upon personal and private behaviour or relationships. This is necessary, given the ways in which the women's movement differs from more conventional collective action. The movement has never had an organisation, in the sense of a single over-arching or peak organisation which brought together all those who supported feminism. It may have come close to one in the early 1970s, in the form of the women's liberation movement. Even at the time, however, many women who subscribed to the ideas of feminism remained outside the movement, and from the late 1970s it has incorporated many different groups, from women's committees in local authorities to those involved in peace camps such as Greenham Common to the Working Mothers' Association. The tactics employed by feminists have ranged from conventional lobbying of decision-makers, to 30,000 women linking hands around American nuclear bases, to the setting up of refuges for victims of domestic violence. Ideologically, the movement encompasses those who conceptualise their fight as being all about equal rights, particularly in the workplace, to those who believe that lesbianism is an essential prerequisite for true feminism. It is perhaps not surprising that such a variety of motivations and behaviour should have inspired different interpretations. Before analysing these, however, it is necessary to summarise the more important developments that have taken place over the last three decades.

It is generally accepted that the second wave of feminism in Britain was stimulated by the upsurge of interest in revolutionary socialism and libertarianism in the late 1960s that centred upon the Vietnam war and is now referred to in shorthand terms as the student movement. Much of the intellectual impulse came from America, where the interest in feminism was, somewhat ironically, stimulated by the leading role played by men in the student movement and the earlier civil rights campaign. The movement became visible at a national level in 1970 when the first National Women's Liberation Movement Conference was held: four basic demands were agreed — equal pay, equal education and opportunity, extensive nursery provision, and free contraception and abortion on demand (financial and legal independence for women and no discrimination against lesbians were added in 1974, freedom from intimidation by threat or use of violence or sexual coercion in 1978). From the outset, however, such nationally coordinated mobilisation was the exception rather than the norm. Instead, the movement developed through small groups, based on locality, occupation or existing political allegiances. Although many of the early activists were also active in left-wing politics, ranging from the Labour Party and trade unions to the revolutionary left groups, and sought to give these a feminist perspective, their message fell on largely barren ground. Notwithstanding some successes within the trade union movement (on issues like equal pay and conditions of work), the Labour Party was locked in internal struggle over the best strategic response to a Conservative government and, in any case, was perceived as too bureaucratic to be a very attractive prospect to those whose prior political experiences were in the libertarian left. The more extreme left organisations not only tended to view feminism as something of a distraction from the fight against capitalism but were, if anything, even more prone to sectarianism and rigidly formalised processes of decision-making. Instead, women turned to a form of mobilisation that was at one and the same time more diffuse and more specific than activism within the existing political institutions.

Diffuse in that in its early years, simply coming together as women within their own 'spaces' (be they local groups in mainly urban areas, or groups within institutions and professions) was the key ingredient in developing a feminist consciousness. Although it was not to last long, in the early to mid-1970s 'sisterhood'—taking this to mean a recognition that all women were to varying degrees the victims of oppression, and a determination to remedy this—was a sufficiently exciting ideology to mask any disagreements over how or why such oppression occurred. There is little in the way of precise data, but hundreds of local groups sprang up during the 1970s, with many of them establishing women's centres which not only provided a meeting place but also published newsletters, organised cultural activities, and generally acted as a resource base for local activists. Little attempt was made to establish national coordination, although communication between groups was certainly facilitated by the launch of *Spare Rib* magazine in 1972.

Out of this plethora of small groups came initiatives on single issues such as domestic violence, rape, abortion and health. Some took the form of creating a physical space—for example, the creation of refuges for victims of domestic violence (a British innovation which later spread to America). These multiplied to the extent that, in 1975, a National Women's Aid Federation was established to act as a coordinating body. By 1977 there were almost two hundred refuges in the UK, and they have survived the vicissitudes of fragmentation in the women's movement since, with there being the same number in England alone by the 1990s. Rape Crisis Centres started to emerge at a local level from the mid-1970s on (offering victims phone counselling and support groups); they also have survived into the 1990s. The issue of abortion did not give rise to much activity at the local level, because the legislative changes of 1967 (David Steel's Private Member's Bill on abortion, and the NHS Family Planning Act allowing local authorities to provide contraceptive aids and advice), although falling short of 'abortion on demand', were sufficient to make other issues seem more pressing. Although there were marked variations between different regions of the NHS, the 1967 Act was implemented more liberally than might have been expected, with some 14% of pregnancies being terminated by 1972. When the 1967 changes were threatened, however, in the form of another Private Member's Bill in 1975, the women's movement responded with one of its relatively few instances of nationally-organised protest. The National Abortion Campaign was created, drawing together existing local women's groups, and also establishing its own network of groups within the Labour Party, trade unions and urban areas. As well as lobbying within these institutions and encouraging supporters to put pressure on their constituency MPs, the Campaign mounted a national demonstration which attracted some 20,000 people—relatively small in comparison to some of the demonstrations organised by CND in the 1980s, but nevertheless the biggest demonstration on a women's issue since the suffragettes.[3] When the provisions of the 1967 Act were yet again threatened in 1979, the National Abortion Campaign (in conjunction with the TUC), mounted a protest march with some 100,000 participants. While this kind of mobilisation was taking place at the national level, women involved in local groups made the connection between reproductive rights and preventative health care, and began creating local self-help groups aimed at providing an alternative to the male-dominated view of women's health needs emanating from the established medical profession. Many of these followed the American example and evolved into 'well-women' clinics in the 1980s; they also set the context within which loosely-knit groups within the medical profession (such as Women in Medicine and the Association of Radical Midwives) emerged, determined to put the feminist perspective upon the agenda of medical community.

This is not the context in which to undertake a detailed account of the multifarious activities undertaken by the movement during its first decade. Suffice to say that, by the beginning of the 1980s, there were estimated to be some 10,000 committed activists and a further 20,000 active on a more intermittent basis.[4] Yet the movement was facing two problems. One was that—precisely because it engaged in such a variety of activities, from women's theatre groups or the creation of women's studies courses in higher education to conventional lobbying of local and national politicians or protest demonstrations—its impact on British society was arguably more marked in the cultural sphere than the political. Feminism was certainly on the agenda in terms of causing people to question popular attitudes, but (with the exception of some trade unions) it had yet to make its mark on the mainstream political parties and major interest groups. The other problem was that the movement itself was undergoing some major internal disagreements over ideology and tactics.

Different viewpoints were evident within the women's movement from its inception. To adopt the commonly used terminology, there were at least three different perspectives by the mid-1970s. 'Liberal' (or 'Equal Rights') feminists' perception of the situation was that equality of opportunity between the sexes was the important goal, and that legislative and representational change was the most important target; their attention was focused on institutions. 'Socialist' feminists were also concerned with the poor deal that women received in the workplace but argued that this was another instance of the oppression which was an integral feature of capitalism, that women had to work with other exploited sections of society, and they placed particular stress on mobilising among working-class women to this end. As far as both groupings were concerned, there was nothing inherently wrong with cooperating with men to achieve their aims. 'Radical' feminists, in contrast, took a more fundamental view. They saw patriarchy rather than class or institutional barriers as the cause of the problem. Their argument rested on an assertion of difference, that women were different from men, that men had power over women and would continue to exercise that power because it benefited them—unless women (and only women) mobilised to fight against the patriarchal attitudes which permeated British society.

Such differences were easily tolerated in the early years: 'In the beginning all socialist-feminists were radical feminists and all radical feminists were socialist-feminists; or rather the two strands had not yet separated out as distinct currents.'[5] It is worth noting that in the smaller women's groups, usually located outside the major conurbations, such tolerance persisted throughout the seventies and into the eighties. In the larger groups, however, disagreements became bitter to the point that the movement held no more national conferences after 1978. The differences were both ideological and tactical, with the radical feminists arguing that political separatism was the only way forward. Seeking representational advances within mainstream political institutions, as prioritised by liberal feminists and seen as part of a wider struggle by socialist feminists, was not part of their tactical repertoire. For them, such parties and institutions were hopelessly imbued with male values and interests. The answer lay in interpersonal and women-only group activities rather than the institutional sphere, and radical feminists prioritised such activities as rape crisis centres and women's refuges. Theory and practice became self-reinforcing, as such activism increased their concern with male violence. The result was a strong current of opinion among radical feminists that lesbianism was the mark of a true feminist. The move from political to sexual separatism split the women's liberation movement; some left, and those who remained were unable to agree on strategies of action. Nor was this the only division. Towards the end of the 1970s, black women began to articulate a dissatisfaction with the wider women's movement. Their argument was that feminism, as conceptualised by the movement, was essentially a white women's movement (and, indeed, well-educated, middle-class white women at that). Black women argued that they faced problems their white sisters did not—ranging from discrimination in employment to immigration and (especially in the Asian community) a hostile reaction from members of their own community when it came to questioning traditional family relationships. The Organisation of Women of African and Asian Descent was created in 1978, but by 1982 even this had split as women of Afro-Caribbean and Asian descent could not agree upon priorities and tactics. The emergence of a black lesbian grouping in the early eighties produced yet more divisions.

By the beginning of the 1980s, the movement no longer had a single core. This did not mean it was paralysed, however. Activists may have been unable to agree on a strategy, but this did not stop them from pursuing their own different strategies for empowerment. Although many women turned to interaction with established political institutions during the 1980s and 1990s, protest and associated 'unconventional' political activities did continue. One of the best known was the Greenham Women's Peace Camp which, whilst it certainly reflected the ethos of radical feminism, also attracted women from throughout the movement and mobilised many new supporters. The protest (against the siting of American cruise missiles in Britain) began in 1981 and originally included a small minority of men, but became a women-only action in 1982. There were various reasons for this, ranging from essentially tactical arguments that the exclusion of men would heighten the contrast between the non-violent direct action of the protesters and the (male) authorities, to ideological perspectives which equated nuclear weapons with patriarchy and male violence.[6] A combination of mass actions (30,000 women 'embracing the base' in 1982; 40,000 in 1983) and smaller-scale initiatives (numerous invasions of the base) secured at least as much media attention as anything the much larger CND was doing at the time. Of course, it can be argued that the Camp was not specifically a feminist project, in the sense of being concerned with women's rights, but a powerful symbol of women's determination to act autonomously, and there are many anecdotal accounts of the powerful consciousness-raising impact it had upon those who partici-pated. It may have acted as something of a spur for another instance of mass collective action by women in the 1980s, Women Against Pit Closures.[7] Taking place in the context of the 1984–85 miners' strike, this took the form of women mobilising in support of their male relatives, including mass demonstrations attracting around 10,000 women, a network of support groups and local rallies. The movement petered out with the ending of the strike, though it was revived to some extent following the 1992 decision to close many of the UK's major pits. Like Greenham, however, its significance in this context was not so much the impact (or, rather, lack of it) on the policy issue involved as in the reinvigoration it gave to women's belief in their capacity for autonomous direct action.[8]

Confirmation that direct action remained part of the women's move-ment tactical repertoire can be seen in the strategies adopted by the various groups campaigning on the issue of pornography since the mid-1980s. Inspired by the Labour MP Clare Short's Indecent Displays Bill in 1986, the anti-pornography campaign has utilised both conventional tactics such as lobbying of Parliament and the media, but also direct action in the form of demonstrations and picketing of retailers which stock pornographic magazines. Further evidence that the movement was still capable of organising direct action on a national scale came with the attempt in 1987 by Liberal MP David Alton to gain parliamentary approval for a Private Member's Bill reducing the 28-week limit on abortion to 18 weeks. The National Abortion Campaign immediately joined forces with the Abortion Law Reform Association and the Women's Reproductive Rights Campaign to form the Fight the Alton Bill (FAB) campaign. At its height, FAB had over 150 local branches or groups throughout Britain, and was able to mount a national demonstration to coincide the Commons second reading of the bill (which subsequently fell), even though this was on a significantly smaller scale than the demonstrations of the 1970s.

Direct action, then, remained a characteristic of the movement during the 1980s, but the largest mobilisations were of women protesting about issues which were wider than those articulated by the women's liberation movement of the 1970s; gender-specific issues did not inspire 'unconventional' protest in the way they had during the previous decade. One reason for this may well have been a reflection of a degree of success; attitudes had changed since the inception of the movement — as the British Social Attitudes Survey concluded in 1988, 'Britain seems to be much more egalitarian now on women's issues than it was twenty years ago'[9] — reducing the sense of urgency. Another reason was that it was clear by the 1980s that institutional and legislative innovations like the Sex Discrimination Act and the Equal Opportunities Commission were falling far short of delivering equal rights and opportunities for women. An implementation gap was evident, and that was something best addressed from within the system rather than outside. In short (and to oversimplify), if the 1970s was a decade of getting women's issues onto the political agenda of the mainstream established political institutions, the 1980s was one in which the issues were pursued within those institutions.

One area that was of particular importance was the development of Women's Committees in local authorities. Although these originated largely as the result of pressure by socialist feminists active in the Labour Party and trade unions, radical and liberal feminists were also involved, and the Committees saw their task as facilitating the mobilisation of women from all wings of the movement. The first full Committee to be formed (as distinct from informal working groups) was the Greater London Council Women's Committee in 1982 — control of the GLC having fallen to the Labour group under the leadership of Ken Livingstone the previous year. Others soon followed, although they were virtually all found in Labour-controlled authorities and then only around a quarter of those.[10] These Committees sought to influence the internal practices of local authorities (for example, conditions of employment and appointment procedures) but also the provision of services such as child-care, women's health issues, and liaison with police authorities over domestic or other threats of violence to women. Many have not survived into the 1990s, not least because of high profile criticism from both the Conservative Party and the media over decisions to fund lesbian groups, but their emergence marked the engagement of what had been an autonomous liberation movement with mainstream institutions of the state.

The Committees themselves were, of course, to some extent a reflection of increasing engagement with the Labour Party and trade union movement. It was during the 1980s that the Labour Women's Action Committee was formed, which campaigned within the Labour Party—partly to give some real power to the women's organisations which had existed for over sixty years but only operated under the sufferance of the party's National Executive Committee, and partly to introduce new initiatives such as the compulsory inclusion of women candidates on all parliamentary candidate selection short-lists. A similar process took place within the unions, as women pressed for (and achieved) a change of attitude towards the TUC Women's Conference, persuading their male colleagues to treat this as a serious political forum; and at the same time they mobilised within individual unions, as a result of which many unions adopted new policies on such issues as equal rights, maternity provision and sexual harassment in the workplace. Indicative of their success was the creation of an Equal Rights Department by the TUC in 1988.

Such advances were facilitated by factors outside the Labour and union movement, not least the commitment of the newly-formed Social Democrats in 1981 to equal opportunities policies and compulsory short-listing of women parliamentary candidates (both of which survived the subsequent merger with the Liberals); given the potential electoral threat Labour saw in the Liberal/Social Democrat Alliance in the mid-1980s, this was clearly a spur to action on the part of the Labour movement. The process was somewhat delayed by internal party politics, as the Labour Women's Action Committee was perceived by the party leadership to be closely associated with the 'Hard Left' (especially the Militant Tendency) within the party—who were, of course, the prime target of the leadership between 1983 and 1987. It was only towards the end of the decade, when the leadership was clearly winning its battle with Militant, that it was prepared to respond to demands from Labour feminists.

Response then, however, verged on the dramatic. A Shadow Minister for Women was named in 1989. The 1990 Annual Conference agreed that within the next ten years at least 40% of all representatives on all the party's important policy-making bodies (including the NEC and the new National Policy Forum) would be women, and set a target of at least half of all Labour MPs being women. To this end, it was agreed in 1990 that henceforth all ballot papers cast by members of the Parliamentary Labour Party in elections for the Shadow Cabinet had to include votes for at least three women, or they would be rejected as invalid—and, despite some rumblings of discontent within the PLP, this was increased to four in 1993. At constituency level, it was agreed in 1988 that henceforth the selection of parliamentary candidates would be subject to the requirement that all short-lists had to include at least one woman. The 1993 Conference took this one stage further, deciding that there would be women-only candidate short-lists in half of the party's 'winnable' seats — that is, marginals and those where an incumbent Labour MP retires — and this was confirmed at the 1994 Conference after an extensive debate. The leadership changes during the early 1990s have not impeded this process; John Smith upgraded the post of women's officer; and although there were initial fears among some women activists that Tony Blair might not share Smith's commitment to prioritising this aspect of the party's transformation, such apprehensions have subsided.

Even the Conservative Party has made some response to pressure from the women's movement. A ministerial group was established in 1986 with the task of considering the effect of all proposals for legislative change on women, and John Major upgraded the status of this group to a Cabinet committee in 1992. Beyond that, however, it has to be said that the government's response has been limited to protestations of support for equality of opportunity, with little in the way of concrete action.

There is much to suggest that such progress within the political parties is reflecting rather than leading public opinion. A major study of participation in Britain in the mid-1980s found overwhelming agreement (92%) with the proposition that women should enjoy equal opportunities, with over 40% expressing strong agreement. Relaxing restrictions on abortion also found favour with over 48%, although only 13% thought it very important. Altogether, some 46% agreed with both propositions, and could be regarded as having pro-feminist values. Moreover, the study suggests that support for such values is relatively dispersed among the population. More were from the working class than the salariat; almost a third were men; almost 90% were not graduates; their age profile matched that of the total sample. Nor were such outlooks found only on the left of the political spectrum; although over 14% were on the 'far left' and 37% identified with the Labour Party, there is also a strong contingent from the centre and the right of the political spectrum, with 34% identifying with the Conservative Party.[11] The British Social Attitudes Surveys produce a similar picture; whilst just over half the respondents in 1984 agreed with the idea that a husband's role was to earn the money and a wife's to look after the home, by 1989 only a quarter agreed and over half disagreed; around 90% thought that the job of a councillor or MP was equally suitable for men and women.[12] Having said this, attitudinal change is not necessarily synonymous with behavioural change. The same surveys show that only around half of those who agree that domestic responsibilities should be equally shared actually practice this. Nor should we forget just how much progress has yet to be made in the public sphere; at the beginning of 1995, for example, women accounted for 50% of the work force but only 9% of MPs, 7% of the senior judiciary, 9% of the senior civil service, 3% of company directors and 5% of university professors.

If the women's movement can take heart from the progress made to date, there is clearly a long way to go before its objectives could be said to have been fully achieved. Yet, on the face of it, the movement has significantly declined during the nineties. *Spare Rib* ceased publication in 1993. Lovenduski and Randall's impression at the end of the 1980s — 'everywhere we went, except Scotland, we encountered a sense that numbers of activists were falling, local women's newsletters were folding, old networks were breaking down' — is confirmed by more recent surveys which suggest that, despite widespread agreement with the aims of the women's movement, the younger generation born since the seventies tends to see the movement as 'extreme, man-hating and separatist'.[13]

One reason for apparent decline may be that women are still active in the 1990s, but in other movements and protest networks. There is little quantitative data available as yet, but clear impressionistic evidence that women are playing at least as much of a role as men, if not more so, in recent protests over Animal Rights, transport policy and the Criminal Justice Act. Women are prominent in groups such as Earth First, for example — radical environmentalists who accuse groups such as Friends of the Earth and Greenpeace of having become bureaucratised and over-cautious, and who have taken the lead in non-violent protest over new motorway constructions at Twyford Down, Solsbury Hill and the M11 extension in East London. Women have been equally to the fore in the recent wave of protests over the export of live animals. It is not just the case that the gender balance in such mobilisations is far more equal than in more conventional politics. Women's participation is also important in that it is freely acknowledged by men in such movements that they have learnt a lot from the women's movement, especially in terms of non-hierarchical decision-making and non-violent direct action. The fact remains, however, that the women's movement as such is far less visible than it was. This gives rise to two questions — did the women's movement of the 1970s and 1980s set about its task of changing British politics and society in the 'right' or 'best' way, and what are the prospects for the future?

Even disregarding those who disagree with its aims, the women's movement has certainly not lacked its critics. We have already noted the internal divisions within the movement between those adopting radical, socialist and liberal perspectives, each ready to criticise the others. More detached criticism has come from sympathisers outside the movement, particularly those whose experience has been in the American women's movement. From an American perspective, the British women's movement tends to be seen as commendable for the degree of commitment it has inspired, but regrettably insistent upon ideological purity at the expense of coalition-building which would result in pragmatic gains. Gelb's observations are characteristic: she has argued that the failure of the British women's movement to construct a national organisation which could then engage in dialogue with policy-makers at the national level has resulted in 'a strangely limited vision of feminist goals and ideals which, in fact, produces less societal change than might be expected'.[14] To be fair, she stresses that any movement can only be assessed within the context of its political opportunity structure[15]—meaning both the institutional factors like electoral and party systems, and the prevailing cultural attitudes which characterise different political systems. She notes that the British system is much more closed and inflexible than the American, and that there are consequently less opportunities to forge alliances with parties which have stronger ideological imperatives than their American counterparts or to influence administrators who operate in a centralised system rather the multi-level openings which are a feature of the American federal system. Nevertheless, the point remains: if the British women's movement had been less concerned with developing theoretical analyses of the causes of their subordination and prepared to bury their differences and work together (and, at least in the case of radical feminists, work more closely with male sympathisers), might not the movement have achieved more in the way of concrete changes and done less to apparently alienate the younger generation?

A counter-argument is provided by continental European commentators, who tend to assess social movements not so much by their impact upon political institutions and public policy as upon culture and ideas in society. They make the point that social movements may well have instrumental motives, as in seeking to achieve legislative change, but they also have non-instrumental goals which are concerned with 'living out' the cause. Melucci, for example, argues that it may be necessary to analyse the visible aspects of movements (such as protests and similar mobilisations), but it is not sufficient. Analysis which examines only the overt interaction of movements with the political system overlooks 'the network of relationships which constitutes the submerged reality of the movements before, during and after events'.[16] In other words, he is arguing that movements do not just exist in the dimension of public actions, but also in the dimension of everyday life. They aim to change attitudes as well as public policy, and interpersonal and small group interaction is a vital component of this. It follows that the organisational and tactical repertoires of movements should be assessed not just as means to an end (change in public policy) but as ends or goals in themselves.

The women's movement may well have inhibited its impact upon mainstream institutions by choosing to remain localised rather than national; non-hierarchical rather than bureaucratic; loosely networked rather than coordinated by a peak organisation performing an aggregative function; and purist rather than pragmatic—but this strategy is not without its advantages. The very lack of a structure meant that it was to able to survive the disputes of the late 1970s, which a more conventional organisation almost certainly would not, because there was no hierarchy within which to pursue them. Fragmentation is a disadvantage if one views the goal as impacting directly upon mainstream political institutions; but if , following Melucci, one views the raison d'être of a social movement as challenging the dominant values and cultural codes in society, then such fragmentation enriches a movement. It is the sign of a movement preoccupied with identity. The women's movement has been, and is still trying to create a new identity in society and getting the rest of society to accept this.

Fragmentation is understandable in a movement centred upon claims to a different identity and experience, as distinct from a particular policy or issue. Once women started to assert their difference from men, the way was open for women to assert their differences from each other. Identity politics may militate against coalition-building within the movement, and between the movement and established actors in the political process, but it expands the ideological parameters of the movement. The more women moved from a concern with equality to the assertion of difference, the less radical (and thus more acceptable to the mainstream) arguments for equality appear; what was formerly contestable—the claim to equality—is now common ground. Women have argued with each other, but this has acted as a catalyst for the creation of a strong self-interest in demanding at least the lowest common denominator of agreement, equality of opportunity and treatment. The activists of the last twenty years have failed to act in concert but, by their constant striving to question their own ideology, they have changed the consciousness of the vast majority of women in the UK, and not a few men, and this is now reflected in the promises held out by the Labour Party.

The American analysis emphasises the visible, quasi-formal interactions between the movement and the established political authorities, and it is true that ideological disagreements have divided the movement, and rendered the development of such connections more difficult. The European analysis stresses the importance of new meanings of social reality being developed and expressed in private as well as public life, as it is out of this that widespread challenges to dominant cultural values emerge, and it is equally true that the multifarious disagreements within the women's movement over the last twenty years have given it an intellectual dynamism and vitality not found in other movements which stress policy change rather than identity. The American perspective can be criticised for concentrating upon how the movement interacts with political authorities and for overlooking why the movement exists at all—where it is coming from. Similarly, the European perspective directs our attention to the underlying source of visible mobilisation but has little to say on where it is going.

There is, however, a sense in which both these perspectives, and that of conventional pressure group theory, can be synthesised. It lies in the concept of collective identity. What is sometimes lost sight of in discussions of social movements is that, in comparison with the peace or environmental movements, the women's movement has the potential to develop a strong sense of self-interest, as distinct from more altruistic motives. If the consciousness of a collective identity can be formed, then women's awareness of their common interests as women, rather than as members of a class or ethnic group, may well influence their political behaviour and partisan loyalties. If so, then established institutions like parties and unions will move towards accommodation of women's issues almost regardless of how fragmented the movement is. The movement may not perceive itself as a conventional pressure group; but if identity motivates partisanship, then those seeking votes will treat the movement with as much regard and respect as more conventionally organised groups.

The worrying aspect for the movement is that such argument may have been stimulating but appears to have communicated a negative image to the younger generation. If, as seems the case, the autonomous women's movement has largely disappeared, and the succeeding generation does not wish to revive something they see as unnecessarily strident and separatist, then from where will the driving force come to ensure that the agenda continues to expand and that such promises are kept ? Social movement are like icebergs — the visible 10% is important, but without the underlying 90% it will melt away. The identity-centred politics of the women's movement has put equality firmly upon the political agenda; out of the disputes between radical, socialist, black and lesbian definitions of feminism has come a core of agreement, a collective identity centred upon women's rights to equality. It has not been cost-free, however; with the exception of solidarity on the basis of sexual orientation, the foundations of the movement are withering. Without the stimulus of women coming together in autonomous groups to push forward arguments about the higher ground of difference and the need to recognise it, it might be easier for parties and governments to come to view the lower slopes of equality as too much of an uphill struggle to pursue.

---

1   Such terms are open to different interpretations. I am using definitions advanced by Dahlerup, Lovenduski and Randall: 'feminism — ideologies, activities and policies whose goal is to remove discrimination against women and to break down the male domination of society', D. Dahlerup, *The New Women's Movement: Feminism and Political power in Europe and the USA* (Sage, 1986) p. 6. 'Women's movement — all those individuals, networks, organisations, ideas and practices that espouse feminist values and goals', (J. Lovenduski and V. Randall, *Contemporary Feminist Politics*, (Oxford University Press, 1993). This does not necessarily incorporate 'Third Wave' feminism as enunciated by Camille Paglia, Naomi Wolfe and Katie Roiphe, which argues that women can deny themselves opportunities by acting the role of victim, but my main concern here is with the experience of the British women's movement from the early 1970s to the early 1990s.

2   M. Diani, 'The Concept of Social Movement', *The Sociological Review*, 1992, p. 14.
3   D. Marsh and J. Chambers, *Abortion Politics*, (Junction Books, 1981), p. 47; J. Lovenduski and J. Outshoorn (eds), *The New Politics of Abortion* (Sage, 1986).
4   D. Bouchier, *The Feminist Challenge* (Macmillan, 1983), p. 177.
5   E. Wilson, *Hidden Agendas* (Tavistock), p. 99.
6   For the camp, see J. Liddington, *The Long Road to Greenham* (Virago, 1989); for the relationship between CND and the Greenham women, see P. Byrne, *The Campaign for Nuclear Disarmament* (Croom Helm/Routledge, 1988).
7   See L. Loach in H. Benyon (ed), *Digging Deeper: Issues in the Miners' Strike*, (Verso, 1985).
8   Cf. Lovenduski and Randall, op.cit., p. 124.
9   R. Jowell, S. Witherspoon and L. Brook (eds), *British Social Attitudes: Fifth Report* (Gower, 1988), p. 193.
10 Lovenduski and Randall, op.cit., p. 151.
11 G. Parry, G. Moyser and N. Day, *Political Participation and Democracy in Britain* (Cambridge University Press, 1992).
12 L. Brook et al, *British Social Attitudes Cumulative Source Book* (Gower, 1992).
13 G. Sianne and H. Wilkinson, *Gender, Feminism and the Future* (Demos, 1995).
14 J. Gelb, 'Feminism and Political Action', in R. Dalton and M. Kuechler, *Challenging the Political Order: New Social and Political Movements in Western Democracies* (Polity Press, 1990) and 'Feminism in Britain: politics without power?', in D. Dahlerup, op.cit.
15 Cf. H. Kitschelt, 'Political Opportunity Structures and Political Protest', *British Journal of Political Science* (1986).
16 A. Melucci, op.cit., p. 44.

Quotas for Women: Fair Representation?

BY JUDITH SQUIRES

ON TUESDAY 25 July 1995 Tony Blair announced that after the general election the Labour Party would abandon its policy of insisting that some constituencies choose their candidates from all-women short-lists. He claimed in a Press Association interview that 'the process has not been ideal at all and that is accepted by the most vociferous supporters of the proposal'. Though 'not ideal' it was nonetheless argued by Blair that as a result of the adoption of the policy: 'We will have increased radically the number of women standing and we will have made the quantum leap that we wanted to make.' This statement infuriated many within the party, notably Clare Short, Labour's Shadow Minister for Women and one of the strongest advocates of the quotas policy, who have declared their intention to fight for its continuation. In the face of this challenge, Tony Blair prevaricated on the issue of the future for quotas within the party. So what was this policy; why was it adopted; and why is there now such conflict over whether it should be continued? Here we explore not only the practical operation and implications of the quotas policy, but also examine some of the theoretical issues which underpin its raison d'être. What, for instance, is the status of the claim that we need to guarantee the presence of a certain number of women MPs; what claims are we making about the nature of our representatives when we argue for or against such quotas; and what implications can we glean from this debate about the potential role of our political representatives more generally? In short, what can we learn from the quotas debate about who our representatives are representing and how?

Quotas: the policy

The process of implementing quotas for women, involving drawing up all-women short-lists in half the marginal and vacant seats for the next general election, was agreed by the Labour Party in 1993. The principle of quotas in the Labour Party was first agreed at Annual Conference in 1989. The reasons for the decision were widely perceived to include: the lack of real progress in terms of women's representation at any level of the party; the experience of socialist parties in other countries, which had used quotas to increase the number of women in their own organisations; post election research in 1977 indicating that a key problem was women's perception of Labour as a male-dominated party; the belief that creating more positions of power and responsibility for women within the party at all levels would not only to be more equitable but might bring significant electoral rewards.

After the Annual Conference of 1989 there was a period of consultation with party organisation and affiliates. The 1990 Conference moved beyond the 'in principle' debate of the 1989 to endorse a far-reaching programme of quotas. It adopted a 40% quota for the National Executive Committee, Constituency Labour Parties, branch officers and delegations. It further adopted the target of 50% women in the Parliamentary Labour Party over the next ten years or three general elections. The 1991 Conference went on to vote through rule changes concerning all levels of the party, with 3,536,000 votes for and only 144,000 against. Following recommendations made in a consultative process the Conference of 1993 endorsed rule changes implementing quotas for the Conference Arrangements Committee, National Constitutional Committee, Regional Councils and the European Constituency Labour Party. The decision was made to implement the following: a target of 50% women candidates in all seats where a Labour MP is retiring, and 50% in the most winnable seats; regional consensus meetings to agree which of such seats would have all-women short-lists; the NEC to intervene if consensus on reaching the target was not achieved, to lay down which seats would have all-women short-lists; a range of supportive measures for women candidates.

The practical implications of these policies are roughly as follows: for the next general election half of all constituencies with vacant seats have been asked to select candidates from all-women short-lists. In the 1992 election, Labour chose 138 women candidates, of whom 101 were in seats where they faced hopeless odds, and 37 were elected to the House. In the light of the quotas policy, the following outcomes were predicted. Firstly, as a result of quotas being adopted in seats were a Labour MP is retiring: 'If women are adopted for half the Labour inheritor seats, we would expect that one average about 15 new women Labour MPs would enter the Commons via this route in the next general election, at most 25.' Secondly, in the most winnable seats: 'If won by strong Labour challenges, the number of new women on the Labour back-benches could rise by 11 in the average election, and by at most 28 if there is a strong swing to Labour.' Overall, Pippa Norris has estimated the potential change thus: 'On the basis of postwar electoral trends we could probably expect the number of women Labour MPs to increase from 37 to about 63, or at most 75, in the next general election. If women made no significant gains in other parties, the proportion of women Members of Parliament would increase from about nine to 15%.'[1]

Responses to this strategy from other parties have been unsurprisingly negative. Replying to an Opposition-led debate of women's issues in March 1995, David Hunt, then chairman of the Cabinet committee on women, said that Labour was interested only in quick fixes. He condemned the party's policy of women-only quotas for the selection of Labour parliamentary candidates saying: 'Labour's fixation with window dressing just grows more embarrassing.' He went on to warn the Labour Party not to confuse 'gender politics with gesture politics', insisting that positive discrimination in favour of women could have diametrically the opposite effect. Diana Maddock, the Liberal Democrat spokesperson on women's issues, also denounced the quotas policy, saying: 'We want equal treatment for women not special treatment. Our aim is equality of opportunity, not equality of outcome.'[2] In these statements we find a clear manifestation of the difference of ethos within the parties regarding the concept of equality: the Labour Party manifesting its tradition of endorsing equality of outcome as a desirable goal, in addition (or, at times, rather than) the equality of opportunity traditionally favoured by the other parties.

What is interesting about these reactions is that they focus exclusively on quotas in terms of the equality issue of fairness for the individual women seeking selection. They do not address the issue of the representativeness of the candidate and the justice to the electorate of being represented fairly. Whether the quotas policy would indeed secure a fairer representative system is, of course, also open to debate, but it is interesting to note that the critics of the policy within the parliamentary debate have tended to focus on the equality of opportunity/equality of outcome aspects rather than the representation aspects. Yet it is the representation issue which is of greater theoretical import.

The issue of fair representation in relation to quotas has however been addressed within the Labour Party itself. The NEC statement following the 1994 Conference made no mention of the issue of fairness to individual women candidates but focused instead on the issue of fair representation of the female electorate: 'Conference reaffirms its view that if the Labour Party is truly to reflect the communities it seeks to represent there must be a significant improvement in the level of women's representation in Parliament.' This statement would seem to imply that the adoption of quotas was motivated primarily by a concern with the representativeness of the party's candidates vis-à-vis particular sections of the electorate. Such a concern is in keeping with the culture of the Labour Party, in that recent surveys of MPs indicate that Labour politicians are much more likely to see themselves as group representatives than are their Conservative colleagues who tend to stress the public service role more strongly.[3] This would indicate that significantly different perceptions of what it is to represent others exists between the political parties. This difference of party culture generally and of the understanding of the nature of representation in particular has unsurprisingly influenced the different party responses to the issue of quotas policy.

Yet, in addition to the cultural ethos of the Labour Party which renders it open to the logic of group representation, there are also more

pragmatic reasons which have led certain of its members to advocate a
quotas policy. The much debated phenomenon of the gender gap has
provided a further concrete reason for its concern at this point to make
itself 'truly reflect the communities it seeks to represent' in terms of
women's representation. It is been shown that Labour faces lower levels
of support among women than among men: women were eight percentage points less likely than men to be Labour voters at the time of the
1992 election (although this figure varies according to age-group). It is
argued by Sharon Witherspoon in a report for Clare Short that: 'Gender
differences in voting behaviour are systematic and statistically significant. And because women and men constitute roughly half of the
electorate, bringing women's voting behaviour closer to that of men
could constitute an important source of additional votes for Labour.
For instance, if women had voted Labour in the same proportion as
men in 1992, Labour would have had 40% of the vote, instead of 36%,
and the Conservatives would have had 39% of the vote, instead of
43%.' These figures lend support to the quotas policy via the following
form of reasoning, as expressed by Barbara Follett: 'In 1992 the swing
to Labour in all key seats was 3.6% but in the seats contested by women
it was 4.0%. There is also some evidence to suggest that women are
more likely to turn out to vote if the candidate is female. With a gender
gap 6 points in the Conservative's favour, Labour is going to need every
woman candidate it can get.' Despite that fact that the evidence Follett
refers to is disputed and that many claim that there is no difference by
gender after controlling for region and type of seat[4] the belief that
increasing the number of women candidates might help address the
'gender gap' has proved an important factor in rallying support for the
quotas policy. Thus there are both cultural and pragmatic reasons why
the Labour Party should be interested in group representation when
other parties are not, and should perceive the quotas debate in terms of
such representation when others perceive it primarily in terms of
equality of opportunity.

   The advocates of the quotas policy within the Labour Party itself
have tended to invoke both the principled and the pragmatic arguments
interchangeably. Note that the reasons cited for the adoption of the
policy by Conference involved not only the assertion that this would
bring about a more equitable situation, but that it might bring significant electoral rewards as well. In other words, there was a clear, though
perhaps not clearly perceived, concern with three distinct issues: the
fairness of treatment of the women who wished to pursue careers as
politicians; the responsiveness of the party to the female electorate in
terms of the representation on offer; the potential electoral success of
the party if it could appeal more effectively to the female electorate.
Thus the Labour Coordinating Committee state in 'The Case for
Quotas': 'The LCC has long believed that it is vital that women's
representation in the Party is increased, both in the interests of fairness

and because it will increase Labour's chances of winning elections.' It continues: 'Quotas are the only proven way to secure equality of representation', and 'Labour need women's votes to win power.'

The unquestioned assumption underpinning the debate about quotas is that it matters that there are so few women present in the House. This consensus is fairly new and to be welcomed. But let us not forget that it is important to articulate why it might matter. For this, despite popular assumption to the contrary, is not so clear. One can pinpoint at least three clear reasons which are significantly distinct and which have different implications for our evaluation of a quotas policy as an effective means of addressing them. The first is an argument from justice. This is the argument that sexual segregation is wrong wherever it occurs, thus it is unjust that women should be excluded from the central activities in the political realm. Indeed, given the overarching significance of politics, it is particularly unfair that women should be kept out of this arena. This case for justice, it should be noted, says nothing about what women will do if they get into politics. The second is an argument from diversity and tolerance. This is the argument that women will bring to politics a different set of values, experiences and expertise. Women will therefore enrich our political life, usually in the direction of a more caring, compassionate society. The case for difference, therefore, implies that the mode of politics will change. This argument relies on a cohesive notion of 'woman' and assumes that simply guaranteeing the number of women present can secure the values of the women present. The third is an argument concerning representativeness. This argument claims that men and women have conflicting (or at least distinct) interests and that it is a nonsense to think that women can be represented by men; 'group representation' is required. Thus, the case for representation implies that the content of politics will change.

As more women do actually enter into parliamentary politics in greater numbers within an increasing range of states, these have been subject to extensive empirical research (see also Pippa Norris in this volume).[5] Whilst most studies do indicate that a critical mass of women within a parliament may make a difference to policy attitudes and political procedures, the research has yet to prove conclusively that the presence of women does make in itself a significant difference. Nonetheless, those arguing for quotas frequently invoke all three arguments, and do so without distinction. For instance, Clare Short, Shadow Minster for Women, argued in her 'Briefing for MPs' on quotas: 'It is clear that the selection process so far has excluded women, especially in the most winnable seats. Increasing women's representation in parliament is essential if we are to build a House of Commons which more truly represents the whole population. As more women come into the Commons, the culture will change, the agenda of politics will broaden, and the institution itself will be transformed.' All three arguments are

invoked in turn, with no clear indication that there is any distinction
between them. This is perhaps where much of the ambivalence concerning quotas originates. There are three quite distinct reasons why we
might be concerned to secure more women in Parliament, and commitment to one does not necessarily entail commitment to all. One could
argue in favour of the first form of defence of quotas, whilst rejecting
the second two.

However, the focus here is not on the much-debated issue of justice
in the form of equality of opportunity for women within the professions,
but on the issues of group difference and representation. It is not, of
course, that the former issue is not significant, nor that it does not
properly inform the debate regarding the pros and cons of quotas. It is
rather that it is a debate which has been well-rehearsed; moreover, it is
not specific to the parliamentary process, being of general concern
regarding equity and women's employment prospects. The arguments
from representation on the other hand, raise issues unique to the
parliamentary system, notably how might a party attempt truly to
reflect the communities it seeks to represent; what constitutes fair
representation and what mechanisms might guarantee its realisation? In
placing these questions on the political agenda the quotas debate has
raised profoundly important issues for our parliamentary system, it
should be used to explore issues of fundamental importance to our
understanding of what constitutes political representation itself.

Representation: sources of confusion

Much of the debate surrounding quotas for women has centred around
the notion of fair representation. In Labour Party literature we repeatedly find statements such as: 'Quotas are a proven mechanism for
guaranteeing fair representation for women.'[6] Yet, although a foundational principle of modern democratic politics, the meaning of the term
representation is notably vague, even for a political concept. Consensus
on what might constitute fair representation is thus far from evident.
Until we can be clear what it is to represent another politically, we
surely can not—with any conviction—engage in debate about what
constitutes fair representation, or evaluate the pros and cons of a quotas
policy as a just and effective strategy for achieving this end.

Yet ambivalence, theoretical and historical, surrounds even the
attempt to describe the process of representation. For example, electing
representatives according to geographical constituencies suggests that
those elected are meant to represent, and speak for, an area or a place.
The implication is that interests are relatively homogeneous within
localities, but potentially at odds between them. An alternative view of
representation is Edmund Burke's notion that representatives serve the
interests of the nation. Yet another comes with the party system, which
implies that representatives are representative of their supporters and
ideological allies. Even within our current party system there are clear

differences of opinion as to how representation should operate. For example, there is debate over the degree of autonomy of the representative in relation to his or her electors; whether there is a difference between the representation of constituents' interests and representation of their opinions; and the extent to which it is the function of the representative to promote the national interest rather than the interests of particular constituents. It is largely because of the contested nature of the concept of representation that our MPs can continue to claim to be 'representative' despite the fact that manifestly fail to 'represent' the electorate on most — if not all — of the above criteria.

This strategic definition and use of a political concept for one's own particular ends is of course integral to the very nature of political discourse itself. The concept of representation is an essentially contested one. Dispute over the meaning of such a concept, which is itself complexly interrelated to other contested concepts, is but a surface manifestation of deeper ideological difference. In particular, we might argue that representation can been seen as a sub-category of that most paradigmatically contested concept — democracy. Thus conceptions of representation which have variously been invoked, depending upon the theory of democracy being advocated, include distinct representation (serving the interests of the area); microcosmic representation (personal likeness), service representation (individual casework of constituents), policy representation (equivalence between attitudes of constituents and policy voting of representative), party representation (party standard-bearers) and pluralist representation (of organised groups). Which one holds will, to no small extent, rest upon one's conception of democracy itself.

It is worth noting, as we contemplate the contemporary uncertainty about the nature of representation, that there have been significant historical shifts in our understanding of what the representative nature of the democratic system was in fact about. Indeed, much of the current ambivalence can be traced back to the historical tension between various forms of representation which have developed alongside, but not replaced, pre-existing representative mechanisms. It is not without significance that our current structures evolve out of a system designed to limit the actual influence of the masses and to avoid the 'tyranny' of uninstructed public opinion. Note, for example, that the idea that representation should be based on individuals who would be grouped together in roughly equal numbers emerged only in the late 18th century. Prior to this is was commonly assumed that government, if it represented anything at all, represented property owners. Hence instead of demanding democracy, most 18th century liberals advocated a meritocracy — property-ownership being taken as an indication of political competence: thus women were assumed to be represented by their husbands, workers by their bosses. The mass suffrage movements, demanding working-class and then women's suffrage, challenged this notion. But representation did not become about the representation of citizens as equal individuals, as the contemporary liberal model might imply. The adoption of the party system meant that the embodiment of the popular will was deemed to be located in the party. Thus what representatives were representing here were ideological perspectives and class interest. If there is any continuity to be found in this narrative, it is that there has been no clear unchanging conception of what it is that we require our representatives to represent.

More recently we find a simultaneous appeal to at least three distinct conceptions of what it is that is being represented: interests (based on e.g. economic status and regional location), ideologies (statements of belief) and (following the introduction of the quotas policy) identities (social or ethnic group membership). What has worked to hold the two earlier bases for representation together and elide the crucial differences between them, has been—following and perpetuating the main political cleavages of our society—the dominance of the belief that interests and ideologies will cohere within geographically defined locations. The differences within the electorate that are therefore represented are the difference of economic status manifest between groups which are themselves internally cohesive. This assumption underpins the workings of the current political system in Britain in that our current representatives in Parliament are deemed to represent both their constituents and their party, even as local and party identification becomes less central to citizen's idea of who they are. The introduction of a quotas policy places a third basis for representation on the political agenda and complicates the process yet further. By insisting the one's gender identity also determines one's claim to be representative of one's constituents, a further distinct criteria for evaluating fair representation has been (re-) introduced into the parliamentary process.

To expand this point, we may cite a distinction between interest, ideological and social groups outlined by Iris Young: 'By an interest group I mean any aggregate or association of persons who seek a particular goal, or desire the same policy, or are similarly situated with respect to some social effect ... Social groups usually share some interests, but shared interests are not sufficient to constitute a social group. A social group is a collective of people who have affinity with one another because of a set of practices or way of life ... By an ideological group I mean a collective of persons with shared political beliefs ... The situation of social groups may foster the formation of ideological groups ... shared political or moral beliefs, even when they are deeply and passionately held, however, do not themselves constitute a social group.'[7] The liberal tradition which underpins the rhetoric of our political system has notably extolled the virtue of representing people of the basis of individual ideas, not social grouping: interests and ideologies not identity. The representation of women secured via quotas, on the other hand, institutionalises a social group identity which is a biological given and so (arguably) not amenable to erasure.

Representation: conceptual clarification

'Learning what representation means and learning how to represent are intimately connected.'[8] The first definition of representation given by Hanna Pitkin is representation in the sense of the descriptive representation of identities, where representativeness is used to indicate that a persons share some of the characteristics of a class of persons. Thus we might talk of a representative sample, and demand that the legislature, if it is to be representative, is to be a mirror of the nation. Second, there is symbolic representation: indicating that a person symbolises the identity or qualities of a class of persons. Thus we might say that a queen represents her people. The third is where a representative denotes an agent who acts on behalf of his or her principal, as when we speak of a lawyer representing her client.

Iain MacLean offers a similar distinction to Pitkin's active and descriptive conceptions of representation in his distinction between principal-agent and microcosm forms of representation.[9] Principal-agent representation occurs when one person acts on behalf of one other, or when the agent acts in the principal's interests. Microcosm representation occurs when, in John Adams' words, the legislature are 'an exact portrait, in miniature, of the people at large, as it should think, feel, reason and act like them.' In other word, a group is representative if the sample includes the same proportion of each relevant subgroup as the population from which it is drawn. Such subgroups are usually assumed to be age, sex, class, racial division. Anne Phillips too makes a similar distinction within representation in her formulation of what she calls the 'politics of ideas' and the 'politics of presence'.[10] Both conceptions of representation can be applied to representatives, though they may conflict — representatives could conceivably be a microcosm of society in every relevant respect and still fail to do what the voters want. Conversely, they could do what the voters want without being statistically representative of them. In practice they usually fail to do either. The key difference here is whether one looks at the composition of Parliament to determine its representativeness, or whether one looks at its decisions.

In the quotas debate it would seem that its advocates are firmly endorsing a microcosm conception of representation, arguing that what matters is the number of women in Parliament in relation to the numbers of women in the population. Fair representation would therefore seem, in this context, to mean microcosm representation. Thus Clare Short, in a speech to the 1994 Labour Party Conference: 'I am one of the 167 women who have ever in the history of Britain been elected to the House of Commons. When you consider that we elect 650 MPs every time, this figure is an outrage. It means that our parliament is not representative of the country, and that our democracy is incomplete.' She also said: 'The beauty of the all-women short-list —

unlike the one woman on a short-list formula—is that it guarantees a real political choice to the local party, and it guarantees an increase in women's representation.' What is meant here is clearly that quotas guarantee an increase in the number of women present within Parliament. No guarantees can be made, through these mechanisms alone, that the concerns or interests of women constituents will be represented more effectively, as would be required in the principal/agent conception of representation. Many advocates of quotas, of course, imply that we will more adequately realise the principal/agent conception by ensuring that the microcosm form of representation is guaranteed. But this hope is based upon an assumed, and highly tendentious, direct correlation between gender (or 'presence') and interests (or 'ideas') which, in practice, is far from evident (Mrs Thatcher's failure to promote what some perceived to be women's interests being a clear manifestation of problematic status of the general assumption).

Microcosm: group 'presence'

Throughout this century there has been a growing interest in non-geographical communities as the basis for representation. Such interest develops out of a recognition of the importance of an emerging cultural politics of difference or identity politics. The distinctive feature of this is a rejection of the monolithic and homogeneous in the name of heterogeneity. The cultural politics of difference perspectives are commonly underpinned by a theory of subjectivity which is firmly critical of the classical liberal abstract individual. Cornell West perhaps summarises the characteristics of this school of thought best in the following passage: 'Distinctive features of the new cultural politics of difference are to trash the monolithic and homogeneous in the name of diversity, multiplicity and heterogeneity; to reject the abstract, general and universal in light of the concrete, specific and particular; and to historicize, contextualise and pluralize by highlighting the contingent, provisional, variable, tentative, shifting and changing.'[11] Thus, difference theorists and activists work to question many of the basic assumptions of classical liberalism by seeking to recognise 'differences of identity' within our political structures rather than transcend them.

This theoretical movement away from the general, universal and abstract towards the specific, particular and contextual has already characterised numerous current political developments—ethnic, religious, linguistic and gendered. Examples range from the founding of a separatist Maori party in New Zealand in 1979 in pursuit of the recognition of Maori distinctness (linguistic and cultural); the establishment of a Feminist Party in Iceland in 1981; the constitutional debates in Canada concerning appropriate recognition of a distinct French society, and the accompanying debates about separate representation for its Aboriginal population; the formation is the Islamic Parliament in Bradford in 1989 to represent Sunni Muslims, their organic notion of community generating a notion of collective representation which sits at odds with our individualist representative ethos. And finally, of course, the current strategy of the Labour Party to implement quotas for women at all levels of the party and to insist on all-women short lists in 50% of its vacant seats.

Most of these initiatives have been met with a conventional liberal individualist response along the lines that the political institutions of modern representative democracy do not and should not differentiate between citizens on the basis of identity differences: all persons, whatever their social and cultural background should be considered equal before the law.[12] Politics in this model is about transcending difference. It is the function of the state to act neutrally, to safeguard the individual rights of all its citizens. But this response does not begin to deal with the rising demands for group-based special rights, for cultural justice without assimilation and the public recognition of different group experiences and identities. What is more, this theoretical model has always in practice been moderated by the operation of the party system. Thus in reality, certain differences have always acknowledged in that system we call liberal democracy—it is simply that those deemed politically acceptable have been perceived to be those of interests and ideology, not those of identity.

The differences that a polity deems politically pertinent and the representative system that a particular polity adopts will of course be a normative decision influenced by the contingencies of dominant flows of power. The questions about representation that are deemed pertinent within any given polity at any given time reflect and perpetuate the main political cleavages in society, whether language, class, race, center-periphery or whatever. Thus one might argue that in Britain the issues deemed pertinent have been class and party, whilst in Northern Ireland they have been religion and territorial boundaries. Thus we must ask: what are we currently jettisoning from our representative agendas and why? What has our representative system chosen not to represent and for what reasons? Which differences have been articulated with our political structures, and which repressed?

The point then is that difference has always been an issue within liberal democracy. The issue of which differences were to matter politically has always been particularly sensitive. Differences of ideas and interests have been embedded within our representative system. On the other hand, differences of identity and presence have generally been deemed politically irrelevant. Based in a long-admired liberal commitment to tolerance, differences of identity have been claimed to be transcended in the political: firmly jettisoned from the public-political arena into the sphere of civil society. This allowed us to claim that we had moved from the illiberal discrimination on the basis of differences of identity to the (morally superior) liberal transcendence of identity differences. However, the 'cultural politics of difference' movements (within which the feminist arguments for quotas fall) would have us question the ethical and political desirability of this move. Here we find an endorsement of a second shift in relation to the political role of difference. This shift tends to be characterised as a move away from the liberal transcendence of identity difference to the radical democratic recognition of cultural differences, and sometimes even towards the demand for self-determination.

One needs to explore the potential benefits and hazards of moving from the representation of interests to the representation of identities; from the endorsement of a principle/agent conception of representation to a microcosm conception. What is there to commend it? On this, Hanna Pitkin was clear: 'Think of the legislative as a pictorial represen-tation or a representative sample of the nation, and you will almost certainly concentrate upon composition rather than its activities.' Such an over-emphasis on who is present in the legislative assemblies, she fears, will divert attention from more urgent questions of what the representatives actually do. Therefore activities rather than characteris-tics matter. Fair representation can not be guaranteed in advance; it can only be realised through responsiveness and secured by constitutional constraint. The quality of representation is here thought to depend on tighter mechanisms of accountability that bind politicians more closely to the opinions they profess to represent. Is this argument persuasive? Does microcosm representation have something to recommend it? In the context of our debate about the quotas policy, would the Labour Party's stated concern to guarantee a fairer representation be more effectively secured by addressing the mechanisms of accountability between representatives and the electorate or by specifying the desired composition of the representative body?

Amongst the most interesting and influential theoretical writings to have emerged recently on this issue, and possibly one of the strongest theoretical basis for defending the quotas policy on the basis of fairer representation, is to be found in the work of Iris Young. What characterises her distinctive contribution is the argument presented for group representation. This rests on the claim that existing electoral and legislative processes are unrepresentative in the sense that they fail to reflect the diversity of the population in terms of presence, leading her to demand that a certain number of seats in the legislature be reserved for the members of marginalised groups. This call is made on the assumption that under-representation can be overcome only by resort-ing to guaranteed representation and that representing difference requires constitutional guarantees of group participation within the parliamentary system. Groups who have suffered oppression of disad-vantage need guaranteed representation in order that their distinct voice be heard.

A politics of difference, she argues, requires the participation and inclusion of all groups by different treatment for oppressed or disadvantaged groups. This rejection of the assimilationist ideal is based in a belief that attachment to specific traditions, practices, language and other culturally specific forms is a crucial aspect of social existence. In this her argument is echoed by Charles Taylor's critique of 'difference-blind' theories which are in fact frequently (or possibly inevitably) a reflection of one hegemonic culture: 'Consequently,' he argues, 'the supposedly fair and difference-blind society is not only inhuman (because suppressing identities) but also, in a subtle and unconscious way, itself highly discriminatory.'[13] A truer manifestation of equality of respect would involve a recognition of the intrinsic value of the survival of the integrity of diverse cultures. Recognising the equal value of different cultures involves not only letting them survive, but acknowledging their worth. The question is this: what would such a recognition of worth entail in the practical arrangements of our representative system?

The answer given by Iris Young that a democratic public should provide mechanisms for the effective recognition and representation of the distinct voices and perspectives of those of its constituent groups that are oppressed or disadvantaged. Such group representation, she claims, implies institutional mechanisms and public resources supporting: self-organisation of group members so that they achieve collective empowerment and a reflective understanding of their collective experience and interests in the context of the society; group analysis and group generation of policy proposals in institutionalised contexts where decision-makers are obliged to show that their deliberations have taken group perspectives into consideration; group veto power regarding specific policies that affect a group directly, such as reproductive rights policy for women, or land use policy for Indian reservations.

Young rejects the strict principal/agent conception of representation. She argues that she is seeking specific representation not for interest groups or ideological groups, but for social groups: 'Social groups usually share some interests, but shared interests are not sufficient to constitute a social group. A social group is a collective of people who have affinity with one another because of a set of practices or way of life; they differentiate themselves from or are differentiated by at least one other group according to these cultural forms.' In making this distinction, it is differences of identities, rather than interests or ideologies, that are her concern in relation to our representative structures. In this, Young is clearly advocating what Anne Phillips has called a 'politics of presence' rather than a 'politics of ideas'. Yet, intriguingly, she does not go on to endorse a simple microcosm vision of representation, in the sense that representatives would be proportional to the polity. She notes that 'proportional representation of group members may sometimes be too little or too much at accomplish that aim.' and continues 'allocating strictly half of all places to women might be more than is necessary to give women's perspectives an empowered voice, and might make it more difficult for other groups to be represented'. It would appear that Young is not advocating a microcosm conception of representation after all, but a symbolic conception.

In this she is not alone; others have recognised the importance of the symbolic to the issue of group representation. Given this, I think it interesting to return momentarily to Pitkin, who notes that 'since the connection between symbol and referent seems arbitrary and exists only where it is believed in, symbolic representation seems to rest on emotional, affective, irrational psychological responses rather than on rationally justifiable criteria'.[14] Any attempt to answer the question whether political structures were representative, on this symbolic conception of representation, would therefore be highly subjective, offering little basis for constitutional guarantee.

Thus there are obvious tensions within this argument. Having endorsed a conception of difference as fluid and heterogeneous, Young nonetheless wants to hold onto the notion of there being definable and discernible women's perspectives; and, having argued for a politics of recognition, she nonetheless does not want to demand strict numerical presence. But who might constitute the group whose subjective assessment of representativeness is to count politically? Or, what would constitute recognition in this symbolic sense and who would determine its fulfilment? Given the critique of impartiality one must question whether there remains any basis for believing that a polity might secure mechanisms of (symbolic) representation that everyone, in all their diversity, feels to truly recognise their particularity. Thus, despite the evident appeal of Young's perspective, the problem with this type of attempt to simply graft identity politics onto our existing mechanisms of representative government are clear. The most immediate might be summarised thus: firstly, underpinning the argument for such representation is the assumption that people cannot empathise across lines of difference. This can lead to factionalism and the politics of the enclave. Secondly, the assumed sameness and cohesion within the groups merely replicates the assumption of sameness within society that group representation advocates want to criticise. Thirdly, mechanisms of accountability are hard to realise when one's constituents are self-defined identity groups with no formal membership mechanisms. We could continue: how are we to decide which groups should be entitled to group-based representation? Why privilege women as such a group? Are we asking that a group should be represented in proportion to its numbers in the population at large, or that there should be a threshold number of representatives? Is it important that representatives belong to one's group, or that they are elected by one's group? The upshot of such questioning may well be that this form of identity thinking ultimately leads to the notion that nobody can represent anyone else at all.

The problems facing Young's attempt to represent our identities within existing 'representative' structures are those inherent in dicing with the dangers of essentialism and factionalism. When formalised into the structures of state-based representation, such a group-based micro-cosm or symbolic representation can rigidify what are actually very fluid identities; it can lead to attempts to represent us on the basis of one aspect of our identities only; and it raises the serious question of whether the recognition of differences of identity thus formulated involves relinquishing the pursuit of any common perception of the justice of political structures.

The implications of this theoretical debate for the more concrete issue of the Labour Party's policy on quotas for women, are primarily twofold, one pro, one con. On the one hand, the cultural politics of difference perspective attunes us to the importance of recognising identity differences within our political structures rather than attempt-ing to transcend differences through the rhetoric of liberal neutrality and universality. As such, this perspective should make us more sceptical of those who claim that justice necessarily implies formal neutrality and that fair representation inevitably means not discriminating (positively or negatively) between men and women when selecting political candi-dates. Given the history of women's low participation within the formal mechanisms of politics it is clearly possible to argue that women constitute precisely one of the disadvantaged social groups which Young argues should be allocated special representation rights. On the other hand, given the fluidity and complexity of each of our identities, to claim that women as a group share a collective set of interests, or a common cultural perspective, which can be effectively represented only by other women, is to endorse a form of essentialism which rigidifies what are very fluid differences and dichotomises what are actually multiple perspectives.

The Labour Party's quotas policy is a clear move to introduce a microcosm form of representation into the House of Commons which has previously rejected this form of representation in favour of the principal/agent model. As such, it represents a significant departure for our political system, and one that has both strengths and weaknesses in relation to what has gone before. It is true that the Labour Party has a history of endorsing certain forms of group representation (such as affirmative action for trade unionists given resources to help bring 'working men' into parliament), but to date these have applied to interest and ideological groups only. The introduction of mechanisms for securing social group representation is a significant departure within our House of Commons (though perhaps not so within the House of Lords, based as it is, in part, on the inclusion of certain groups by virtue of their social group status).

On balance, there are valid reasons for endorsing the principal/agent conception of representation, rather than microcosm or symbolic rep-resentation. Given the desire to recognise difference more fully within our political system and address the justice issue, yet to avoid some of the potential pitfalls of microcosm representation, could we therefore recommend other strategies open to the Labour Party following the next general election and its potential abandonment of the short-lived quotas policy?

Representing difference without quotas

There are other proposals which attempt to recognise the importance of symbolic or microcosmic representation, thereby acknowledging the politics of presence, without falling into the traps of fragmentation and essentialism. Given the Labour Party's ambivalence about its own quotas policy it might be worth exploring these options rather more carefully than has previously been the case.

Some radical options involve relinquishing the procedures of election. John Burnheim, to take one notable example, argues that interests are better protected when we are represented by those who share our experience and interests, and that this similarity of condition is a far better indicator of representativeness than whether people might share our rather shaky opinions. He proposes that decision-makers should therefore be chosen by lot as a 'statistically representative' sample of the various groups concerned in the decisions.[15] James Fishkin, to take another example, argues for random sampling as a way of combating the power of money and the media in current elections. He proposes a mixture of deliberative opinion polls and the jury principle to replace current representative structures.[16] Both of these proposals have something to recommend them, but alone will not address the range of concerns raised by the politics of difference theorists.

More pragmatically, many have advocated the adoption of multi-member constituencies and a party lists system as a mechanism for achieving greater recognition of difference within one's political structures. Proportional representation is thought to allow for a greater inclusiveness of candidates for election by making under-representation in the nomination process both more visible and more accountable. Thus, party lists systems make for a more balanced line-up of candidates. Electoral systems make a big difference to the composition of legislatures. Countries with proportional representation and large numbers of representatives in districts are the leaders among democracies in the proportions of women in parliament. Political parties have an incentive to place women on their lists to broaden their appeal, whereas in single-member constituencies, political elites have a disincentive to risk backing a woman candidate (or any candidate perceived to be a risk).[17] Systems that allow for diversification and fragmentation generally are able to address the relative absence of women and minorities within the political system, without resorting to the entrenchment of such identities within existing party selection procedures.

In addition to these mechanisms for representing difference, we might also reflect more specifically on the sites of representation. It is interesting to note that most of these proposals for altering our representative structures remain firmly wedded to the nation-state as the site of representation. We might usefully ponder the benefits of subsidiarity to this discussion (see also Brown and Meehan in this volume). Multiple sites of representation would allow for multiple criteria of political difference to be accommodated. Indeed, it is somewhat surprising that much of the cultural politics of difference literature has taken the nation-state for granted as the site of the political, omitting to draw upon political writing which has pointed to the inadequacies of this partial conception of the political.[18]

Thus the recognition that there are plural strategies for fair representation, and that they may not be compatible is crucial. It allows us to move beyond the either/or of liberalism and a cultural politics of difference with regard to strategies of representation. The claim here is that neither will be successful in isolation and that both will be more adequately realised if they are clearly distinguished and pursued independently, preferably in different spatial arenas. Moving towards mechanisms of representation for particular societal structures may be one possible route of exploration for territorial, state-based representation may no longer by sufficient, if ever it was. We are now at a historical moment when we could think about disaggregation representation into structures which map onto particular networks of interests and reformulate the relationship between representation and place quite radically.[19]

In this context, the strongest argument to be made for realising group representation arising from a concern with the cultural politics of difference is neither the simple replacement of a principal/agent conception of representation with a microcosm or a symbolic conception, nor the current uneasy attempt to realise all three forms of representation within a single electoral system. Rather, I would argue for the imperative of recognising the plurality of sites of political activities and the diversity of forms of representation appropriate to each. No single conception of representation will do all the work we require of it. No single political arena is able to embody all the forms of representation demanded by recognition of both self-interests and self-images in their fullest diversity. General and local elections are a blunt form of representation, ever less able to represent the diversity and multiplicity within and between people. Tinkering with these structures will not begin to address the challenge posed by the new cultural politics of difference. A more expansive version of representation is needed, concerned not solely with parliament, but with the wider institutions of governmentality.

1   P. Norris, 'Labour Party Quotas for Women' in D. Broughton, D. Farrell, D. Denver and C. Rallings (eds), *British Elections and Parties* (Frank Cass, 1994).
2   *The Times* 8.3.95.
3   See P. Norris and J. Lovenduski, *Political Recruitment* (Routledge, 1995).

4 See I. Crewe, P. Norris and R. Waller, 'The 1992 General election' in P. Norris et al, *British Elections and Parties Yearbook 1992* (Harvester Wheatsheaf, 1992).
5 See S. Thomas, *How Women Legislate* (Oxford University Press, 1994); A. Mazur and D. McBride Stetson (eds), *Comparative State Feminism* (Sage, 1995).
6 R. Brooks, A. Eagle, C. Short, *Quotas Now: Women in the Labour Party* (Fabian Tract, 1990).
7 I. Young, *Justice and the Politics of Difference* (Princeton University Press, 1990).
8 H. Pitkin, *The Concept of Representation* (University of California Press, 1967).
9 I. MacLean, 'Forms of Representation and Systems of Voting' in D. Held (ed) *Political Theory Today* (Polity Press, 1991).
10 See A. Phillips, *The Politics of Presence* (Oxford University Press, 1995). See also Norris and Lovenduski op.cit.
11 C. West, *Keeping Faith* (Routledge, 1993).
12 See J. Rawls, 'Justice as Fairness: Political Not Metaphysical', *Philosophy and Public Affairs* (1985); R. Dworkin 'Liberalism' in S. Hampshire (ed), *Public and Private Morality* (Cambridge University Press, 1978); B. Ackerman, *Social Justice and the Liberal State* (Yale University Press, 1980).
13 C. Taylor, op.cit.
14 Cf. R. Goodin, 'Convention Quotas and Communal Representation', *British Journal of Political Science*, 1976; also W. Kymlicka, *Multicultural Citizenship: A Liberal Theory of Minority Rights* (Blackwell, 1995).
15 J. Burnheim, *Is Democracy Possible?* (Polity Press, 1985).
16 J. Fishkin, *Democracy and Deliberation: New Directions for Democratic Reform* (1991).
17 P. Norris, 'Women's Legislative Participation in Western Europe', *West European Politics*, (1985).
18 C. Pateman, *Participation and Democratic Theory* (Polity Press, 1970) and P. Hirst, *Associative Democracy* (Polity Press, 1994).
19 Cf. D. Massey, *Space, Place and Gender* (Polity Press, 1994).

Women Politicians: Transforming Westminster?

BY PIPPA NORRIS

THE last decade has experienced significant breakthroughs for women in British politics. There have been remarkable gains in local government. Women are about one quarter of all local councillors.[1] In London, one of the best areas for female representation, women have grown from one quarter of all local councillors in 1960 to one third in 1994. In line with most other countries, women in Britain do better at local than national level. Nevertheless, the traditional male grey suits which dominated Commons backbenches for centuries have gradually come to be displaced by more female members. From 1945 to 1983 there were about two dozen women MPs (under 5%), with some peaks and troughs in these figures. In 1987 the number of women members almost doubled, to 41, before rising to 60 in the 1992 general election (9.2%). We can not predict future trends. Nevertheless given past patterns of turnover, plus Labour's policy of all-women short-lists in half their target seats, the proportion of women MPs seems likely to rise, possibly to about 15% in the next general election.[2]

The focus here concerns the implications of this trend: what will be the impact of women's contribution to British public life? In particular, if the number of women at Westminster continues to increase, will they change politics due to their political attitudes, policy priorities, or legislative styles and roles? Here opinion is sharply divided, there are a variety of unstated and often contradictory assumptions underlying the writings on women and politics, and little systematic evidence in Britain. The aim here is to clarify this question by briefly summarising the existing debate in the literature re-examining the evidence based on the attitudes and behaviour of British politicians, and considering the consequences for representative democracy.

Theories of women's contribution to public life

Arguments for bringing more women into public life rest on a variety of normative and empirical claims (See Squires this volume). John Stuart Mill stressed the need to incorporate all talent in Parliament to help solve the nation's problems. Given the clear disparity between women as citizen and decision-makers, there are the simple grounds of equity and justice. Many feel that the absence of such a major sector of society undermines democratic legitimacy and public confidence in institutions. These arguments become more compelling if, in addition, women bring important perspectives and priorities which are currently underrepresented in the policy-making process. One common argument which underlies much popular discourse is the claim that women speak 'in a different voice', whether based on biological, psychological or sociological theories of gender differences.[3]

The most plausible account is provided by sociological theory, based on three core assumptions. First, in society as a whole most women's and men's lives continue to diverge sharply. Structural differences stretch from cradle to grave: from women's upbringing and education, their primary roles as care-givers within the family, their marginalisation and occupational segregation within the paid labour-force, and even their patterns of health and longevity. Second, it is assumed that these differences will lead to a distinctive women's perspective on many major issues facing society. These range from more commonly defined 'women's policies' like reproductive rights, women's health care and the provision of nursery places, through less obviously gendered concerns such as public transportation, environmental protection and Northern Ireland. Lastly, given this distinctive political perspective, an effective democracy requires that the voices of women should be heard in the policy-making process (see also Squires in this volume).[4] By electing more women to public office, feminists argue that women would represent other women, articulate women's concerns, and change the nature and direction of public policy.[5] Since women's interests are themselves varied and divergent, divided by the major cleavages in society of class, race and region, we cannot assume that a few female MPs will be able to articulate the interests of all women. Nevertheless, more women at Westminster would, it is argued, gradually come to reflect the diverse concerns of society as a whole. Members as varied as Diane Abbott, Theresa Gorman, Gillian Shephard and Clare Short can each articulate different dimensions of women's experience in Britain today.

There is nothing novel about this perspective. Today the claim focuses on gender and ethnic representation, although in the past it was commonly heard in terms of class interests. The Labour Party was founded at the turn of the century as the political voice of the trade union movement, on the grounds that the Liberal and Conservative parties did not share, and could not represent, the concerns of working men. The rationale for regional parties rests on the same grounds: that representatives from Scotland or Wales can express the distinct concerns of citizens in these regions.

Based on this argument, many expect women members to make a distinctive contribution at Westminster through their policy priorities as well as attitudes, and their styles of leadership. Some of the most heated battles in politics revolve around the policy agenda: which problems are seen as most important and deserving of government action. In this regard, it is felt that women will give greater priority to issues involving women, children and the family. In addition, other problems may be redefined to incorporate a gendered perspective. Women may have distinctive interests in a wide range of issues; examples include homelessness, public transport, and crime. Moreover, in terms of personal style, some expect that women will introduce a 'kinder, gentler' politics, one characterised by cooperation rather than conflict, collaboration rather than hierarchy, honesty rather than sleaze.

The debate in the literature

Research, mainly derived from other countries, has failed to resolve this debate. Some studies have stressed women's distinctive contribution to elected office, others have emphasised the similarities among women and men politicians, while still others have suggested that gender differences in politics are contingent upon their broader institutional context.

The literature in comparative politics lends credence to claims that women have a distinctive policy agenda. American studies have shown that, compared with men, women in Congress and State legislatures are far more supportive of women's rights, and are more likely to sponsor bills in health, welfare and consumerism.[6] Scandinavian research found a gender-related division of parliamentary activity in terms of tabling motions, parliamentary questions and speeches. In the early 1980s women MPs in Finland and Norway were more likely to ask parliamentary questions in the sphere of reproduction (such as about the family, health, housing, the environment and consumer policy), while men were more likely to ask questions about production (such as the labour market, communications, fiscal policies and energy). Where 'women's questions' were raised in Scandinavian politics, it was invariably women representatives who raised them.[7] Studies of the European Parliament found that when sex equality issues were discussed, this was due to initiatives by women members.[8]

Other evidence indicates a gender gap in general political attitudes and behaviour. American women in elected office have been found to be more liberal than men within the same party in their voting records and attitudes towards issues such as the environment, welfare and military spending.[9] Previous studies of British MPs found that women within each party were more left-wing and supportive of feminist values than men, while they were also more likely to prioritise social policy issues.[10] Many personal anecdotes, though little systematic evidence, suggest that women have a different personal style of politics.[11] There is a widespread popular perception that women politicians are more compassionate, ethical and collaborative than men.[12] In 1992 and 1994 women running for Congress often found it advantageous to campaign as outsiders ready to clean up 'politics as usual'. This does not suggest that gender is the only factor influencing women politicians. Rather, given the competing claims of different constituencies, this claim is that gender is one factor affecting legislative behaviour alongside others like party, interest group affiliations, ideology, cohort of entry, status, region and seat.

Nevertheless, there are considerable grounds for scepticism about claims that women politicians will transform politics. We cannot assume that gender differences in the United States will necessarily be replicated elsewhere, nor that mass-level differences will necessarily affect the elite. Recent research suggests that the last three decades saw increasing similarities between Scandinavian women and men MPs in their political communications.[13] Comparative studies of female leaders, such as Benazir Bhutto, Corazon Aquino and Margaret Thatcher, have usually stressed that they are highly diverse and difficult to classify as a group in their career patterns, leadership styles and policy agendas.[14] Perceptions that women politicians are more ethical or compassionate may be based on deep-rooted social stereotypes which need to be challenged rather than reinforced.[15] Previous work on the British Parliament found that in the 1970s few women entered politics with the primary intention of representing women and their interests, and women's interventions in debates or questions were unlikely to take up exclusively 'female' issues.[16]

Even if women politicians enter politics driven by different goals, there are strong institutional constraints on how far individual members can attempt to challenge the dominant policy agenda or parliamentary procedure without being marginalised politically. Backbenchers may find they have little room for independence, given the strength of party discipline. In this view, the argument for electing more women needs to be based on different premises, such as the contention that the democratic legitimacy of Parliament is undermined if it fails to include representatives from all section of society.[17] According to such arguments we should not expect women politicians to behave any differently to their male counterparts or evaluate them against a different, possibly higher, standard.

The last perspective in this debate is 'critical mass' theory, which suggests that political behaviour is shaped by its structural context. Based loosely on a 'new institutionalism' perspective, this theory stresses that politicians respond strategically to the opportunities around them. In this view, few gender differences in legislatures will be evident so long as women remain a distinct minority. But the situation may be transformed once women reach a critical mass.[18] Dahlerup identified four types of situation: uniform groups, totally dominated by one group; skewed groups with minorities below 15%; tilted groups have minorities up to 40%; balanced groups with ratios within 60:40.[19] She suggests that as parliaments in Scandinavia have shifted from skewed to tilted groups, there have been changes in the political culture, dominant discourse and policy agenda.

The theoretical basis for this argument can be applied to any arena, whether management, academia or politics, where the 'in-group' perpetuates and reinforces the dominant culture, smothering 'out-groups' from challenging institutional norms and procedures.[20] Members of minority groups have to internalise institutional norms for successful entry and career promotion. Women have to 'go along to get along', as do members of minority parties, regions or interests. In this perspective, so long as women remain a skewed group at Westminster, even if they have a distinctive set of priorities, we can not expect them to behave any differently from other members. But once they become a tilted or even balanced group, then we might expect a gradual transformation of the mainstream policy agenda.

To re-examine the empirical basis for these theories, we can turn to *The British Candidate Study*, a major survey of politicians and party members in the 1992 general election.[21] For the sample of British politicians, we combine the survey of 1,320 MPs and parliamentary candidates (with a response rate of 69%), and 361 applicants who failed to become candidates (with a response rate of 55%). Although not confined to parliamentarians, this has the advantage of including a broader sample of those currently aspiring to power and sufficient numbers of women to provide a more reliable analysis than one confined to women in the House of Commons. Throughout the analysis it is assumed that party will prove the major fault line in British politics, so we are concerned with comparing gender differences within and between the major parties. Most of the analysis is based on simple frequency distributions, summarised by the Percentage Difference Index which represents the percentage in favour minus the percentage against each item. This has been standardised so that a positive figure represents a more left-wing response.

Political attitudes

First, turning to attitudes toward women's rights, where we might expect to find the clearest evidence for gender differences, where do women and men stand within each party? The survey included items concerning domestic violence, marital rape, abortion rights and equal opportunities for women. The results in Figure 1 reveal a striking pattern: across all four items women proved consistently more strongly in favour of women's rights, with the largest gap within the Conservative Party. On the issue whether equal rights for women had 'gone too far', for example, male Conservatives tended to agree with this statement while female Conservatives disagreed. The gender gap was usually clearest between parties, but it occasionally overrode party divisions. For example, on the question of abortion rights and domestic violence, women Conservatives proved more strongly in favour of women's rights than male Liberal Democrats.

Turning to the major economic issues facing Britain, the survey used trade-off measures to gauge attitudes towards nationalisation versus privatisation, taxes versus services, inflation versus unemployment, and

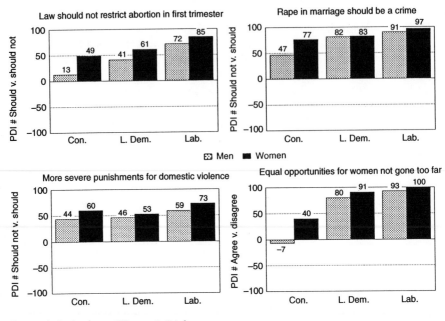

Figure 1. Attitudes to Women's Rights

trade union power. There are all issues which featured prominently in the classic left-right divisions between parties and voters in the last general election. The results in Figure 2 suggest that the gender difference on these issues was more modest, with party proving the best predictor of attitudes. Where there was a gender difference within parties, however, women tended to be slightly more left-wing on all the items except trade union power.

The literature suggests that social issues are an area where we might expect a significant gender gap. To measure social attitudes, the survey included items on equal opportunities for ethnic minorities, the encouragement of private medicine, whether welfare benefits have gone too far, and the use of the death penalty. These items revealed (see Figure 3) that the major cleavage lay between the Conservatives and the parties in opposition. Yet within parties, where there was a modest gender difference, as before women were slightly more left-wing/liberal than men.

The last set of attitudes concerns foreign policy, including Britain's nuclear weapons, levels of defence spending, European integration, and Britain's international links with Europe and America. Security and defence issues are ones where previous studies have found women to be more pacific, and where the parties have taken distinctive policy stands. The results in Figure 4 confirm that women are significantly more unilateralist within each party. The pattern is less clear cut on defence spending, where the previous pattern is reversed in the Conservative

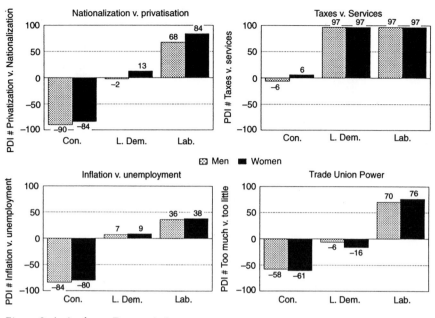

Figure 2. Attitudes to Economic Issues

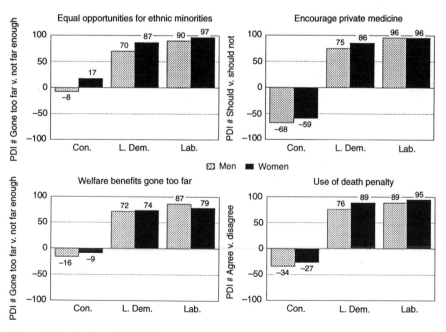

Figure 3. Attitudes to Social Issues

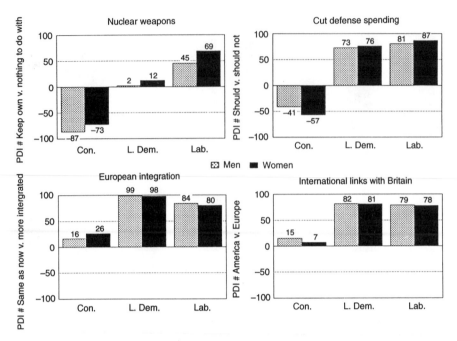

Figure 4. Attitudes to Foreign Policy Issues

Party. Europe has proved an issue bitterly dividing the Conservative Party, precipitating its leadership contests. The nuances of measuring attitudes towards Europe are complex, and the BCS survey indicates that to the extent that Conservative women are divided on this issue; notwithstanding Theresa Gorman's outspoken contribution to the debate, there are more Eurosceptics among the men.

On the basis of this evidence we can conclude that across a range of major political issues, not surprisingly party proves to be the best predictor of attitudes. But this does not mean that gender is irrelevant, as some have assumed. If selection meetings pick more women, they are selecting candidates who tend to be located on the more left/liberal side of their party. Moreover, while modest gender differences are evident across most items, the strongest gender gap relates to issues of women's rights. If these attitudes influence the behaviour of MPs in parliamentary questions, debates, Private Members Bills, legislative amendments and the process of policy formulation within parties, the entry of more women members may well have an impact on the policy-making process.

Policy priorities

But will women influence not just the direction of the policy agenda, but also which items are seen as important? To examine policy priorities, the BCS survey used an open-ended question asking politicians to specify 'the three most important problems facing the country at the present time in order of priority'. These responses were classified into 90 minor sub-categories, then collapsed into three major categories concerning economic, social and foreign policy issues. The results were then transformed into weighted scales reflecting the priority given to the issue, (first issue = 3, second issue = 2, third issue = 1). These weights were then combined with the number of times each issue was mentioned. For example, someone who said that unemployment (weighted 3), interest rates (weighted 2) and inflation (weighted 1) were the three most important issues, in that order, was scored highly on the economic priority scale (total score of 6). It should be noted that there were party differences within each major category, e.g., in the economic category Labour were more likely to prioritise unemployment while Conservatives mentioned business confidence or inflation more frequently. Someone who thought education (weighted 3), unemployment (weighted 2) and electoral reform (weighted 1) were the most important would be given a lower score (2) on the economic priority scale. The scales were then used as dependent variables in a standard regression analysis controlling for the party, elected status and social background of politicians (see Table 1).

1: Gender and Policy Priorities

	Economic	Social	Foreign	
Party	.35**	.30**	.15**	Conservative/other party
Incumbency	.18**	.04	.03	MP/non-elected
Gender	.07	.11**	.04	male/female
Race	.05	.01	.01	white/non-white
Class	.02	.01	.03	working/middle-class
Graduate	.05	.06*	.06*	graduate degree/none
Age	.03	.06*	.02	years of age
Religion	.02	.04	.01	belong to religion/none
Union	.09*	.07*	.01	union member/not
Income	.06	.09*	.05	household income (categories)
R2	.17	.12	.04	total variance

Note: OLS regression analysis with standardized beta coefficients.
See text for the construction of the scales.
Q. 'What would you say are the three most important problems facing the country at the present time? Please list in order of priority . . .'
** = sig p. .01   * = sig p. .05
Source: BCS 92 (N. 1681)

The results in Table 1 indicate that party proved the best predictor of policy priorities, with each party emphasising their areas of greatest strength. Not surprisingly, Labour politicians were far more likely to express concern about social issues like education, pensions and the health service, while the Conservatives were more likely to rate highly foreign and defence issues like European Monetary Union and Eastern Europe. Similarly, the minor parties emphasised issues like the environment (the Greens), or constitutional reform (the Liberal Democrats and the Scottish Nationalists).

After controlling for party and incumbency, gender proved to be significantly associated with the priority given to social policy issues. That is, in the open-ended questions women were more likely to express concern about issues like welfare services, poverty and health. Yet it should be stressed that these differences concerned general social policy priorities. Only two or three women politicians spontaneously mentioned issues which related more specifically to the agenda of the women's movement, such as equal opportunities for women, the provision of nursery schools or tax relief for childcare. In response to the question about 'the most important issue facing the country' politicians tended to reflect the main issues on the public agenda during the general election campaign, where women's issues did not feature as a major part of the debate. It is possible that a different response might have been forthcoming from alternative measures, such as a question about what problem politicians would focus upon if they had the opportunity to sponsor a Private Members Bill.

Legislative styles and roles

The last issue relates to styles of political leadership and legislative roles. As mentioned earlier, one of the most contentious matters of dispute concerns whether women bring a more compassionate, caring and collaborative approach to the way they conduct politics. Certainly, perceptions by party members support these images. Members were asked whether a man or a woman candidate would have a range of qualities, or whether there would be no difference. The most common response was gender-neutral, but where differences were perceived these confirmed common gender stereotypes. Women candidates tended to be seen as more caring, practical, approachable, honest, principled, and hardworking. In contrast, men were seen as more ruthless, ambitious, tough, effective and decisive.[22]

But do these images reflect social stereotypes or reality? This is a difficult issue to evaluate as there is little systematic evidence. One indicator is the priority MPs gave to different legislative roles. By legislative roles we mean the activities which politicians perceive as appropriate and the priorities they allocate to different aspects of their work in Parliament (Legislative votes are the most important dimensions of behaviour, but roll call analysis is not employed here given the constraints of party discipline in the British Parliament). The focus on legislative roles seeks to understand motivation by linking cognitive goals with personality predispositions. Roles shape what politicians do, how they do it, and why they think it appropriate behaviour. Work at Westminster involves many different tasks: attending parliamentary debates, dealing with individual case-work, appearing on the media, developing party policy, answering constituency mail, holding surgeries, scrutinising legislation in select committees, attending local party meetings, and so on. Political careers are not clearly defined, there are no established qualifications or agreed job specifications. Given a hundred and one demands on their attention, MPs can priorities their roles in many different ways.

Many differences have been noted in the roles British MPs adopt. These differences have been explained by party, type of constituency and political generation.[23] But gender may also influence the roles MPs adopt. Do women members choose to work in select committees while men prefer the cut and thrust of parliamentary debate? Do men spend more time on legislation while women prioritise constituency case-work?

To gauge roles, the BCS measured how politicians prioritised 14 different tasks ranging from speaking in Parliament to holding constituency surgeries, supporting the party leader, working with interest groups and dealing with the press. Responses were subject to factor analysis to see if they were structured in a consistent fashion.[24] This analysis revealed three primary dimensions of legislative roles, which accounted for 43% of variance. Respondents saw themselves primarily as constituency workers, party loyalists or parliamentarians.

The largest group, *constituency workers*, gave the highest priority to helping people with individual problems, holding regular constituency surgeries and representing local interests in Parliament. In personal interviews Labour and Conservative MPs often mentioned that public service to the community, helping with particular problems of social services or pensions, and looking after people, was one of the most rewarding parts of the job:

'First of all there's the constituency work. I enjoy it, the social worker side of it, looking after people's individual problems. That's a chore for a lot of colleagues. Its not a chore for me; its a pleasure.'

'I think I've got abilities to help people—part of my job, I mean, I'm a lawyer, and I'm a commercial lawyer, but inevitably in the law there's quite a strong element of helping people, whether you're acting for people or whether you're assisting, and I enjoy that aspect of it, and as I went on with being a candidate and doing more and more constituency related work, the more I realised that I really enjoyed that element—the element of assisting people.'

'I've always had a great desire to be of service, I feel this very strongly—service to the public. I don't profess to be very skilled at lots of things but one thing. I always like to help people, so I think perhaps the constituency side has more attractions than anything within the executive as it were, so I think the key thing was public service.'

In contrast *parliamentarians* gave greater priority to broader legislative activities within the House, such as speaking in debate, working in parliamentary committees and dealing with the media. For these people, Parliament was seen as the place to get things done, the national forum to debate the great issues of state, the main check on the power of the executive. The clearest expression of the parliamentary category came from Conservative MPs like the following:

'Power, in so far as one ever has power in any democracy, is at the centre and if I want to influence the nation's affairs this is the place I have to get to.'

'One sees all the big decisions taken in Parliament, and I became more and more interested in that . . . I think that's where you get things done, where you change things, where you can work for people most effectively.'

Some liked debates while others preferred the quieter committee work behind the scenes, whether select or standing committees:

'I do a lot of standing committees, bills going through line by line. I enjoy these more than I enjoy the chamber. Chamber's quite fun, but it's a theatrical thing rather than, in my view, about government.'

Lastly, *party loyalists* placed the greatest stress on their role as party representatives, whether as standard bearers at election or supporters in the Commons. This group gave high priority to sustaining the party leader, defending and developing party policy, and voting the party line in divisions. For some applicants, the election was primarily about party not personal victory:

'I felt that I'd something to offer the Labour party. I felt that the experience that I'd got on the City Council, my energy and enthusiasm—I felt that I could win a seat for Labour.'

'I thought that I could win the seat for the Labour party—proved to be right, and I feel I can do the job as well as anybody else can.'

In order to examine whether gender had an impact on the roles politicians thought appropriate, the battery of items on legislative activities were used to develop standardised summary scales, based on each role, ranging from 0 to 100. The results of the regression analysis in Table 2 show that gender proved significant across all three roles, with more women than men giving high priority to constituency work.

2: Gender and Legislative Roles

	Constituency Worker	Party Loyalist	Parliament	
Party	.03	.21**	.01	Conservative/other party
Incumbency	.03	.01	.10*	MP/non-elected
Gender	.11**	.06*	.11**	male/female
Race	.01	.01	.04	white/non-white
Class	.04	.06	.03	working/middle-class
Graduate	.05	.03	.05	graduate degree/none
Age	.01	.05*	.05	years of age
Religion	.08*	.07*	.03	belong to religion/none
Union	.13**	.17**	.12**	union member/not
Income	.04	.11**	.02	household income (categories)
R2	.03	.07	.04	total variance

Note: OLS regression analysis with standardized beta coefficients.
Q: 'In your view, how important are the following parts of an MPs job?'
See text for the construction of the scales.
** = sig p. .01   * = sig p. .05
Source: BCS 92 (N. 1681)

Moreover, this pattern was confirmed by evidence about the number of hours which members said they devoted to different activities at Westminster and in their constituencies. As shown in Table 3, male MPs thought they devoted about 29 hours per week to constituency work, while women MPs estimated they spent substantially longer, about 36.5 hours per week, on constituency activities. The biggest contrast was in the hours spent on casework helping individuals with such problems as housing, social services or welfare rights. As further evidence, women also estimated that they received far more letters from constituents (121 per week) than men (87 per week). In contrast male MPs spent more time on party activities, especially informal meetings with other members and in backbench party committees. There were fewer differences in parliamentary hours, except that women spent marginally more time in debates while men favoured work in select committees.

3: Hours Per Week on Parliamentary Work

	Men MPs	Women MPs	Diff.
Dealing with constit. casework	14.1	20.8	6.8
Holding constit. surgeries	3.0	3.8	.8
Attending other constituency functions	4.9	5.6	.6
Travelling time to constituency	6.7	6.3	.5−
Constituency sub-total	28.8	36.5	7.7
Attending local party meetings	2.4	2.1	.3−
Backbench party committees	2.7	2.0	.7−
Informal meetings with MPs	5.9	3.7	2.2−
Meeting group representatives	3.6	3.6	.1−
Party sub-total	14.6	11.4	3.2−
Parliamentary debates	7.8	8.9	1.2
Standing committees	4.0	3.6	.4−
Select committees	2.2	1.2	1.1−
Parliament sub-total	14.0	13.7	.2−
Total hrs p. w. work as an MP	65.5	75.4	9.9

Conclusions

The debate about bringing more women into Parliament raises complex issues. There is a strong argument that the legitimacy and authority of Parliament is undermined if it fails to reflect the diversity of British society. In the classic view of representative government, Parliament should be the main debating chamber for the nation, the forum where all voices are heard. On symbolic grounds alone, the case can be made for increasing the number of women MPs in Britain. Yet the substantive argument is harder to sustain with good evidence. The results of this study suggest that gender influences policy attitudes, priorities and legislative roles. Women tended to give stronger support for issues of women's rights, they express greater concern about social policy issues, and they give higher priority to constituency casework. This gender difference should not be exaggerated, since, as might be expected in

British politics, party proved the strongest divider among politicians. The gender gap among politicians was often modest. Nevertheless, the study suggests that the election of more women to Westminster has the potential to make more than just a symbolic difference.

1 J. Lovenduski and P. Norris, *Gender and Party Politics* (Sage, 1994), p. 44.
2 P. Norris, 'Labour Party Quotas for Women' in D. Broughton et al, *British Elections and Parties Yearbook 1994* (Frank Cass, 1995).
3 Cf. R. M. Kelly, M. A. Saint-Germain and J. D. Horn 'Female Public Officials: A Different Voice?' *Annals of the American Academy of the Political and Social Science* 1991.
4 Cf. A. Phillips, *Democracy and Difference* (Pennsylvania State University Press, 1993).
5 S. J. Carroll, *Women as Candidates in American Politics* (Indiana University Press, 2e, 1995).
6 S. Thomas *How Women Legislate* (Oxford University Press, 1994); D. Dodson and S. J. Carroll *Reshaping the Agenda: Women in State Legislatures* (CAWP, 1991); S. Thomas and S. Welch, 'The Impact of Gender on Activities and Priorities of State Legislators', *Western Political Quarterly*, 1991; B. Reingold, 'Concepts of Representation among Female and Male State Legislators', *Legislative Studies Quarterly*, 1992.
7 T. Skard and E. Haavio-Mannila, 'Women in Parliament' in E. Haavio-Mannila et al, *Unfinished Democracy: Women in Nordic Politics* (Pergamon Press, 1985).
8 E. Vallance 'Do Women Make a Difference? The Impact of Women MEPs on Community Equality Policy' in M. Buckley and M. Anderson (eds), *Women, Equality and Europe* (Macmillan, 1988).
9 S. Thomas, *How Women Legislate*; (Oxford University Press, 1994); S. Welch, 'Are Women More Liberal than Men in the US Congress?' *Legislative Studies Quarterly* 1985; D. Dodson and S. J. Carroll *Reshaping the Agenda: Women in State Legislatures* (CAWP, 1991); S. J. Caroll, D. L. Dodson and R. B. Mandel *The Impact of Women in Public Office* (CAWP, 1991); P. Norris, 'Women in Congress: A Policy Difference?', *Politics* 1986; D. W. Cantor and T. Bernay, *Women in Power: The Secrets of Leadership* (Houghton Mifflin, 1992).
10 P. Norris and J. Lovenduski, *Political Recruitment: Gender, Race and Class in the British Parliament* (Cambridge University Press, 1995), pp. 218–24.
11 L. Witt, K. M. Paget and G. Matthews, *Running as a Woman: Gender and Power in American Politics* (Free Press, 1994).
12 P. Norris and J. Lovenduski, *Political Recruitment*, (Cambridge University Press, 1995) p. 135.
13 L. Karvonen, G. Djupsund and T. Carlson, 'Political Language' in L. Karvonen and P. Selle, *Women in Nordic Politics: Closing the Gap* (Dartmouth, 1995).
14 F. D'Amico, 'Women National Leaders' in F. D'Amico and P. Beckman (eds), *Women in World Politics* (Bergin and Garvey, 1995); M. A. Genovese (ed), *Women as National Leaders* (Sage, 1993).
15 J. E. Williams and D. L. Best, *Measuring Sex Stereotypes: A Multinational Study* (Sage, 1990); L. Huddy and N. Terkildsen, 'Gender Stereotypes and the Perception of Male and Female Candidates', *American Journal of Political Science*, 1993.
16 E. Vallance, *Women in the House* (Athlone Press, 1979).
17 A. Phillips, *Democracy and Difference* (Pennsylvania State University Press, 1993).
18 Cf. V. Sapiro, 'When Are Interests Interesting?', *American Political Science Review*, 1981.
19 D. Dahlerup, 'From a Small to a Large Minority: Women in Scandinavian Politics', *Scandinavian Political Studies* 11(4).
20 V. Klein, *The Feminine Character: History of an Ideology* (Routledge and Kegan Paul, 1946).
21 For details see Norris and Lovenduski, op.cit.
22 Norris and Lovenduski, op.cit., 1995, 135.
23 D. D. Searing, *Westminster's World* (Harvard University Press, 1994).
24 For details see Norris and Lovenduski, op.cit., 1995, 221.

Women MPs and the Media:
Representing the Body Politic

BY ANNABELLE SREBERNY-MOHAMMADI AND KAREN ROSS

REPRESENTATION has two central dimensions: political speaking for others, and mediated presentation through word and image.[1] Recent feminist theory has explored the gendered nature of democracy and the public sphere,[2] and the gendered dynamics of political representation in Britain and elsewhere.[3] But there has been a notable lacuna in analysis of the other form of representation, the manner in which the mediated presentation of politics is gendered, and its implications for representative democracy at large and specifically for strategies to increase women's political participation. Work in political communication has tended to lack a gender dimension, while feminist work on the media has tended to focus on entertainment formats, rather than the 'fact-based' genre of current affairs that address the viewer as a gendered citizen.[4] A recent overview of research work on television and gender representation reinforces the historic emphasis toward entertainment rather than factual programming.[5] Yet, the media have considerable power to frame our understanding of public life, set the agenda of policy issues and influence the political process.[6] In the on-going struggles to get better gender representation in the political sphere, insufficient attention has been paid to media content and its possible effects on aspiring candidates, political activists or the electorate at large. Both the manner in which issues relevant to women are framed and the way in which those active in public life are represented may play crucial roles in the formation of public opinion in general and the mobilization of women voters in particular. Indeed, recent research does suggest strong public expectations of differential competencies and interests between male and female candidates.[7] The double gendering at work—in both the gendered nature of representational politics as well as the gendered nature of media coverage—must be analysed together.

As research on the interface between women, media and politics begins to develop, the most common way to explore these issues has been to analyse media content. Early research evidence from both print and broadcast news media suggested that women were invisible in news coverage, famously summarised as their 'symbolic annihilation'.[8] Later work has focused on stereotyping, negative women-as-victim coverage, and a gender imbalance in the amount of coverage given to male and female political leaders.[9] Often the limited and negative coverage of women can be explained by the gender imbalances within the media industries, which are most skewed in the area of news and current affairs.[10] Hence the argument is made that more women reporters and newscasters might provide better coverage of women in politics. But another, more subtle line of argument is challenging the too-easy assertion of negative coverage. By showing that coverage is indeed different for men and women leaders and that the media may send mixed signals, some negative and some positive, the way is opened for a more nuanced assessment of gendered media representations and strategies to improve them.[11]

Here we analyse perceptions of media coverage by women MPs (who still comprise less than 10% of British MPs): how they view their own coverage, what impact they feel it has, and any strategies they have developed to cope with the media.[12] All 63 women MPs were invited to take part and 28 agreed to be interviewed (22 Labour, 6 Conservative). They are not necessarily representative of all women politicians, although there is a surprising coincidence of views on some issues among this group, which includes left-wing and right-wing socialists and wet and dry Tories. All direct quotations are from Labour MPs except where specifically labelled otherwise.

Media reporting on politics: the tabloidization of news

Our interviewees broadly acknowledged a tendency toward the 'tabloidization' of both print and broadcast media, a phenomenon already widely analysed in the academic literature.[13] They viewed this as part of the growing commercialization and trivialization of the news media:
'I think the whole of the media's agenda now is based on the 15-second attention span. It is impossible to develop an argument about anything in 15 seconds.'

Trivialization, hype and sensationalism were felt to characterize political reporting, all anathema to sustained debate about serious public issues, and as the journalistic framing intrudes more, so political actors are silenced:
'The commentating has become more intrusive, actually talking over what people are saying as if the commentator knows more than the person speaking, as if they are more important.'

Concern over the downgrading of political news and its increasing tabloidization is not gender-specific, many of the women referring to work carried out by Jack Straw MP which looked at the way in which political reporting in the press had fared over the past fifty years.[14] He found that a steady decline had taken place over the half-century but that between 1988 and 1992 reporting in the broadsheet press had significantly reduced, in some cases to a quarter of the space previously allocated to such stories.

A number of our interviewees were concerned about the adversarial nature of British politics. They were even more worried that this is mirrored by a confrontational media approach which gives the impression that politics is only about argument, that all parties are constantly locked in permanent and irreconcilable conflict. This is largely to do with the nature of political reporting and what television in particular selects to broadcast. Most people's visual access to the Palace of Westminster is via the televising of Parliament, but the tendency is to broadcast only the most combative and theatrical aspects of the parliamentary process, that is, Prime Minister's Questions on Tuesdays and Thursdays. These two very brief sessions are thus seen as representative of the way in which Parliament operates, with constant shouting, heckling and general bad behaviour:

'Those who wish to be outrageous are outrageous at 3.30 on Tuesdays and Thursdays when they know the whole world's watching. The usual clowns play to the gallery, those who want to make outrageous accusations do so under the cloak of privilege.' (Conservative)

As many women pointed out, this is a very narrow aspect of the business of the House and much more work takes place in committees, some of which are open to the public, where a more consensual style of politics is typical. The programme formats of *Question Time*, *Newsnight* and *On the Record* continue the aggressive interrogation and the adversarial politics, hardly conducive to sustained analysis of policy issues. The emergence of the 'star' interviewer was regarded as antithetical to proper political debate as audiences tune in to listen or watch popular interviewers such as John Humphrys, Jeremy Paxman or David Frost score points rather than engage in serious politics. To get on *Breakfast with Frost* or be interviewed by John Humphrys on the *Today* programme means that a politician has really hit the big-time and interviewers seem to deliberately cultivate an aggressive posture to make more entertaining programming. Women politicians lamented the good old days of serious political reporting but did not think that a return to those (perhaps mythical) halcyon days was remotely likely. Male politicians' own ambivalences toward increasing numbers of women politicians means that some 'women-bashing' copy may originate from deep within the party structure itself, on both sides of the House. A review of press reporting of the Labour leadership elections in 1994 brought the irresistible conclusion that many of the anti-Margaret Beckett stories had impeccable socialist sources.[15]

Many women MPs were very concerned about the impact of such negative political coverage on public attitudes. Media strategies that construct all politicians as self-serving self-publicists ripe for bringing down a peg or ten are hardly conducive to building public confidence in elected representatives or political institutions. Some argued that the media actively restrict access to information:

'The public are extremely selectively informed. When I hear the press rabbiting against censorship, the press are the censors, the media are the censors. They decide what we'll know, what bits of the news will be shown, what bits of the news will be hyped, what will be tucked away on page 10 and what will not be reported at all.'

However, some politicians do not help their own cause:
'The media is publishing what it hopes will sell its newspapers and the thought of some torpid and seemingly irrelevant debate about something or other is not very interesting. You only have to look at Maastricht. It was all about what the rebels would do, but nobody in the populace at large had a clue what was going on. Even the Chancellor of the Exchequer said that he hadn't read the treaty and when you've got that level of admission from someone who you would have thought would have read it, then the public at large are entitled to think that it doesn't really matter about the detail, what matters is the fun and games part of it. The media dictates that focus, but they are ratings-driven and they are only going to publish what they think people will want to read.'

A number of women pointed to the extreme partiality and danger inherent in a lobby system which tends towards the use of very few legitimate sources whose limited views may well provide a misleading spin on policy. Lobby correspondents are not that interested in back-benchers, unless they want to make trouble and then they deliberately court dissident opinion. Journalists may talk to only a few people before coming to a conclusion about what is going on:
'You see it in the lobby here, every day between 2.00 and 2.30, they tend to talk to a very limited number of people and there are some people giving out information on our side, for instance, who give it from a very specific point of view and that can be dangerous because it gives a false impression.'
'The ordinary man or woman in the street who is not an expert in health or in education or any of these things, listens to a reporter condensing something that has been said in the House or by a particular politician into what he wants the people to hear, not reporting actually what was said and that is a tremendous power. And I regret that that power is not being used wisely or carefully.' (Conservative)
These women MPs felt that the criteria for selection of events as newsworthy, the manner of framing the news and the agendas set were mainly structured through broad economic pressures and somewhat misguided, self-fulfilling perceptions of audience interest; there was very little comment about political bias in the media, or the possible relationship between patterns of media ownership and the nature of political coverage.

Many recognised the paradox between their critique of the media and their need for publicity, and difficulties of gaining access to the media were frequently mentioned. Some, particularly those with constituencies outside London, have a strong sense that 'the media' is largely driven by a small coterie of London-based media folk who meet an equally small group of predominantly male politicians at various functions. The exclusion of women's political voice is thus a function of privileged connections:

'There is very much a London-based cocktail scene where people meet up at parties. I think that the media is very much determined by a London-based group of journalists who are very much into that scene.'

'There are a group of a few hundred men and lots of them went to Oxford and Cambridge together and they are in the Labour Party, in the lobby and in telly and it's a sort of brotherhood, very informal, with a few outsiders mixed in, but who take on this ethos, and they think that people like them are rather good. And they don't know they're doing it, it's such a strong bias. They think they're terribly clever and meritocratic and that all this women's stuff is a bit silly really.'

The old-boy network operating between journalists and politicians is a major obstacle to the easy integration of many women MPs. The London scene with its class biases disbars some women in other ways. When the pressures of family life and the onerous demands of constituency politics are added, the difficulties of finding the time and the means to cultivate friendly media contacts are substantial.

Despite their generally negative views on the media, the crucial role played by broadcasting and the press in giving publicity to politicians, particularly backbenchers, was widely acknowledge. Women MPs are all too aware of the consequences of not conforming to what the media want. One of the media rules is that in order for backbenchers to get any kind of publicity they must say controversial things, particularly if they take a line which is against their own party:

'The media are always looking for an angle, a story and therefore the way in which they report is to sensationalise everything that comes up or they try to find an angle which fits the editorial perspective of the paper ... so they want pictures, they want spicy stories. So whatever you say, it's not enough to be making good points. You must be prepared to say inflammatory things, to rant and rave, before you'll get column inches.'

'If I was interested in getting my face on the box, which is the only realistic way of being noticed in politics, I would have to make a noise, say embarrassing things, say controversial things, talk about national apple day, sing Yellow Submarine in Latin. Do any kind of stunt that people notice. Anything but be a sober politician making a reasonable, decent and interesting point in the Chamber, and that's wrong. Politics is being turned into an entertainment.'

For backbenchers media opportunities offer mixed rewards. It was vital for their work to be reported on as a way of letting constituents know what they are doing and to ratchet up their own standing in their parties, but the constant danger is that journalists and news producers edit their speeches and use one sentence which does not make sense out of context, so that they end up appearing stupid or confused. In an era of presentation politics and an apathetic polity, many women MPs felt that their constituents only believe MPs are actually doing their job when they see them on the box, even if they could not remember what they said but did recall their hairstyle:

'I don't trust them [the media]. I think they are totally untrustworthy. I think that the media will use us for their own ends. I would not trust anybody not to reveal something if it suited them; even if it was supposed to be in confidence, they would use it. I do not trust them to record what I have said accurately, in that it would be a snatch here and a snatch there out of context which will then give a totally different impression of what I wanted to say.' (Conservative)

'The approach is invariably that you are trying to hide something, that you are concealing something, that you are a phoney. On many occasions I have wondered why I bothered to give an interview at all because they didn't really need me. They had already written the piece.'

While some commentators may well be right in suggesting that the burgeoning of media outlets has created many more media opportunities for politicians to sell their slickly packaged messages, more access also means more chances of misrepresentation. Though Franklin argues that politicians 'use' the media for their own ends much more effectively than the other way round, his thesis is most persuasive when 'politicians in government', or even 'government frontbenchers' is read instead of politicians as a whole.[16] Apart from a select core, the majority of Britain's 651 MPs remain photo-opportunity virgins as far as the national media are concerned. Backbench invisibility is slightly less of a problem for women MPs because of their novelty value, although, as with head-counting women in the media more generally, the problem is not so much the extent of coverage but rather what kind of coverage they receive.

A nice bit of skirt: the dress of power?

Leading on from a discussion of the power of the image in influencing political messages, most women politicians believed that their outward appearance is the focus of considerably more media attention than befalls their male colleagues. Women reported the way in which the media always includes the age of women politicians, what they look like, their domestic and family circumstances, their fashion sense and so on:

'I don't know whether it is deliberate or it's so ingrained, but a woman's appearance is always commented on, her age is always commented on, her style of dress is always commented on. That never happens to male politicians, ever, unless they have made a particular point about their style but then they are presented as extreme, exceptions that prove the rule. Women are never the right age. We're too young, we're too old. We're too thin, we're too fat. We wear too much make-up, we don't wear enough. We're too flashy in our dress, we don't take enough care. There isn't a thing we can do that's right.'

Older women recognise that while they might be past the age of provoking the media's interest in them as sex object, such a focus is still a significant problem for younger colleagues. For some, dressing in certain ways was a conscious strategy designed to encourage the perception of themselves as 'serious' politicians:

'I think that it is something that women have realised, perhaps in the Labour Party more than elsewhere, that if you want power you have to look as if you are entitled to power . . . the fact of the matter is that you never get taken seriously unless you are someone who dresses in a fairly establishment way.'

'We are always approached as being suspect women if there aren't certain rules of presentation that are observed.'

Women were irritated with this inappropriate focus on their sartorial style and the spurious links made between outward appearance and ability to do the job. Several women suggested that on any day of the week, male colleagues are to be found with lank and dirty hair, dandruff on their collars, stained ties and looking as though they had slept in their suit. They felt that if a woman were to appear in the House of Commons in a similar state of dishevelment, she would make front-page news and her suitability as MP would be rapidly questioned. Thus a woman politician is always described as such, her gender always the primary descriptor. She is defined by what she is not. She is not simply a politician (male as norm) but a special kind of deviant professional, a woman politician, unable to escape the general objectification of women as subjects for the male gaze:

'I think that men's sex hardly enters into it when they're in politics, no one thinks of them like that until they've transgressed, like three in a bed or that minister who had a child and tried to keep it hidden, or Paddy Pants Down, then suddenly there's a moment when something to do with sex happens and men are in the public eye, but only when they've been caught out. All the rest of the time, they are mainstream serious politicians and sex has nothing to do with it. But I think that women politicians are there and the minute anyone wants to be critical in any way, their looks or the fact that they are a woman instantly sexualises them and so their sexuality is part of them all the time that they are being commented on, for good or ill. They might say "attractive" or "unattractive" or "lumpy" or "man-hating" and she might be talking about policy on Northern Ireland. Of course it's all linked to the idea that women are their bodies for men and men fancy them or not.'

The media tendencies toward privileging form over function, presentation over policy, increasingly means that all politicians are subject to the tyranny of telegeneity and must surrender to sartorial scrutiny, not only women. Yet while there are sufficient 'pretty-boy Blair' stories to make it increasingly so, the objectification of male politicians in this way is still noticeable because of its infrequency, whereas for women politicians it is, on the contrary, the rule. One study of women MPs found that press interest in women's appearance was a source of constant complaint among respondents, including a recognition that such preoccupations could lead to women and their achievements being trivialised.[17] Similarly, a study of women members of the Israeli Parliament in the early 1990s reported that respondents criticised the way in which national media marginalised women, both in their extended interest in clothes and appearance and persistent interest in aspects of women's personal lives.[18]

The frames of gendered discourse

Not only the image, but the language used by the media to describe them is also perceived to be very different to that used about men. Confounding the boundaries of 'normal' female aspirations and role-types carries with it social penalties which often speak in the register of hysteria or aberration. The women MPs identified a number of specific language strategies which are routinely employed by the media to describe themselves and their activities. Helen Liddell reported her surprise at the way in which contestants in the Monklands East by-election, in which she was the eventual winner, were reported in the press:

'Fighting in a by-election, I was struck by the barrage of sexist comment. Because three of the four candidates were women it was described as the "menopausal contest" by a number of commentators and the most vicious articles written about me then, and since, were written by women journalists.'

Looking particularly at the way in which newspapers frame women in their narratives, it is argued that 'women are represented in an unfavourable light and that men are characterised by mentions of occupational and political success. Taken all together, the discourse of the newspaper media handles men and women in terms of different sets of categories, different stereotypes, and it seems very likely that discrimination in discourse helps maintain intellectual habits that promote discrimination in practice.'[19]

'If a woman goes out at 6'o'clock in the morning to clean offices to keep her family together, to raise her children, she will be presented as a heroine. If she wants to run that office she will be presented as an unnatural woman and even worse, as an unnatural mother.'

'They like us as a change from the chaps, as long as we aren't as grey as most of them. They like us to fulfil their obligation for a "token woman". But they usually trivialise us unless we are Cabinet ministers. Women with brains and balls are still an anomaly but at least we get more "shouts" than the men.' (Conservative)

'Of course I have a view about what the media think women politicians are like, what they ought to be like. If you do something different, you're a problem, but then if you fit in with the stereotypes you're a problem. I think that generally the media have a problem dealing with women. They either treat us like men or as lightweight. They have a long way to go before they treat us as people with views who happen to be female and are happy being female.'

The respondents felt that women M.Ps were often described in highly emotional and much less favourable terms than men:

'I don't know how many times I've been described as having my claws out, instead of saying here's a woman being robust, which is what they would say about men. Who would describe a man's claws being out?'

Some women politicians related anecdotes about specific run-ins they had had with the media, often with the local press. In one case, where two MPs shared a local authority area, the local newspaper always referred to the woman by her surname alone while referring to the man as Sir X or the MP; similarly, when the woman MP asked a question, 'it's written up as an outburst. X makes statements and I make outbursts.' Anne Clwyd was sacked in spring 1995 from the Shadow Cabinet for making an unauthorised trip to Turkey and Iraq. While Clwyd took her punishment on the chin, her male colleague and travelling companion, Jim Cousins, defended his decision to go on the visit by insisting that he went to 'protect' her against the rebellious hordes. Yet Clwyd had been to Iraq on many occasions, including when Saddam Hussein was bombing the Kurds, and she had not needed protection on any of those occasions.

Goes with the territory

To a large extent, women believed that the media's interest in them as specifically women politicians went with the territory; putting themselves in the public eye inevitably invited a certain amount of interest which could and sometimes did lead to a more intrusive scrutiny. This has resulted in women being circumspect about taking up media opportunities when they are presented. One politician was asked by a breast cancer campaign group to launch a new screening initiative which would require her to wear a T-shirt with the message 'feel me regularly' emblazoned across her chest; she declined.

Most women preferred live interviews where there was limited scope for creative editing, and studio discussion programmes where there was a genuine sense of debate. However, some with experience of the interrogation interview believe that presenters will often see women as easy targets for bullying, particularly as women have generally had far less match-practice than male panelists and are more likely to follow the rules, unlike the men who, when interrupted, will simply shout more loudly. But even extremely experienced women can be on the receiving end of macho posturing. During a broadcast of *Question Time* (May 1995), Clare Short was treated very rudely by the programme host, David Dimbleby, and was so outraged that she felt compelled to remonstrate publicly with him:

'Well, I must say, I haven't been treated like that for a very long time and there was something peculiar going on. I don't think it was just about being a woman, it was also about class. I was treated very rudely and I had about 50 or 60 letters afterwards from members of the public saying, I'm not Labour but what a rude man, and people stopped me in the street and said what's he got against you? The net result, certainly from the mail, is that it did me more good than harm. They give you a hard time and they think they're so clever. They can goad you into aggressive behaviour and then turn round and say, isn't she aggressive? They put you on the spot behaving like that, but then people find out what you're made of.'

A gendered news agenda

The media help to establish the parameters which structure public thinking about the social world. Media practitioners are heavily involved in gatekeeping public access to information, with a judicious editing decision here, the selection of a particular image there.

Men predominate in the news media and the vast majority of the owners and controllers of media institutions are men. The way in which politics is reported is significantly determined by an orientation which privileges the practice of politics as an essentially male pursuit. As a recent report by the Women's Broadcasting Committee, a campaigning group of women journalists, concludes, 'We know from our own observations that the news the country is given is largely what is considered newsworthy by men—produced, directed, edited and shot overwhelmingly by men.'[20] Far from being neutral then, the classic claim of 'objective journalism', the imagery and language of mediated politics is heavily gendered, supporting male as norm and regarding women politicians as novelties. Interestingly, women MPs felt that women journalists did not write more favourable copy than their fellow male journalists:

'There was an article about me by a woman journalist, and it was a perfectly sympathetic piece and she wrote something that was meant to be flattering—that I was sexy or attractive or something—and I thought, good heavens, this is a woman journalist. Women don't talk about each other like that. They might say "wears striking elegant outfits" or something; we might say that about each other. But this was her writing like a man. It was an extraordinary thing to do. She obviously felt she had to take on that male stance.'

Yet, despite their own often trenchant critiques of their media coverage, few women MPs were willing to accept that they were especially trivialised or domesticated by the media's treatment of them. Most thought that all politicians are seen as fair game by the media and that politics as a practice is trivialised, not necessarily women politicians. While this may be broadly true (and a disquieting trend in political journalism), the consequences for women are probably far graver. Similarly, the press strategy of using women politicians' first names was often seen as a positive construct, in that it makes them seem much more accessible than male counterparts to their constituents and the public more generally. None believed that this more personal approach has the effect of undermining their power base. Here, as elsewhere, their arguments support a more nuanced line that the coverage women politicians receive is not simply 'sex-stereotypical' or negative, although it is indeed different from the manner in which male politicians are represented.[21]

Women politicians were quite resistant to the notion that they might be personally and negatively affected by the media's style of reporting, a somewhat contradictory position considering the significant role they believe the media play in shaping public attitudes and adversely affecting the democratic process. It is almost as if their belief in themselves as true professionals, and their sure knowledge of their own integrity, would protect them from falling victim to the media's excesses. They uniformly believed that while the media's attention to their appearance might be irritating, it was better than not being reported on at all. There are still sufficiently few women MPs for them to be seen as a novelty and therefore of more interest to the media than their backbench male colleagues and that was generally perceived to be a good thing. In other words, no publicity is bad publicity. These perceptions of women MPs could usefully be read against a systematic study of British media representation of male and female political figures, research still to be undertaken.

Other research evidence, however, suggests that such touching faith in their own invincibility may well be misplaced. In a study of women voters, participants were shown pictures of men and women of different ages, with different styles and in different settings, and were asked which ones were the politicians: most of the participants chose the well-dressed older men.[22] Similarly, a growing body of work in the US suggests that the way in which the media favour male politicians and political candidates in their reporting may seriously disadvantage women politicians' status and career aspirations.[23]

Women politicians blame the media for the general decline in political reporting but then articulate all sorts of excuses to explain why it happens: that journalists want to write longer, in-depth stories with more background but the sub-editor will not allocate the space; or that journalists do not deliberately practise gender exclusion by always interviewing male sources but deadline pressures block their creativity in finding a less well-known woman as spokesperson, expert or commentator; or that the media are better tuned to public opinion than are politicians and that gender biases only reflect the norms of the wider society; or that men (including journalists, editors, politicians) do not realise the sexism in their behaviour or language because such is the extent of socialization that these are entirely unconscious.

The woman MPs interviewed pointed out many of the key issues addressed by feminist work in this field. They acknowledged that content is broadly sexist, framing them essentially as women, only secondarily as party politicians; yet they also freely admit the politician's need for publicity and that backbench women are often far more in the media's vision than their male counterparts. They seemed to welcome the growth of more women reporters, yet readily acknowledged that women journalists are socialised into the masculinist norms of the news industry and often find it hard to report in a different frame.

Perhaps political women really do believe what they say about the journalistic motivations behind the discursive framing of women, or perhaps their generous readings of unconscious sexism are a survival mechanism, an acknowledgement of their need for the media's patronage. But there are serious dangers in such complacency. The apparent blindness of Labour women MPs in particular to the biases inherent in the political economy of the British media, and the possibly politically expedient uses of the gender card to criticise the party, suggest a worrying naivety about the nature of political communication.[24] There are clearly insufficient women in positions of power, yet it is not at all clear how far a gender-based solidarity can transcend party-political lines and have an impact on a conglomeratised press. While all women politicians continue to make excuses about male-dominated media, and do not take seriously the problem of sexism in media reporting, it is difficult to see how media-ted images of themselves will change or how strategies can be developed that challenge such gendered coverage. Hence women MPs will continue to be seen as diversions from the serious male game of politics, casually commodified by media images of their neatly crossed legs and no interest in their sharply tuned minds. Women still have a long way to go to represent themselves.

1 G. C. Spivak, 'Can the Subaltern Speak?' in C. Nelson and L. Grossberg (eds), *Marxism and the Interpretation of Culture* (Macmillan, 1988); J. Squires, 'The Cracked Mirror: The Future for Representation', *Demos*, 1994/3.

2 A. Phillips, *Engendering Democracy* (Polity Press, 1991) and *Democracy and Difference* (Polity Press, 1993); S. Benhabib, *Situating the Self* (Polity Press, 1992).

3 J. Lovenduski and P. Norris (eds), *Gender and Party Politics* (Sage, 1993).

4 J. Corner, 'Meaning, genre and context: the problematic of "public knowledge" in the new audience studies' in J. Curran and M. Gurevitch (eds), *Masss Media and Society* (Edward Arnold, 1991).

5 B. Gunter, *Television and Gender Representation* (John Libbey, 1995).

6 J. Keane, *The Media and Democracy* (Polity Press, 1991).

7 K. F. Kahn, 'The Distorted Mirror: Press Coverage of Women Candidates for Statewide Office, *Journal of Politics*, 1994.

8 G. Tuchman, *Hearth and Home: Images of Women in Mass Media* (Oxford University Press, 1978).

9 L. Rakow and K. Kranich, 'Women as Sign in Television News', *Journal of Communication*, 1991 *Arriving On the Scene: Women's Growing Presence in the News* (Women, Men and Media, 1994).

10 G. Dougary, *The Executive Tart and Other Myths: Media Women Talk Back* (Virago, 1994); M. Gallagher, *An Unfinished Story: Gender patterns in Media Employment* (Reports and Papers on Mass Communication, UNESCO, 1995).

11 P. Norris, 'A Splash of Color in the Photo Op: 'Women Leaders Worldwide' in P. Norris, *Women, the Media and Politics* (Oxford University Press, 1995).

12 This study draws on a research project (Women, Politics and the Media) at the Centre for Mass Communication Research, University of Leicester. A. Sreberny-Mohammadi, 'Women Talking Politics', *Perspectives of Women In Television* (Working Paper 9, Broadcasting Standards Council, 1994); K. Ross, *Women and the News Agency: Media-ted Reality and Jane Public* Centre for Mass Communication Research, University of Leicester, 1995) and 'Gender and Party Politics: How the Press Reported the Labour Leadership Campaign, 1994', *Media, Culture & Society*, 1995/3.

13 R. Negrine, *Politics and the Mass Media* (Routledge, 1994).

14 J. Straw, *The Decline in Press Reporting of Parliament* (unpublished report).

15 Ross, 1995, op.cit.

16 B. Franklin, *Packaging Politics: Political Communication in Britain's Media Democracy* (Edward Arnold, 1994).

17 J. Fowler, *Women in Politics: A Fair press?* (MA thesis, University of Sheffield, 1995).

18 D. Liran-Alper, *Media Representation of Women in Politics: Are they still 'domineering dowagers and scheming concubines?* (paper to the IAMCR/AIERI Conference, 1994).

19 R. Fowler, *Language in the News: Discourse and Ideology in the Press.* (Routledge, 1991).

20 Women's Broadcasting Committee, *Her Point of View*. Women's (Broadcasting Committee/Bectu, 1993).

21 P. Norris (ed.), *Women, the Media and Politics* (Oxford University Press, 1995).

22 P. Hewitt and D. Mattinson, *Women's Votes: the Key to Winning* (Fabian Research Series, 1989).

23 K. F. Kahn & E. Goldenberg, 'Women Candidates in the News: An Examination of Gender Differences in US Senate Campaign Coverage.' *Public Opinion Quarterly*, summer 1991; Kahn, op.cit. 1994.

24 G. Bedell, 'Pass the Sick Bag, Emily.' *The Independent on Sunday*, 29.1.95.

Women and Change in the Labour Party 1979–1995

BY SARAH PERRIGO

IN 1979 gender could hardly be said to be an issue in the British Labour Party. Yet by 1995 the party had a Shadow Minister for Women, a detailed strategy for developing and implementing policy aimed specifically at women, and most controversially had approved and begun to implement a quota system for the selection of parliamentary candidates. In order to understand this change we need to analyse the dynamic that developed as women's mobilisation in the party interacted with the alternative strategies that Labour adopted to revive public support in the face of successive election defeats.

The initial impetus for change came from women party members. As Joni Lovenduski has noted, parties do not move on gender issues until they are pressed.[1] Until the late 1970s there was neither significant pressure nor any real incentive for the Labour Party to take gender issues seriously. There was no competition from other political parties on women's issues. Further, despite the widespread mobilisation of women in the feminist movement, there was little attempt by women influenced by feminism to exert pressure directly on the political system.[2] In fact, the British women's movement was extremely sceptical of working though political parties, which were viewed as bureaucratic and incapable of responding to their needs. By the late 1970s this attitude began to change. The women's movement was fragmenting and losing direction. The election of a Conservative government and a deepening economic crisis also highlighted the weakness of a strategy of working outside the political system. A number of women influenced by feminism joined the Labour Party and began to work with sympathetic party members to feminise it.

From 1979 women have mobilised to demand a voice in decision-making and changes in the political agenda. They have sought increasing representation, shifts in the party programme and changes in its structures and organisation. They have proved to be highly skilled organisers. They have mobilised resources, they constructed allies in and outside the party, and have proved adroit at adapting their strategies to the imperatives of intraparty politics. However, whilst a necessary condition, the mobilisation of women is not sufficient to explain the changes that have taken place. The strategies that women have adopted, and the nature and timing of the party's response, have to be understood in the wider context of the crisis of the Labour Party. Since 1979 the Labour Party has been under enormous pressure to modernise in order to counter successive electoral defeats, increasing party competition and a declining membership. On the one hand, this situation has been advantageous for women. They have been able to use the modernisation process, and the impetus it has generated for internal party change, to press their own agenda. On the other hand, those forcing the pace of party change have had very different agendas. Women have been both constrained by and forced to adapt their own strategies in order to influence those other agendas.

Most theories of party change assume that parties are instrumentally rational and will change and adapt to changes in their environment in order to maximise votes.[3] However, the political significance of environmental changes are far from self-evident; particular responses are always contested.[4] Further, as the 'new institutionalists' have pointed out, parties are not just electoral machines; they are specific institutions with their own histories, ideologies, cultures, factions and coalitions. The ways in which parties respond to changes in their environment and the pace and direction of the change is always partly constrained by their internal organisational characteristics.[5]

The dynamics of change in the Labour Party since 1979 clearly illustrate the complex relationship between changes in its external environment and its response. Change in policy and internal organisation has not been smooth or linear. At all stages, change has been contested as it has threatened vested interests, traditional alliances or ideological positions. This is evident both in terms of the party's response to crisis since 1979 and in its response to women's demands. The different ways in which the party has responded to the crisis have provided different structures of possibilities for women to press their claims.

We can identify three distinct periods, each of which has provided a specific set of opportunities and constraints for women activists.

Between 1979 and 1983, the party moved to the left. This provided the initial context for women's mobilisation. The period provided important new opportunities for women to articulate their demands. The second period, between 1983 and 1987, provided a very different environment where the political priorities of the leadership and that of women appeared to be distinct or even incompatible. In this period the party leadership response could be described as one of containment. The third period, since 1987, has provided the most favourable context for women as the party strategy of modernisation and the demands of women have become increasingly congruent. Before exploring the strategies women adopted in each of these periods, the party's response and the distinctive gender party dynamic that developed as a consequence, it is necessary to describe the nature of the Labour Party in 1979. In particular, it is necessary to identify those characteristics which have historically made it difficult for women to establish gender as a salient political issue.

The Labour Party in 1979

Before 1979, the Labour Party was not a favourable site for gender struggles. It was an extremely male dominated party. Though women constituted around 40% of the membership they were grossly underrepresented in the Parliamentary Labour Party, as local councillors and as party officers.[6] In 1979 only 3% of Labour MPs and 11% of conference delegates were women. They occupied a mere seven of the 29 seats on the National Executive Committee, five of which were actually reserved for women.[7] The party's organisation, traditional alliances and culture all played a part in perpetuating this male domination.

Though ostensibly open to men and women on equal terms, the Labour Party was structured by deeply held assumptions of gender difference which had the effect of privileging the male as the political actor. In historical terms, women were not key actors in shaping the party. A culture rooted in the experience of male trade unionists developed which was extremely conservative in its attitudes towards women members. Drucker has argued that what he call the ethos of the party, that is its traditions, beliefs and ways of doing things, are crucial to understanding the behaviour of members.[8] What he failed to notice about this ethos was that it reflected a traditional, familial and paternalistic gender order in society in which men and women occupy different spheres. The model of the political activist, central to both party ideology and its ethos, was the male unionised worker. Women, on the other hand, were defined as wives and mothers, as supporters rather than actors in their own right. This culture was deeply entrenched in the party organisation, helping to structure its beliefs and determine the behaviour of its members.

In terms of organisation and the decision-making process, the Labour Party remained very similar to the party that was set up in the 1918 constitution. Though it presented itself as a democratic, mass-membership party, it was neither a typical mass-membership party nor was it very democratic. Its leadership has paid very little attention to individual members.[9] The federal structure of constituencies, affiliated socialist societies and trades unions virtually assured the domination of the trades unions over individual members. The unions were crucial to the party, providing most of its finances and the bulk of the membership. The constitution guaranteed them a good deal of power through their block vote at Conference and their representation on the NEC. Although the party formally assigned sovereignty to its members through the party Conference, in reality it was ruled by a coalition of parliamentary and trade union elites. Unions also had an important role in selecting parliamentary candidates and, as delegates to Constituency Parties, in determining the political agenda of the constituencies.

The most powerful affiliated unions were those representing workers in heavy industry and manufacturing, overwhelmingly male in membership, the leadership almost exclusively so. They strongly shared the culture of masculinity and gender difference noted above. It was the culture of the unions that also determined Labour's bureaucratic and rule-bound ways of working in branches, constituencies and at Conference. Heavily influenced by the rule books of the trades unions the party rules required a long apprenticeship to be used effectively. Moreover, knowing the rules and how to use them entailed forms of ritualised behaviour which fostered feelings of fraternal solidarity and tended to exclude women as outsiders in the political game.

The majority of women members were originally integrated into the party through the women's sections, which were set up under the 1918 constitution. This institutionalised separate spheres and served historically to cut the majority of women off from the main party organisations. The women's sections had no direct powers of decision-making themselves, nor direct representation on the decision-making bodies of the party. (Although five places were reserved for women on the NEC, they were chosen by the annual Conference, which ensured that only those acceptable to the unions were elected.) Women who had political ambitions had to compete in predominantly male structures where they faced a pre-structured masculine bias. This bias continued to be effective even as more women became active in mixed Constituency Parties after 1945 when the women's sections declined in importance. Concepts of what constituted a good candidate for office and what had priority on the political agenda continued to reflect masculine assumptions even though men might differ widely on aspects of party policy and ideology.

Ideology has been the principal basis for internal divisions. The party has always been divided between left-wing socialists and more pragmatic revisionists and right-wingers, giving rise to factionalism and conflict, a situation exacerbated by the federal structure of the party and its complex system of representation and delegation. For most of its history, the potential instability threatened by ideological factionalism was controlled by the dominant alliance of a pragmatic parliamentary leadership and key trade unions. Ideological discourses, whether left-wing socialist or a more pragmatic 'labourism', were constructed almost exclusively around conceptions of class and class interests in which gender divisions were unimportant. If gender was irrelevant to ideologies, it was also irrelevant to the alliances constructed around them.

To some extent these features were being undermined before 1979. The socio-economic composition of the party had been changing significantly since the 1960s. There was a marked decline in the traditional working-class membership and a corresponding increase in members who were better educated, predominantly professionals employed in the public sector, often referred to as the 'new middle class' or the 'new urban left'.[10] The nature of affiliated trade unions was also changing with the growing importance of public sector unions and

unions with a significant female membership. However, the impact
these changes had on the party, its culture and organisation was
extremely limited until the 1980s.

1979–1983: new opportunities

The crises Labour was to be plunged into after the defeats of 1979 and
1983 were already apparent in the 1970s. There was a growing
disenchantment among many in the party with the postwar 'social
democratic consensus' in the face of economic crisis and declining
electoral popularity. The failure of Labour governments to implement
radical policies despite manifesto commitments caused a real disillusion-
ment with the parliamentary leadership and led to increasing factionalism between left and right, between older working-class and younger,
often professional middle-class members, between some Constituency
Parties and their MPs, and between trade union members and their
leaders. Demands grew not just for a left agenda and an 'alternative
economic strategy' but for internal party reform to democratise it and
ensure that its leadership was more accountable to members. The
Campaign for Labour Party Democracy and the Labour Party Coordinating Committee, founded in 1973 and 1978 respectively, pressed for
change but until 1979 this was successfully resisted by the leadership.
Defeat in 1979 strengthened the left and led to some significant changes
to the party constitution, including the mandatory reselection of MPs.
The traditional coalition between the parliamentary leadership and key
trade unions fell apart, a crisis of leadership which Michael Foot could
not overcome. The party became increasingly characterised by organisational instability and ideological polarisation. In 1981 after the special
conference at Wembley adopted a new method of electing the leader, a
number of influential members left to form the Social Democratic Party.

The shift to the left was an important inducement to a number of
women, who identified with both socialism and feminism, but who
hitherto had remained outside, to join the party. With its stress on
democracy and a radical socialist agenda, the left seemed to offer new
possibilities for the development of a party which would take feminism
seriously. Their immediate aim was to work with women in the party
sympathetic to feminism to challenge the party's attitudes towards
women and make gender a salient political issue. The very turmoil the
party was in opened up spaces for achieving these goals. The loss of
leadership control made it easier for women to work with left-feminist
groups outside the party. In order to avoid factionalism and infiltration
by the extra-parliamentary left the leadership had in the past rigorously
enforced rules circumscribing members' links with outside organisations. Its ability to enforce these was considerably weakened between
1979 and 1983.[11] The disintegration of the coalition between the
parliamentary leadership and the unions, and the fluidity of new
coalitions, further opened opportunities for women to construct alli-

ances. The ideological ferment caused by disenchantment with social democracy also stimulated a real debate within and outside the party about the future of socialism. This offered some space for a socialist feminist discourse to emerge which challenged the left's exclusive concern with class. Numerous journals carried articles on women and socialism. The impetus for reform of the party's constitution offered women a further opportunity to press for organisational changes that would benefit them.

One of the first signs that women were making an impact came though the increased activity of the party's women's organisations. Active in the 1920s and 1930s but increasingly moribund in the postwar period these were revitalised. The women's conference became a focus for women's organisation and networking as well as for the development of policy. At the same time, women used the multiple channels available in the party to raise gender issues and contest the masculine culture in all the party organisations.

One important group to emerge in the early 1980s was the Labour Women's Action Committee. Its demands included a debate at the annual Conference on five resolutions passed by the women's conference and election to the seats reserved for women on the NEC by the women's conference, which would make them accountable to women members rather than to the party as a whole. It also demanded the inclusion of at least one woman on all short-lists when parliamentary candidates were selected. A further sign of activity was the development of women's initiatives in local government.[12] Some Labour-controlled authorities attempted to develop a kind of local socialism in opposition to the Conservative government. Amongst other things, they introduced women's committees, with a brief to develop equal opportunities for women employees of the council, to involve local women in decision-making processes, and to improve services to women in the community. Though these initiatives were confined to a fairly small number of authorities, such as the Greater London Council, other London boroughs and a few large cities, they did give women's issues a platform in some local parties. The initiatives themselves were generally the result of pressure from women councillors and party members networking with feminist groups in the community. To an extent, these efforts became discredited after 1983 as the party leadership distanced itself from what the media called 'loony left' councils. However, the model of women's committees did provide ideas that reappeared in proposals for a Ministry for Women in the mid-1980s.

In terms of party policy, the initial mobilisation of women had some tangible results. 'Labour's Programme 1982' was a real breakthrough. For the first time, an official Labour policy document seriously analysed the problems facing women in society and offered some radical solutions, including a major expansion of child-care, a positive action policy for women at work and the strengthening of Britain's sex equality legislation. Though some of the commitments were watered down in the 1983 manifesto, the ideas continued to inform Labour's programme for women into the 1990s.

Women were less successful in obtaining organisational reforms. To the extent that the constitutional reforms of 1979–81 shifted power in the party away from the Parliamentary Labour Party to Constituency Parties and to party activists it may have widened the scope for women activists. However, neither of the two rule changes did much to enhance women's representation. The mandatory reselection of MPs (1979) had the potential for increasing the representation of women in Parliament, but only if it had led to an increased turnover of Labour MPs (incumbency is a major barrier[13]) and women were then preferred to men. This it failed to achieve: between 1979 and 1983, only eight MPs were deselected, and only one woman, Clare Short was selected as a replacement. The altered election system for the party leader (1982) did even less for women. By giving the trade unions 40% of the votes in the electoral college it strengthened the power of the unions who were opposed to the demands of women.

None of the specific Labour Women's Action Committee's demands were met. One reason for this was that the CLPD and campaigns for constitutional reform relied on the support of important sections of the trade unions which were reluctant to support the collective representation of women, as that would have reduced their own powers. Further, by the time women were beginning to be organised the momentum for constitutional reform was rapidly dissipating. The fragile left coalition was itself fragmenting and the acrimony that followed the 1982 Wembley conference with the establishment of the SDP, convinced both the trade union and the parliamentary leadership of the need to call a halt to any further reforms.

The mobilisation of women did however stimulate the NEC in 1984 to appoint Jo Richardson as a spokesperson on women's rights and to produce a 'charter for equality for women in the party' which urged all sections to appoint women's officers and to examine their procedures to see if they discriminated against women. The real weakness of the charter was that although it urged positive action to encourage the increased participation of women in party affairs, it did not compel them to take such action. Though the leadership was forced to respond to the demands of women by placing women's issues on the agenda in the party programme and by expressing support for increasing their participation, there was a great deal of resistance to moving beyond rhetoric.

On the one side, the entrenched culture of masculinity and the vested interests of men in the party constituted formidable barriers to any form of positive action. On the other, though women had begun to mobilise, their support was limited. The alliance with the left was itself problematic. Despite its radical pretensions, the left was not seriously concerned with women's issues except in so far as they could be used to further its own ends. The ideology of the left and its practice continued to marginalise women and gender issues. Neither could women activists at this stage count on the support of the majority of women party members. It is clear that gender solidarity cannot be assumed in advance; it has to be constructed. Women in the party were not a unified group. Many had strong identities as party women which seemed to conflict with organising around womens issues. Older, working-class women in particular often perceived the language and style of feminism to be patronising, even offensive. Those who identified with the feminist agenda tended to be young, articulate and well educated. They were often insensitive to the experience of other women in the party and lacked the political skills to appeal to the wider constituency of women.

By 1983, it is difficult to point to any real changes in response to the demands of women, with the significant exception of the party pro-gramme. The programme was important in that it was the one part of the left agenda that was not repudiated later. It also signified a departure from the past, where party documents rarely mentioned women or their interests. If the activity of women brought no other tangible results, it did lay the groundwork for the wider mobilisation that took place in the years that followed. Women at least had a toe-hold on the agenda and were beginning to understand the need to work through the party and its rules, which was to become crucially important later in the decade.

1983–1987: containment

Labour's defeat in the 1983 election was devastating. Michael Foot resigned and Neil Kinnock was elected leader by a comfortable majority. He inherited a party badly demoralised and in disarray. Its programme had been decisively rejected by the electorate and it faced serious competition from the Social Democrats in alliance with the Liberals. The clear priority for Kinnock was to re-establish the authority of the leadership, shift control of policy-making back to the Parliamentary Party, marginalise the left and purge extremists held responsible for the appalling election performance. This agenda was to preoccupy the leadership until the election of 1987 and was to delay any significant response to women's demands. Nevertheless, a number of changes occurred during this period which forced Labour to attend to the demands of it's women members.

First, there was an element of party competition from the SDP which appealed to women members and voters. It introduced a gender quota at the short-listing stage in parliamentary candidate selections.[14] The Social Democrats also made much of their claim to be a new kind of party, modern and open as compared with Labour, which they por-trayed as concerned to protect the vested interests of a narrow group of organised male workers. To counteract this, the Labour leadership became concerned with image in general and its male-dominated image in particular. This trend increased significantly after 1987.

Second, the mobilisation of women gained momentum and won new bases of support. The Labour Women's Action Committee mounted a highly effective campaign around its demands for collective representation. It distributed model resolutions, forced debates at national conference, and organised alternative women's slates for NEC elections. It also worked through the NEC's women's committee to press its claims on the party leadership. The result of this was to widen and deepen the debate about women in the party. Support, which had previously been confined to middle-class feminists primarily identified with the left, spread to include significant sections of the wider membership. Though the number of Labour women MPs remained low after the 1983 election, the new intake included younger women like Clare Short and Harriet Harman who were sympathetic to women's demands and joined Jo Richardson to press their claims.

Even more important, women began to obtain some support from the trades unions. Women had been campaigning in the trades unions since the late 1960s for changes in union policy to meet the needs of women workers and for increased representation. The growing crisis in the union movement in the 1980s led its leaders to become more receptive to these demands. The combined effect of Conservative economic policy and industrial relations legislation led not only to a dramatic decline in union membership but to a significant shift in union power away from the traditional male-dominated industrial unions to those of the service sector with substantial female membership. In response, unions were forced to adapt to accommodate the needs of women members. A consequence for the Labour Party was that a number of union leaders began to add their voice to the debate on gender and representation. At the same time, women in the party began to work more closely with union women to coordinate their campaigns.

The party leadership faced a real dilemma in how to respond. On the one hand, it was still engaged in a struggle to reorganise the party internally, as well as to expel militants and isolate the hard left. The leadership tended to identify women activists and particularly members of the Labour Women's Action Committee, with the hard left and was therefore reluctant to make any changes to party structures that might enhance their influence. On the other hand, the pressure to offer something was growing. The party responded with a policy of containment, a strategy that allowed it to be seen to be acting positively whilst containing the more radical demands of women and isolating those they considered extremists.

The positive response was the proposal for a Women's Ministry. In 1986, Jo Richardson introduced a discussion document entitled

'Labour's Ministry for Women's Rights', and in 1987 the NEC endorsed the proposal which was given a great deal of publicity. At the same time, the leadership tried to drive a wedge between what it saw as extremists and the more moderate women in the trade unions by reforming the women's conference to curtail the powers of constituency delegates. As late as 1987, the NEC refused to allow the National Labour Women's Committee to participate in the Policy Review on the grounds that they were unrepresentative left-wing women. Clearly, purging the party of extremism took priority over increasing women's representation. It was not until the leadership had established firm control over the party that it was prepared to consider the latter. Only then, in any case, could it risk internal party reforms which would challenge significant vested interests.

1987–1995: *from rhetoric to action*

The election defeats of 1987 and 1992 led the party to accelerate the modernisation process begun between 1983 and 1987. The trends towards centralisation and the professionalisation of the party organisation continued. Greater attention was paid to public opinion research and the use of professional image-makers. Women were not formally represented on the Policy Review that followed the 1987 defeat but its final report, 'Meet the Challenge, Make the Change', did include a number of important commitments to women, including equity in taxation, a strengthening of sex equality legislation, an expansion of nursery provision and a minimum wage. Criticism that women had not been formally involved led to a women's monitoring committee being set up, chair by Jo Richardson. The 1990 publication, 'Looking to the Future', demonstrated a greater involvement of women and spelt out in some detail the proposed Ministry for Women, with Cabinet status for the Minister for Women.

In 1992 the party introduced a number of policy forums for developing policy. Though none has a special responsibility for women's policy, each has a brief to consider the implications of policy for women. The forums were set up after the party had agreed to the implementation of a quota of women throughout its organisations: in consequence, women constitute 40% of the membership. It is anticipated that their presence, along with the increased presence of women in the Shadow Cabinet and the NEC, will have a significant programmatic impact. Clare Short, the present Shadow Minister for Women, is undertaking a wide consultation with party members on Labour's strategy for women and has set up regular seminars with women academics.

The leadership's concern with the electorate's perceptions of the party dictated its attitudes. The evidence of the party's Shadow Communications Agency, advertising consultants and commissioned opinion polls all suggested that it continued to be seen as insular, backward-looking and in the pocket of the unions. The main aim of internal party reform was to transform this perception; to move away from a party of 'vested interests' towards a more open, pluralistic party based on individual membership. To this end, the leadership sought to distance itself from the unions, to reduce their powers in party affairs and to shift power away from constituency activists towards the 'ordinary' member. The increased attention paid to party image and opinion polls led the leadership to make links between this agenda and the representation of women. Research carried out by the Shadow Communications Agency after the 1987 election suggested that the party's male image was still a key problem.[15] This view was reinforced after the 1992 election when polling data demonstrated that a gender gap which had closed in 1983 and 1987 had opened up again. The data suggested that if women had voted Labour in the same proportion as men, then Labour would have won in 1992.

Once the party leaders were convinced of the connections between its modernisation strategy and the demands of women, they responded much more positively. The party quickly moved from a rhetorical commitment to increased women's representation to support for positive action through setting targets and training for women, and finally to positive discrimination through a quota system. Women were quick to respond to the increased receptiveness of party leaders. The Labour Women's Action Committee dropped its demands for collective representation and the empowerment of the women's organisations and began to develop a strategy for increasing the individual representation of women, clearly more congruent with the party's modernisation strategy.

This change of strategy was not universally welcomed by all women activists. Some opposed what they saw as a narrowing of gender struggles to issues of individual representation and the focus on increasing the numbers of women MPs which, they argued, would only benefit a small number of middle-class women. There was also a feeling, not unreasonable, that gender issues were being hijacked by the party leadership for purely electoral reasons rather than out of any real commitment to women. Nevertheless, there is evidence that most women welcomed the leadership's more positive attitude. There was further evidence, at least amongst Labour women, that there was strong support for the introduction of positive action.[16] In 1988 a Labour women's network was established. It used extensive contacts to encourage women to stand for office. After 1992, influenced by the success of the women's campaign in the Democratic Party in America, an 'Emily's list' was set up to provide both financial support and training for prospective parliamentary candidates.

Party modernisers had for some time been concerned to reform the party's candidate selection procedures. They were strongly opposed by the trades unions and constituency activists. In 1989 the party Conference approved a rule change which replaced selection through the

General Management Committees of Constituency Parties by an electoral college in which the unions held 40% of the votes and the individual members of the CLP the other 60%. In 1993 the party finally, by a narrow margin, approved the introduction of one person one vote for the selection of prospective parliamentary candidates.

In 1987 the party adopted a rule change for the compulsory shortlisting of a woman if a woman had been nominated. When this failed to have a significant effect, pressure intensified for some form of positive discrimination. In 1990 the party Conference responded by a far-reaching programme of quotas throughout all the party organisations. The resolution also proposed the introduction of a quota system into candidate selections, with the target of securing 50% female representation in the Parliamentary Labour Party within ten years, or over the period of the next three elections, whichever proved the shorter. The decision to introduce quotas was the result of a remarkably effective campaign by organised women directed at all sections of the party. That it obtained NEC approval was, however, as much to do with the instrumental rationality of the party leaders once they were convinced that increasing women's visibility would further Labour's electoral fortunes. The defeat of the party in the 1992 election only served to strengthen this view.

After 1990 the party moved quickly to introduce quotas into party delegations, for the National Executive Committee and for officer posts in branches and constituencies. The Parliamentary Labour Party also introduced a quota for elections for the Shadow Cabinet. The real problems arose in implementing the quota for parliamentary candidates. Labour's selection process is decentralised and Constituency Parties have zealously defended their freedom from interference by the centre. No attempt was made to enforce the quota in the selection process in the 1992 election. However, the NEC did encourage Constituency Parties, where there was no incumbent, to adopt all-women short-lists. Although the number of Labour Women rose from 21 in 1987 to 37 in 1992, few constituencies were prepared voluntarily to consider an all-women short-list. The policy of persuasion had little impact on local parties, suggesting that even though the leadership of the party was convinced of the need for some positive discrimination, this was not shared by activists, particularly in safe seats.

It was not until 1993 that the party conference finally agreed a mechanism for introducing quotas in candidate selection. Support for this was the outcome of a successful alliance between party modernisers and women activists: women agreed to support the resolution to introduce one-man-one-vote (OMOV) on the condition that the resolution to implement quotas was also supported.[17] The agreed procedure was that half of the constituencies with safe vacant seats and half of the constituencies with marginal seats must adopt all-women short-lists for the next election. If this is fully implemented, Norris and Lovenduski estimate that the number of Labour women MPs would rise from 37 in 1992 to between 60 and 75 at the next general election.[18]

From late 1994, the party has organised regional 'consensus meetings' to decide which constituencies should have all-women short-lists. Anticipating more resistance from the safe vacant seats, the consensus meetings began with the marginal seats. Levels of resistance have varied according to the marginality of the seat and whether the previous candidate was supportive of the policy. By mid-1995, almost all the regions had decided on the marginals to have all-women short-lists and most of these had either selected or were in the process of selection. Real resistance, however, can be expected from the safe vacant seats. By mid-1995 only two of these had agreed to adopt all-women short-lists. There are signs of a backlash developing as men who had hopes of inheriting seats realise the implications of the quota system, a backlash which has been encouraged by adverse media publicity and by the public criticism of the system by prominent party elder statesmen including Neil Kinnock and Roy Hattersley. However, both women activists and the party leadership anticipated resistance and it is unlikely that the party leadership will fail to implement a policy which is clearly of mutual interest.

Conclusion

There is no doubt that the Labour Party has changed since 1979 in response to the demands of women. Labour's crisis and the strategies the party has adopted to restore its popularity have provided women with new opportunities for mobilisation; opportunities they have used very effectively. Successive election defeats and the consequent impetus towards radical reform have provided an increasingly favourable terrain for women to press their claims. They have been able to take advantage of the crisis to construct new alliances, first from the left and later from party modernisers. Internal party reforms, in particular the weakening of trade union and constituency activists' powers, will over time help make the party's internal culture less exclusive and masculine.

It is clear that without the organisation of women, party modernisers would not have taken gender seriously. However, in order to be effective women have also had to adapt their strategies. Inevitably, as the debates on gender reached a wider audience in the party and began to involve different actors, such as trade unionists, MPs and the party leadership, the nature of debate has altered in ways which were more congruent with those groups. Above all, women have had to adapt their strategy to fit with party modernisation. Modernisation has, however, been a top-down process, dictated by the party leadership for instrumental reasons. This has led to a certain cynicism about the party's commitment to women and an unease at the ways in which women's demands have been linked to modernisation. Given that gender issues cross cut other divisions in the party, this tension between women activists and party modernisers is inevitable and likely to continue. Nevertheless, as success on the quota issue demonstrates, women have much to gain from maintaining their coalition with advocates of modernisation.

Of the changes that women have achieved, it is the decision to introduce the quota system that is of greatest significance and is most indicative of the importance the party now gives to women. Though the introduction of quotas would not have occurred without the mobilisation of women, it is extremely unlikely that the party would have agreed to such a controversial measure if it had not been seen as a crucial component of the modernisation strategy.

The implementation of quotas by increasing the representation of women at all levels of the party will do much to transform its masculine culture. Their increased presence in the Parliamentary Labour Party, the Shadow Cabinet, the National Executive and the new policy forums are the most important safeguard to insuring that policy commitments are kept once Labour is in government. Though equality between men and women in the Labour Party has yet to be achieved the implementation of quotas will provide a new context and a more favourable site for future struggles and provide the momentum for a continuing process of mutual accommodation between women and the party.

1   J. Lovenduski, 'Introduction: The Dynamics of Gender and Party' in J. Lovenduski and P. Norris (eds), *Gender and Party Politics* (Sage, 1993).
2   J. Lovenduski and V. Randall, *Contemporary Feminist Politics* (Oxford University Press, 1993).
3   A. Downs, *An Economic Theory of Democracy* (Harper Row, 1957).
4   E. Shaw, *The Labour Party Since 1979* (Routledge, 1994).
5   P. Panebianco, *Political Parties: Organisation and Power* (Cambridge University Press, 1988).
6   J. Hills, 'Britain' in J. Lovenduski and J. Hills, *The Politics of the Second Electorate* (Routlege & Kegan Paul, 1981).
7   V. Randall, *Women and Politics* (Macmillan, 1982).
8   H. Drucker, *Doctrine and Ethos in the British Labour Party* (Unwin, 1979).
9   Cf P. Webb, 'Party Organisational Change in Britain: The Iron Law of Centralisation' in R. Katz and P. Mair (eds), *How Parties Organise: Change and Adaptation in Party Organisations in Western Democracies* (Sage, 1994); A. Ware, *Citizens, Parties and the State* (Polity Press, 1987).
10 P. Seyd and P. Whiteley, *Labour's Grass Roots* (Clarendon Press, 1992).
11 L. Minkin, *The Contentious Alliance* (Edinburgh University Press, 1991).
12 J. Edwards, *Local Government Women's Committees* (Avebury, 1995).
13 P. Norris and J. Lovenduski, *Political Recruitment: Gender, Race and Class in the British Parliament* (Cambridge University Press, 1995).
14 P. Norris and J. Lovenduski, *Political Recruitment*, op.cit., 1995.
15 P. Hewitt and D. Mattinson, 'Women's Votes: The Key to Winning' (Fabian Research Series No. 353).
16 C. Short, J. Richardson and A. Eagle, *Quotas Now* (Fabian Tract No. 541).
17 L. Lovenduski, 'The Case for Quotas' in *Renewal*, January 1994.
18 P. Norris and J. Lovenduski, op.cit.

Public Management Change and Sex Equality within the State

BY HELEN MARGETTS

PUBLIC management approaches in the UK have been revolutionised in the last fifteen years. At the central level, widespread privatization and contracting out of governmental functions has followed on the heels of the Next Steps programme, accompanied by the widespread introduction of managerial techniques and pay reform. At the local level, compulsory competitive tendering and the introduction of purchaser-provider splits have been introduced with the aim of reshaping local authorities as enablers rather than providers. UK reforms fall within a cohort of changes occurring to varying degrees across OECD countries, described summarily as the New Public Management.[1]

Here we investigate what such changes mean for inclusion of women within the institutions of the state. Local authorities were among the leading innovators in equal opportunities policies in the 1980s. The central civil service has developed a reputation for good practice, although improvement at the highest echelons has been slow. Meanwhile a growing literature on state feminism is caught between the liberal feminist assumption that sex equality within the state will continue to improve and the radical feminist claim that the state apparatus is irredeemably gendered. Will the changes in public management, through the disaggregation of governmental bureaucracies, result in alternative organizational structures more conducive to women's inclusion, or will they erode the advances of sex equality policies made in the last fifteen years? The argument made here is that if the gains made so far are not to be lost, then it is necessary to recognise the substantial impacts of public management change and that the two divergent literatures of gender studies and public administration have something to learn from each other.

Sex equality policies in central and local government

A sex equality policy can contain a variety of elements, which may be summarised into three categories: formal elements which address discrimination in recruitment, promotion and grading; informal elements which address discriminatory features of an organisation's culture, such as continuous service requirements, a long-hours culture or a requirement for geographical mobility; and care-related elements which include maternity leave, child-care arrangements, jobshare and part-time working arrangements. These are not exhaustive aspects of a sex equality policy, but rather they are widely regarded to be an essential core. For all three elements, monitoring and review arrangements are crucial in ensuring that a policy is being carried out and is having the intended effect.

Until the 1990s, sex equality policies implemented across local authorities had, while varying widely across authorities, some measure of success. Local authorities were early innovators in equal opportunities, with most developing some form of equal opportunities policy covering race, gender, disability, recruitment, selection and training. Practice was sufficiently successful by 1989 for Joni Lovenduski to observe that local authorities had been in the front line of implementation and are the site of many instances of good practice.[2] While the media have concentrated on a small number of atypical incidents, the academic literature contains studies of good practices, innovative organizational mechanisms for implementing equal opportunities and a number of successful feminist interventions.[3] After 'the tempestuous early years, marked by political controversy and extreme statements, both from supporters and opponents' had passed, Riley observed a 'settling down period' and a 'coming of age' of equal opportunities work in local authorities. Political and executive structures based around women's committees and equal opportunities units were developed in many local authorities, with improvements of nursery facilities and maternity leave. A Local Government Management Board survey in 1993 found that 82% of local authorities had adopted equal opportunities policies, almost all of which covered race, gender, disability and marital status, concluding that the high proportion of authorities with equal opportunities polices demonstrates the long standing commitment in local government to equal opportunities and being good employers. Sex equality policies alone are insufficient, however; implementation is crucial. So the mere fact that a high proportion have adopted policies masks wide variations across local authorities, across service sectors and across manual and white-collar staff. For example, the Equal Opportunities Commission has observed markedly more commitment towards equal opportunities in white collar services than manual services.[4] Manual services in some sectors are worse than others; in building cleaning, policies had not been systematically applied with any commitment. Notwithstanding these variations, however, many local authorities have been described as model employers, some even playing an important role in the local economy as a major (often the largest) local employer in terms of setting standards.

The central civil service built up a reputation as a reasonable equal opportunities employer during the 1970s and 1980s. Commentators have been observing for some time that the centralised recruitment procedures seem to operate without bias. In 1981 Elizabeth Brimelow observed that 'we can accept ... that women are now—and have for some time been—joining the service, at the levels which feed the higher grades, in numbers which reflect their representation among suitably qualified people' and further improvements to the procedure caused Sophie Watson to reach the same conclusion in 1995.[5] Informal and care-related elements of sex equality policies have also improved. In 1970 the Civil Service Department had established a committee, chaired by Mrs E. Kemp-Jones, to look at the employment of women in the civil service. This committee recommended changes in three main areas: increasing maternity leave and allowing unpaid leave for urgent domestic affairs; increasing opportunities for part-time work; and changes in the rules on reinstatement, to make it easier for women to return to suitable work when their children were older. All its recommendations were accepted and implemented. However, the impact of such policies on the numbers of women reaching the higher grades showed virtually no improvement during the 1970s. Elizabeth Brimelow observed in 1981 that ten years on, the results had been negligible. The civil service was still geared towards people who work continuously from recruitment to retirement. Promotion procedures involved informal procedures of assessment of long-term potential which were biased towards men. The Kemp-Jones committee had tried to overcome these obstacles, but implementation had been weak. For the most part, its recommendations were discretionary rather than mandatory, inviting departments to take up mental attitudes rather than asking for specific results.

Measures taken during the 1980s seem to have had more impact. A Programme of Action was first introduced by the Cabinet Office in 1984 and another in 1992. This identified lack of child-care as a continuing barrier to women's progression, recommending changes relating to conditions of service, including extending maternity leave from 44 to 52 weeks; special leave to care for sick children; and a three year right to apply for reappointment to a former grade position where an applicant had accepted a lower grade post because of absence of a vacancy. Government departments were urged to set up equality committees, appoint equality officers and introduce positive measures. By 1989 the overall ratio of male to female within the higher civil service was roughly 12:1 for the senior grades as a whole, with the ratio increasing to about 40:1 for the top two grades.[6] While the figures for 1994, shown below,[7] are not dramatic, they do represent a doubling of the proportion of women employed at senior levels since 1984. However, a 2% increase at Grade 4 is the only evidence of improvement between 1993 and 1994, undermining any confidence that the upwards trend will continue.

Investigating the question whether continuing improvement in the highest grades was likely, Sophie Watson concluded in 1995 that the civil service is unusual in its combination of fairly progressive equal opportunity policies on the one hand and a more than usually exclusive culture on the other: 'anyone who can disguise themselves as the "right

	1984		1993		1994	
Grade 1 (Permanent Secretary)	0	0%	2	5%	2	6%
Grade 2 (Deputy Secretary)	5	4%	10	8%	9	7%
Grade 3 (Under Secretary)	25	5%	46	10%	48	10%
Grade 4 (Deputy Under Secretary)	11	3%	28	7%	35	9%
Grade 5 (Assistant Secretary)	173	7%	388	13%	379	13%
Grade 6 (Senior Principal)	380	7%	672	13%	674	13%

sort of chap" can rise to the top of the civil service.' The right sort of chap was someone who exhibited the characteristics of a strong sense of duty and obligation, reflected in a willingness to be available at any time; the ability to manage feelings; the 'right' class in terms of social background. The exclusionary culture was maintained through the continuing existence of old-boy networks with their origins in public schools, expectations of working late and the perception of part-time hours as denoting a lack of commitment. The type of women who were able to break through the barriers presented by this culture were 'women who came from (upper) middle-class backgrounds, who can learn the codes, behave just like the chaps and who may deploy their sexuality as part of passage to the top'. Such a culture was more prevalent in some departments than others; Watson observed considerable variations in the impact of sex equality policies across departments, with the Home Office and Foreign Office especially resistant.

Local government and the central civil service differ in the extent to which feminist initiatives have provided impetus for the changes that have taken place. In contrast to the local level, there is little evidence at the central level that equal opportunity policy has been influenced by self-identified feminists. Gains have been achieved through liberal equal opportunities policies and a few successful female individuals. One central government official interviewed, when asked if she was a feminist, answered that she was, but not publicly: 'because it sets you up as a target, it is like saying "I am a born again Christian". Neither is there any sign that women have been brought into the civil service because of an identified need for the development of women's policy areas.[8] While the community of the 'Whitehall Village' described (and referred to as 'he') by Heclo and Wildavsky in 1981 might underpin Watson's exclusionary culture, there is no evidence of the 'bureaucratic kinship'[9] structures of feminists that Eisenstein and Watson identified at the central level in Australia, where 'the path followed by feminists has been reliant upon an alliance with the Labour Party and on a decision to take up bureaucratic positions within state and federal administration in order to further the interests of women using the power of the state'.[10] Local government women's initiatives, 'set up largely as the result of pressure from feminist women organized in the Labour Party'[11] might be said to come into this category. In general, at the local level, there appears to have been a strong feminist impetus for policies aimed at improving sexual equality, accompanied by strong organizational resistance and opposition. In contrast, at the central level, Sophie Watson considered that equal opportunity policy was formulated with surprisingly little formal resistance, with respondents believing it merely reflected larger social shifts. Rather, the modest success at the central level has come from generous but non-radical, centrally-implemented liberal sex equality policies combined with the success of a few determined individuals in breaking through the exclusionary culture to the higher ranks.

It does seem that the top-down hierarchical structures of the traditional civil service allowed the top down implementation of sex equality policies during the 1980s, with limited success (in comparison with the private sector) in increasing the number of women at higher levels. It is difficult to generalise across sectors and companies, but from the literature on sex equality at management levels within the private sector it seems that women have penetrated middle-management levels but it remains extremely difficult to reach the top. For management and related occupations, the proportion of women has risen from 11.3% in 1975, to 17.4% in 1986 and 40% in 1991.[12] But there were no woman chief executives among Britain's top 100 companies in 1989 and only 21 out of the 200 largest industrial companies in the United Kingdom had women board members. In total, 24 women were appointed, but the majority, 18, were either part-time or non-executive directors; several of the appointed women had a family connection to the company or a title; and women often hold appointments on boards of a number of companies belonging to the same group or in similar sectors. Commentators identify many of the same obstructions to women's penetration of the highest levels as Watson observed in the highest echelons of the civil service.

The new public management

Since the end of the 1980s and 1990s, local government and the civil service have undergone a period of radical change, centrally directed in both cases. These changes fall within the now widely used term New Public Management. New Public Management changes have been usefully summarised into three broad categories by Patrick Dunleavy: incentivization, disaggregation and competition.[13]

Disaggregation changes involve breaking up public sector bureaucracies into deconcentrated or decentralized patterns of organization aimed at increasing executive autonomy, and a move away from multifunctional organizations to single issue agencies. At the local level, 'provider' functions have been separated into Direct Service Organizations which operate as far as possible along private sector lines. At the central level, administrative functions originally carried out by the major government departments have been hived off into organizationally distinct Next Steps Agencies.

Competition changes are aimed at removing monopolies in the public sector, by opening up tranches of work for competitive tender. At the local level, through various Acts since 1980, Compulsory Competitive Tendering requires local authorities to offer public sector work to private bidders competing against in-house teams, in the form of the Direct Service Organizations. White collar or support services may also be offered for tender. In 1991 the value of work subject to CCT was set to increase by £6 billion a year. At the central government level, Market Testing was introduced in 1991, instituting a similar procedure for the civil service, with targets for departments and agencies. By September 1994, £2.06 billion of activities had been reviewed, with £1.18 billion awarded to external suppliers. Market testing targets were introduced; these were lifted in 1995, but the process continues in an indirect manner; every Agency must carry out a Prior Options Review every five years, a review process during which the agency must first consider abolishing itself, then consider offering itself wholesale for privatization, and finally identify possible areas for contracting out.

Incentivization changes are those which attempt to replace the old public sector ethic by substitutes for the private sector profit motive. For example, in some local authorities performance pay schemes have been introduced. At the central level, the principal changes have been the introduction of performance pay for top officials and the destandardisation of pay, bargaining and personnel policies across departments and agencies. From April 1996 departments will have delegated responsibility for pay arrangements for grades up to and including Grade 6. Civil servants at Grade 5 and above will be offered individual contracts of employment, similar to the rolling contracts used in the private sector. Some 12% of appointments in this senior open structure are now made from outside and this figure is anticipated to rise to about 20%.

New Public Management-type changes are all aimed at running public sector organizations as far as possible along the lines of private sector companies. The emphasis is on increasing efficiency while maintaining quality, and on outcome rather than process, with performance indicators introduced to replace the old public service ethic emphasis on rules and procedures. The reforms are also aimed at reducing the size of local government and the civil service: at local level, local government employment fell by 5% between 1988 and 1993. A 1993 White Paper states that the civil service should number significantly below 500,000 within two years. Market Testing reviews led to a 26,900 reduction in posts (10,600 staff transferred to external suppliers, 3,300 redundancies, the remainder through natural wastage).

So what do these reforms mean for the presence of women in local government and the central civil service? Their full implication will not be known for many years, but there is sufficient initial evidence to make some preliminary predictions.

Disaggregation

At local government level, disaggregation has taken place in a variety of ways,[14] but the most important here is through the creation of Direct Service Organizations, which then compete for contracts tendered under Compulsory Competitive Tendering. Central personnel departments and equal opportunities units have far less influence over DSOs than they had over the more homogenous local authority workforces of the past. As one official put it, 'Departments do not want a central unit overseeing their work; they would rather just do it themselves.' Incentives for DSOs to introduce equal opportunities policies are small; better working conditions entail expenditure which can jeopardise an in-house bid and equal opportunities policies are often be viewed as an expensive luxury when failure to win a bid means extensive job loss. In a major study of the gender impact of CCT, the Equal Opportunities Commission found that in only two out of 39 local authorities studied were equality targets set and progress of the DSOs regularly monitored.[15]

Moves towards disaggregation in central government have been implemented through the Next Steps programme. Executive Agencies are organizationally discrete units falling under the loose control of their parent ministry, and run as far as possible along private sector lines. Out of the 104 agencies created by 1994, only eight were headed by women (including the head of the beleaguered Child Support Agency who subsequently resigned). The main effect of 'agencification' seems likely to be an increase in discretion in the setting and implementation of sex equality policies, as Chief Executives are freer to control matters relating to personnel. Rather than setting up equal opportunities units, the trend appears to be towards identifying key staff responsible for implementing equal opportunities and including equal opportunities in the forward job plans of managers.[16]

The creation of quasi-governmental bodies is another disaggregation change. Governmental functions previously carried out by central government departments or local authorities are divested to newly constituted semi-autonomous bodies. Sex equality policies within these organizations are entirely discretionary. Wider concerns over the accountability of their ruling boards suggest that there is little control over the extent to which women are represented on them. There have been targets for increasing representation of women members of public bodies, as membership seats come up for review, but the argument that there is a dearth of women to appoint, especially in the property world, is often used. In 1987, the Women's National Commission obtained agreement that details of some 50,000 public appointments should be published for the first time and the proportion of women receiving appointments did rise from 18.5% in 1987 to 23% in 1989. These figures mask a large variation across sectors, with public bodies attached to the Ministry of Agriculture, Fisheries and Food scoring only 3% in 1985 and 5% in 1989.

Competition

Changes geared towards increasing competition are having the greatest effect of all on issues of employment. Redundancies within local authorities through the first tranche of compulsory competitive tendering in manual and blue-collar sectors appear to have affected women more than men. There was a 21% fall in employment in manual services across the Equal Opportunities Commission 39 case study authorities between 1988 and 1993. Evidence from this survey, combined with previous surveys carried out by INLOGOV and the Public Services Privatization Research Unit, suggests that across cleaning building, school catering, refuse collection, and sports and leisure management, female employment declined by 22% while male employment declined by 12%. Overall, the greatest impact under CCT has been in cleaning and catering services. Productivity has increased but the profits achieved by Direct Services Organisations and private contractors have largely been at the expense of female part-time workers. In contrast, there has been a small increase in full-time employment for men in these services.[17] The extension of CCT to white-collar services is likely to have a further disproportional impact upon female employment. Areas identified as candidates for contracting out are finance, personnel, legal services, information technology, architecture, engineering, property services, housing management and libraries. The concentration of female employees in these areas is high, around 60% in finance, personnel and legal services, 50% in housing management and 80% in libraries.

Where work is contracted out to private sector providers, the only way that a local authority can influence the way that the staff carrying out the work are recruited, promoted or paid would be by specifying that the successful tenderer must operate a sex equality policy. However, equal opportunities are designated 'non- commercial' matters in the Local Government Act of 1988 and restrictions are placed on their inclusion in the CCT process. There is only one way round the restrictions; local authorities are allowed to introduce 'quality conditions' into contracts, specifying that contractors must be sensitive to their client group, in service delivery areas with high ethnic constituencies for example. In these cases, a limited form of 'contract compliance' is possible, with contractors required in the terms of the contract to ensure that a certain proportion of their employees are of a specified group.

The implementation of equal opportunities policies in local authorities has traditionally rested with equal opportunities units and officers. However, the EOC found that the majority of equal opportunities officers did not initially participate in the compulsory competitive tendering process, the conclusion was that a combination of the legislative framework for CCT, a lack of understanding of the CCT process and the structure of local authorities accounted for this lack of involvement. These factors have combined to produce a situation where CCT officers responsible for the tendering process have usually not sought the involvement of equal opportunities officers; likewise, equal opportunities units have often chosen not to be involved in CCT. As a result, the EOC concluded that equal opportunities were accorded 'no significance' in the preparation of contracts. Its findings suggested that local public service providing contractors tended to have equal opportunities statements but little commitment and did not monitor employment. Interviews since the EOC report suggest that some equal opportunities units are starting to become involved in contract specification by pressing for the 'quality conditions' clause to be included in contracts, but this exception to the restrictions applies only to areas where the client group is largely women.

At the central government level, where Market Testing was introduced several years after CCT, the initial picture seems similar to that observed by the EOC locally (although no analyses have been carried out). Market Testing guidelines allow departments and agencies, subject to restrictions imposed by EC directives; 'to give prospective contractors the opportunity to provide information on their employment practices, including equal opportunities, that such contractors may believe is relevant to their ability to fulfil the contract for which they are bidding', and this clause is deemed by the Office of Public Service and Science within the Cabinet Office to be adequate provision against any worsening of sex equality provision.[18] However, the majority of market testing awards are in areas where such information is unlikely to be regarded as relevant: central administrative tasks such as information technology development, legal services and financial management. For example, in the privatization of the Information Technology Office of the Inland Revenue, in which 2,000 staff were transferred to the computer company Electronic Data Systems, equal opportunity policies are not mentioned in the National Audit Office report covering the sale. The same is true for the sale of the Information Technology arm of the Department of Transport, in which another 320 staff were transferred. Under the European Union's Transfer of Undertakings and Protection of Employment Directive (TUPE), staff who are transferred to a successful contractor retain previous terms and conditions, but in general transferred staff have little protection against redundancies after a period of time in the new company. This period is specified in the contract; only six months in the case of the transfer of Inland Revenue staff to Electronic Data Systems.

Market testing has had a severe effect on civil service morale. It is difficult to see in this organizational climate which individuals or organizational units within departments or agencies will be motivated to lobby for the inclusion of sex equality policies in contracts, whether they are won by private sector providers or by in-house teams. At Whitehall level, there was little of the culture of equal opportunities that existed at the local level. Such equal opportunities initiatives as existed were managed centrally and implemented at the level of whole departments or even the whole civil service. Contracts are managed by burgeoning contract and finance divisions, organizationally distinct from personnel departments and organizationally remote from the Equal Opportunities Unit of the Cabinet Office. There seems little incentive for managers who have equal opportunities monitoring built into their 'forward job plans' to tackle the issue of the equal opportunities policies of private sector providers, especially as this is not one of the issues that is monitored by the Cabinet Office.

Incentivization

The incentivization changes with the greatest impact for sex equality policies would seem to be the 'deprivileging' of public sector workers, changing 'sheltered' pay structures, employment relations and pension rights to more flexible private sector forms which remunerate employees more directly in relation to local conditions and market scarcities. At local government level, there is evidence that Compulsory Competitive Tendering has engendered what the Equal Opportunities Commission termed a 'contract culture', in which it is easier for hours or jobs to be cut and terms of service to be altered. Across all services there has been increased use of part-time workers on short hours. Such changes seem to have affected women more than men, and previous differences in men's and women's pay have been exacerbated under CCT.

At the central level, incentivization changes are undermining the idea of what it means to be a civil servant, in terms of a unified civil service with respect to pay, promotion and grading. Destandardization of pay and bargaining means that existing differences across departments are likely to increase. Previously the Cabinet Office was responsible for overseeing the implementation of the civil service's equal opportunities Programme of Action; now departments and agencies will be responsible for their own policies. The process of extended delegation may jeopardise the progress of future work on the programme, given that the Cabinet Office's influence over individual departments and agencies will be diminished. The new draft contract for top civil servants mentions 'excessive additional hours' and 'mobility', thereby institutionalising one element of the cultural barriers to sexual equality noted earlier. The Office of Public Service and Science has acknowledged that the implications of performance pay for sex equality would require close monitoring; some studies of performance pay in private sector organisations have indicated that 'men were significantly more likely than women to receive awards'.[19]

The trend towards bringing top civil servants in from the private sector seems likely to affect the slow but steady increase in the number of women that have been making it through the civil service career structure to the highest echelons. In 1994 some 12% of appointments in the senior open structure were made from outside the civil service, and the White Paper anticipated that this figure would rise to around 20%. The inclusion of women in these appointments will depend upon availability, and therefore to a large extent on the number of women who have reached board level in the private sector; still extremely low, as noted earlier.

To summarise, changes at both local and central levels break up governmental bureaucracies and open them up as far as possible to competition from the market. At the local level, the most important effect seems likely to be the introduction of a 'contract culture' which erodes the abilities of local authorities to operate sex equality policies within local authorities and leaves any form of regulation of contracts to equal opportunities units with seriously enfeebled legislative tools. In the central civil service, competition changes seem likely to have an even greater impact than at the local level unless individuals are provided with the motivation to make equal opportunities an issue in contract provision. Disaggregation of departments increases the discretionary elements of sex equality policies, already noted as seriously weakening the impact of previous reforms in the 1970s. Incentivization changes seem likely to have most impact at the highest levels of the civil service, eroding previous efforts to overcome informal barriers to women's progression, while actually formalising some of the elements of the 'exclusionary male culture'. As increasing amounts of work are put out to tender, it seems likely that the effect observed by an interviewee in one local authority will be seen in the central civil service: 'the managerial elite stays untouched, and so therefore it is almost inevitable that you are going to end up with slimmer organisations with more men in them.'

Gender research and public administration research

The academic fields of gender studies and public administration remain almost entirely unintegrated, existing as analytically distinct specialisms and barely recognising each other's existence. The burgeoning literature on the New Public Management and administrative reform rarely considers the gender implications of change. Since a special edition on Equal Opportunities Policies in 1989, the journal Public Administration has accorded virtually no space to the subject, and a recent special issue on 'Emerging Issues in Public Administration' in 1995 made no mention of sex equality issues or feminist writing on the state, which has moved from a concentration on the effects of state policies on women to an emphasis on the gendered processes and structures that comprise state institutions.

Similarly, the growing literature within the field of gender studies on state feminism has shown little consideration of public management change and the changing nature of the state. It concentrates on a number of disagreements and controversies[20] surrounding the extent to which feminists should engage with institutions of the state. Liberal feminists such as Moss Kanter argue that once women achieve organizational power, their gender pales into insignificance; thus the way forward must be sex equality policies geared at increasing the number of women at higher levels in organizations. Radical feminist writers such as Kathy Ferguson, argue that bureaucracy is intrinsically patriarchal, and that when women do enter bureaucracies they find themselves 'caught between the instrumentality of male-dominated modes of public action and the expressive values of female-dominated modes of action in the private realm'. Catherine MacKinnon characterises the state as male. Such writers argue a case against bureaucracy and against women's participation in bureaucratic organizations. In contrast, Susan Halford argues that 'feminist perspectives which view "the state" as a functional tool in the hands of patriarchal (and/or capitalist) interests paralyse our understanding of local government women's initiatives and, more widely, of the relationship between gender relations and the state in contemporary Western society'.[21] Those writers who have taken Halford's advice and carried out empirical research in the civil service, for example Cynthia Cockburn and Sophie Watson, have not yet investigated the impact of public management change of the 1980s and 1990s.

Heedless to the intricacy of the state feminism debate, the subject under discussion is slipping away. As the institutions of the state become more and more fragmented, with an increasing number of central and local government organizations existing mainly as contract writers and overseers, opportunities for any kind of centrally directed initiative towards attaining sex equality in the future are diminished. As redundancies continue at the lower and middle levels where women had gained a foothold, and a largely male dominated elite forms a higher proportion of civil servants that remain, the proportion of women penetrating the highest levels seems just as likely to worsen as to improve. The site of action for moves towards sex equality within the state has now changed, with legislative change, regulation and increased monitoring the central areas on which to focus. Any future discussion of the extent to which state processes are gendered will need to take these changes into consideration. If this task is left to the field of UK public administration (which, perhaps not entirely coincidentally, is largely male-dominated), it is unlikely to happen.

---

1 See C. Hood, 'A Public Management for All Seasons', *Public Administration*, 1991/3. C. Hood, *Explaining Economic Policy Reversals* (Open University Press, 1994); G. Jones 'International Trends in New Public Management', LSE Public Policy Group Working Paper, 1994.

2 J. Lovenduski, 'Implementing Equal Opportunities in the 1980s: An Overview', *Public Administration*, Spring 1989.

3 K. Riley, 'Equality for Women: The Role of Local Authorities', *Local Government Studies*, Jan./Feb. 1990. Also A. Coyle, 'The Limits of Change: Local Government and Equal Opportunities for Women', *Public Administration*, Spring 1989 for some problems experienced in implementation of local authority opportunities policies.

4 K. Escott and D. Whitfield, *The Gender Impact of CCT in Local Government* (Equal Opportunities Commission, 1995), p. 167.

5 E. Brimelow, 'Women in the Civil Service', *Public Administration*, Autumn 1981; S. Watson, 'Producing the Right Sort of Chap: The Senior Civil Service as an Exclusionary Culture', *Policy and Politics*, July 1994.

6 K. Dowding, 'The Civil Service' in R. Maidment and G. Thompson (eds), *Managing the United Kingdom* (Sage, 1993), pp. 18–19.

7 Data from Office of Public Service and Science, *Equal Opportunities for Women in the Civil Service Progress Report 1992–1993* (HMSO, 1993); *Equal Opportunities for Women in the Civil Service* (HMSO, 1995).

8 S. Watson, *Playing the State* (Verso, 1990).

9 H. Heclo and A. Wildavsky, *The Private Government of Public Money* (Macmillan, 1981).

10 See 'The Uses of Power: A Case Study of Equal Employment Opportunity Implementation' in H. Eisenstein, *Gender Shock: Practising Feminism on Two Continents* (Allen and Unwin, 1994).

11 S. Halford, 'Women's Initiatives in Local Government: Where Do They Come From and Where Are They Going?' *Policy and Politics*, 1988/4; 'Feminist Change in a Patriarchal Organisation: The Experience of Women's Initiatives in Local Government and Implications for Feminist Perspectives in State Institutions' in A Savage and M. Witz (eds), Gender and Bureaucracy (Blackwell, 1992).

12 See V. Hammond and V. Holton, 'The Scenario for Women Managers in Britain in the 1990s' in N. J. Adler and D. N. Izraeli (eds), *Competitive Frontiers: Women Managers in a Global Economy* (Blackwell, 1994).

13 See P. Dunleavy, 'The Globalization of Public Services Production: Can Government be "Best in World"?', *Public Policy and Administration*, 1994/2.

14 For local government reform see S. Biggs and P. Dunleavy, 'Changing Organizational Patterns in Local Government: A Bureau-Shaping Analysis' in J. Lovenduski and J. Stanyer (eds), *Proceedings of the Annual Conference of the Political Studies Association 1995*.

15 K. Escott and D. Whitfield, op.cit., p. 21.

16 Office of Public Service and Science, *Equal Opportunities for Women in the Civil Service: Progress Report 1992–1993*.

17 Cf. K. Escott and D. Whitfield, op.cit., ch. 8.

18 Reply from Minister for OPSS to Commission for Racial Equality.

19 OPSS, 1933.

20 For review of the literature see M. Savage and A. Witz (eds), *Gender and Bureaucracy* (Blackwells, 1992).

21 S. Halford, op.cit., p. 156.

The Privatisation of Sex Equality Policy

BY IAN FORBES

A WEEK may be a long time in party politics; in equality politics, twenty years is no time at all. In 1975, the passage of the Sex Discrimination Act and the coming into effect of the provisions of the Equal Pay Act marked the effective inauguration of a British sex equality policy, as distinct from those policies which ignored gender or actually promoted sex inequality. That policy took as its main focus the importance of the employment prospects and conditions for women. Education and training were seen as supporting elements in a general attempt to establish equal opportunities for women in need of employment protection, as well as the chance to establish a measure of economic security. Those legal changes were criticised for threatening the very financial survival of businesses both large and small, not to mention undermining the family. At the same time, they were derided by some equality campaigners as mere legalistic sops to liberal conscience. Neither fast nor dramatic changes in the situation of women were immediately forthcoming, but a process was begun that is much easier to appreciate two decades later. British sex equality policy has developed into an interesting and complex phenomenon. It has an identifiable and settled core, based on an entrenched legislative base, as well as a burgeoning set of policy measures with national and European dimensions, and an extensive and varied periphery enlivened by debates touching on most areas of the public and private realms. As a result, the policy arena is now broad rather than marginal and ghettoised, and 'gendered' analyses of public policies are much more likely to be given a hearing. Nevertheless, it is by no means a fixed phenomenon. It is now possible to document some of the practical impacts of an evolving conservative agenda and policy amalgam on sex equality.

We first review general developments in equality policy, then explore the contradictory nature and impact of government policies in the labour market, after which the active and passive parts of the government's approach to sex equality policy in general. The British government presents itself as innovatory and dedicated to the achievement of equality for women. It claims to deliver greater opportunity for women by forcing systemic changes in the operation of various reaches of the labour market. However, the results do not support the chosen policies and bring into question the government's understanding of and commitment to sex equality. Finally, the implications of these developments for the policy environment are discussed.

Equality for women has not been the uniform or evident consequence of the development of sex equality policy, despite a number of changes beneficial to women as a group and some individuals. The institutionalisation of anti-discrimination measures is the principal outcome, but more interesting are the secondary outcomes: the widening of the political opportunity structure for women; the emergence of evidence of the efficacy of policies and their implementation; the experimentation with new methods of introducing change; the shifts of foci for action; and the identification of new areas of inequality or resistance to change.

The development of equality policy

Analysts of the situation of women over the last twenty-five years are frequently struck by the paradox of a welter of progressive changes combined with the almost total rigidity of global patterns of inequality between women and men. Within the women's equality movement, a range of indicators point to the efficacy of efforts to produce substantive change, including, for example, the spread of expertise, the creation of new institutions, the successful application of new approaches, the integration of more women into all reaches of the public and private sectors, the sensitivity to difference and the exploration of new ways to deal with it, mainstreaming and the formation of links with other oppressed and disadvantaged groups. It can also be pointed out that, in legislative terms, the ferment of the 1970s has been followed by the quiet but widespread 'seeding' of all manner of legislation with equal opportunity clauses, such that the principles have become prescriptions embedded in the entire breadth of policy arenas. However, twenty years of equal pay demands, backed by legislation, have produced only marginal changes, and these may be explained by a worsening of employment prospects for men rather than a product of an equality policy. Small and large-scale labour market studies comparing women and men have consistently found the same glaring inequalities, the same patterns of disadvantage, the same structural obstacles. Not that such findings are confined to Britain. Perron's comparative assessment of equal opportunities in employment indicated that there was no great improvement in any of the countries of the European Union in the 1980s.[1] Even so, the United Kingdom came low on her index, despite having the kind of regulatory framework that can be conducive to greater gender equality.

The gains of the last twenty years have generally followed long and lively campaigns to introduce a new issue and move it up the policy agenda. These issues have often reflected their origins in the feminist analysis of the public/private split. In the 1980s, for example, the campaign for gender equality in the public realm was heavily concentrated on employment and pay issues. A large number of women became actively engaged and then employed in implementing equal opportunities policies. At the same time, the private realm was receiving a great deal of attention. Issues such as violence, rape, harassment, abuse, sexual orientation and censorship were forced on to and up the political agenda. The experience in the 1990s, however, is quite different. In the public arena, the gains for women are proving vulnerable. Part-time work for women is increasing, but more as an economic necessity than a route to independence. Low-paid jobs are also increasing, breadwinner women are suffering unemployment, gender segregation is growing within and between occupations, and the class divisions between women are increasing. In the private realm, the radical agenda is under severe pressure, exemplified by a renewed pro-family campaign, tightening of the abortion law and pressure on single mothers from government and its agencies. The effect of this changed climate, the threat to fundamental gains for women, is to reinforce that which came under some challenge in the last twenty years—the notion that employment is the bedrock of women's equality.

The broadening of the equalities movement, encompassing cross-cutting forms of social and political exclusion, has now been met by a challenge to the historically progressive nature of that movement. In the 1970s and 1980s it was possible to conceive of just two modes of equal opportunities implementation—the radical and the liberal. Arguments among theorists and practitioners were largely based on differences deriving from theoretical perspectives associated with Millian liberalism and varieties of socialism and marxism. However, as the departure from the postwar consensus toward the New Right agenda become more evident in the 1980s, so this simple liberal/radical dichotomy became increasingly inadequate to the task of explaining equality policy. The missing dimension stems from the increasingly influential application of a conservative approach to equality of opportunity. This approach, in combination with the development of New Right models of public policy implementation, has led to the emergence of an equality policy with distinctive features. At base, the concept and desirability of equality itself came under sustained attack, and a New Right approach to justice challenged the large measure of agreement between liberals and radicals over the need for law and procedures. In place of the valorisation of women's perspectives, the conservative view of equal opportunity celebrates inequality and claims that the free market produces outcomes that can not technically be found to be unjust. Accordingly, market liberalisation is framed as a policy advance compatible with the (real) interests not just of women, but of society as a whole. In effect, it has placed work for women at the centre of the agenda once more.

The existence of three views of equal opportunities suggests that the analysis of equality policy is intrinsically complex, likely to unearth developments with differing inspiration and pedigree. Some policies will be classically liberal in formulation, others will have radical elements, while more recently we should expect to find policies driven by the New

Right agenda. Equally, criticisms of equality policy come from different directions. Therefore, it is not possible to assume that all 'equality policy' is concerned with a simple kind of equality for women. The message here must be that there is more than one core concept at issue, each of which is understood and gains coherence in the context of others, all of which must remain fluid, to new possibilities of interpretation and application. How can that be done, while still making progress in policy analysis and implementation?

On the basis of general agreement—across the conventional political spectrum—that action needs to be taken in respect of women's position in society, it is unsurprising that discussions of equality policy tend to focus on anti-discriminatory action. Such activity can be undertaken in an infinite variety of settings—family, economy, politics, civil service, the public and private arenas—by a person, a group, an agency, a government, non-governmental actors, states and organisations of states in respect of a range of actions relating to variously defined groups or individuals. Just as anti-discrimination can refer to a wide range of activities, whether such activities are the subject of legislation or not, it is also plain that governments have accepted responsibility for institutionalising various anti-discriminatory measures and have provided a wealth of material for analysis.

In order to have an effective anti-discrimination strategy, three vital components have to work in concert. First, differences in respect of gender and culture must be recognised, in combination with a compelling ethical justification of anti-discrimination through which general agreement on key principles can be established, in order to develop and sufficiently widespread support. Second, a sophisticated body of legislation must be enacted to deal with the specific circumstances within which different kinds of discrimination occur. Third, there must be arrangements for effective action to combat discrimination in all areas of society. These three things, principles, prescriptions and processes—embodying an ethics of difference, anti-discrimination law and equality practices—are the preconditions for successful anti-discriminatory action. Unless they are properly institutionalised, progress can be uncertain and vulnerable to changing circumstances, such as economic downturn or shifts in public opinion. Contradictions and weaknesses in any one of these areas threatens the viability of the overall strategy, and can seriously undermine advances made in other areas. It is far easier to damage an anti-discrimination strategy and its achievements than it is to extend its impact and operation.

The equal opportunities movement in Britain has made its contribution to the setting of the policy agenda in a number of ways. It has undertaken many of the tasks associated with the formation of the ethics of difference, the drive for anti- discrimination legislation and the front-line implementation of equality practices. This movement has never been a single and simple alliance of feminist, anti-racist, disability and sexual orientation campaigners; there have been complementary contributions such that fundamental principles have come to be shared. These are equality, social justice and, most recently, diversity. All are contested terms and draw heavily on liberal traditions of thought. In general, the history of the equal opportunities movement shows that, in philosophical terms, the original, liberal-individualist approach has been augmented by socialist conceptions of the role of economic and social circumstance, and by theories of oppression deriving from feminist and anti-racist political experience. The same is true of equal opportunities policies, which have departed from a liberal-individualist understanding of the most telling means to tackle inequality, and have adopted more group-based, socio-economic perceptions relating not just to equal treatment rights but also to rights to resources. This is true not only in individual countries, but also in the European Union and in respect of other policy areas such as race.

Despite this foundation in progressive liberal ideas, giving way to more socialist or communitarian approaches to inequality, the institutionalisation of anti- discrimination has come under increasing challenge in Britain, exemplified at the public level by largely febrile debates about positive discrimination. In effect, sex equality policies give rise to negative forces, ranging from apathy to outright hostility of elites resting changes in the underlying gender system. It is this dynamic that is explored here. Each aspect of anti-discrimination — principle, prescription and process — is under more or less continuous challenge from pro-feminist as well as anti-feminist elements.

The bedrock of the change process, the ethics of difference built up since the 1960s, is being seriously tested. In the 1990s, the principal vehicle for diluting the acceptance and validation of difference is the view that a harmonious society can only be secured if men and women fulfil the roles laid down by antiquity, function and 'common sense'. This subverts the radical appreciation of difference by reaffirming traditional, sex-differentiated roles for women and men. Central to this is the hegemony of the family as the foundational social form, and the importance of mothering for the well-being of society. These ideas, and the way that women and men reconstruct the associated forms and practices daily, provide a blame-free rationale to defenders of sexism, sexual inequality and injustice. To undermine the ethics of difference is perforce to consolidate prejudice and provoke discriminatory behaviour.

The second area of concern is the legislative base to deal with discrimination. Domestic sources of anti-discrimination regulation are of three types: those which introduce obligations or prohibitions or directly create rights and/or entitlements for individuals; those which instantiate rights and/or entitlements for groups; and those which set objectives and launch programmes, and are therefore intended mainly as guidelines for the responsible bodies — such as government — rather than as sources of individual or group rights. Often it is difficult to determine into which category an instrument falls, in which case court decisions can be a guide. Two associated developments are noticeable here. The increasing impact of the European Court of Justice has led to a greater willingness of domestic courts to find in favour of women (see Collins and Meehan in this volume). Calls for new legislation are commonplace, particularly covering violence and harassment, yet the reaction of the government so far has been to sidestep such demands, with the notable exception of the recognition in law of the offence of rape in marriage. In almost all other respects, the government has remained opposed to legislative change, in the face of repeated demands and even treaty obligations, to the point that Lord Lester has observed that the government's delay in implementing an European Court judgement on equal pay dating from 1982 'amounts to a continuing denial of the effective enjoyment in the United Kingdom of the funda-mental human right to sex equality in pay'.

Overall, the net result after twenty years is a general neglect of foundational legal measures and a failure to introduce new measures. Consequently, available remedies have become divided into three types: the minimally effective, the massively costly, and the virtually moribund. In the process, the developing culture of anti-discrimination and the changing climate of expectation concerning acceptable standards of behaviour have been compromised. The unsatisfactory result is that the laws have been driven into disrepute in the view of opponents and supporters of sexual equality alike. The most powerful institutional force offsetting the inefficacy of domestic legislation is, again in the opinion of Lord Lester, Community law. In his view, it 'has come to the rescue of the scope and substance of our statutes, and it is now addressing key issues about the need for effective remedies. Community law has enabled the EOC and individual women and men to win in the courts what we in the mid-1970s could not win in Whitehall and Westminster.'[2] These words betray the unsatisfactory state of British legislation, indicate the long-standing restraint on equality policy deriv-ing from politicians and civil servants, and suggest that the EU is now a powerful ally to the Equal Opportunities Commission in its attempts to reinvigorate legal remedies and advance sex equality policy.

Other informed critique of existing anti-discrimination policies comes mainly from academics and practitioners, and their critiques are almost always produced by those committed at the level of principles. There is disagreement about law, machinery, speed and spread of implementa-tion, and strategic goals. Hence the appropriateness of affirmative action laws or policies continue to stimulate debate, as do the issues of pornography and reproductive choice.

It can not be assumed that the legislators, or even all practitioners, share the assumptions of those who analyse the institutionalisation of anti-discrimination. This is hardly surprising given the documented absence of women at the top of government and the political hue of the government. While it may once have been accurate to describe men and their government as woefully uninformed about women's inequality, content to keep things as they were, this is no longer the case. Whether for electoral considerations or not, ministers and their civil servants are much less able to ignore the interests demands of women, and are much more likely to be aware that justifications of their policies will be demanded. Under the Conservatives, practical examples of this changing culture would include the tax reform which allowed all women to submit returns in their own right, the introduction of equal opportunities monitoring right across Whitehall, and the creation of a Ministerial Group on Women's Issues. The case of the Ministry of Defence's indefensible policy on pregnant service personnel shows that complacency can be both expensive and embarrassing.

However welcome such changes to the political culture are, the Conservative government has not adopted an anti-discrimination strategy based on liberal and radical approaches. Nor has it drawn wholeheartedly on the established professional expertise. Not surprisingly, its approach to anti-discrimination conforms to its ideological perspective. Conservative thought, with its clear and compelling account of equality of opportunity, is based on core values of stability and order. To maintain order, the conservative wishes to ensure that the right kind of society persists — a society with a stable and functioning hierarchy, where everybody knows their position and associated duties. Such a society need not be static — it is not necessary that individuals are locked into a particular stratum. Conservative proponents of equal opportunities believe that competition breeds improvement: the hierarchy is refreshed by new blood — of the right kind of course. As far as difference is concerned, the conservative holds that society will produce a desirable outcome if it is allowed to sort itself out, free of too much political interference.

Accordingly, the conservative is strongly committed to merit as the foundation of judgement about the suitability of persons to take their place in the hierarchy. Existing barriers to achievement should also be removed without causing any structural change in society. Finally, attention should be paid to the existence of incentive. People should want to benefit from an advantageous position in the hierarchy and anything that reduces their drive to compete should be minimised. Within a New Right or neo-liberal framework, this means a reduction of state interference and a focused vitalisation of market forces.

There is now ample evidence to suggest that the conservative approach to equal opportunities permeates sex equality policy in Britain, severely restricting the ambit of even the liberal approach with its known shortcomings. This development has taken place at the level of central government, and is in direct contrast to developments at local authority and European levels. The impact has been demonstrably negative, despite the fact that the government has sought to cloak its policies in the language of access, independence and equal chances for employment for women. 'Flexible working', for example, is being promoted 'as being both a route to economic recovery and an aid to equality of opportunity'.[3] Faith in the restorative forces of a deregulated labour market clearly takes precedence over policies which focus on need satisfaction or the political demands of women. Instead of enhanced social policies relating to social welfare and better employment conditions, there has been an easing of protection for women and a failure to introduce protection relevant to new labour market conditions. This fits with the aim of encouraging the growth of a low-wage, low-skill economy (or at least the generation of such segments of an economy), and further moves to part-time employment. It is women, especially white working-class women, who fill these posts. Flexible working may be convenient for individual women forced to fill multiple (stereotypically defined) roles, but the effect for women as a group is to entrench the structural inequalities which the 1970s legislation was designed to dismantle. Such developments have to be set against other, more positive readings of equality politics which point to the spread of good practice at institutional level, the expansion of opportunities for women and significant advances in feminist analyses of equality and difference.

The impact on women of the government's free market philosophy can be documented. The philosophical claim that actors entering the market do not intend outcomes to be unjust is deemed to mean that markets per se can not be unjust and therefore should not be constrained by 'social' considerations. Moves to ensure equal pay, better protection for women in employment, access to full-time benefits, maternity and childcare provisions, and interventionist equal opportunity policies are all characterised as socially (even socialist) inspired policies which would detrimentally skew the operation of the labour market and produce results harmful to society's and women's interests. This policy orientation has resulted in acts of commission and omission. First, some legal changes have restricted the ambit of established measures, while others have proven to discriminate against women. Second, since 1979 no substantive new public policy initiatives in relation to sex equality have been generated by central government. Its actions have been confined to introducing better practices within the bureaucracy of government and directly aligning itself with a private enterprise initiative.

The implications for equality policies of a conservative approach may be illustrated by accounts of, first, the impact of legislation specifically aimed to influence the role of local authorities in the labour market between 1980 and 1992, and, second, the government's high profile support for Opportunity 2000 from 1991. These typify the current state of British sex equality policy and highlight its consequences.

The changing culture of local labour markets

In the 1970s and 1980s, local authorities were 'in the front line of implementation' of equal opportunities, providing 'many instances of good practice'.[4] Policies were developed, sometimes disastrously and often controversially, to deal with all the major aspects of discrimination. In the field of employment, it was not unusual for authorities drastically to revise hiring practices and alter the composition of the workforce in favour of previously excluded or disadvantaged groups, such as women, ethnic minorities and disabled people. Such policies were consistent with the letter and intent of existing anti-discrimination laws. Once in employment, these groups were able to benefit from training schemes and relatively favourable terms of work. Since it was not unusual for a local authority to be one of the largest employers in the area, the policies had a direct effect on the local labour market. Some, in particular the Greater London Council, sought to do more, by using their considerable spending power to extend their equal opportunity policies into the community. The means—contract compliance—were relatively simple. Potential contractors were obliged to demonstrate their commitment to the GLC's equal employment opportunity policy, provide details of the current gender and ethnic mix of employers, supply evidence of procedures to ensure fair recruitment, and outline measures to correct any perceived imbalances in the workforce. In this way, authorities were able to exert a disciplinary influence on the labour market and employment practices well outside their own organisations. The effectiveness of contract compliance was limited by the sophistication of the contractual demands, the extra administrative burdens imposed, the willingness of companies to agree to these conditions, and the political outcry from Labour's opponents. By the mid-1980s, the pattern of Labour control meant that many local labour markets, while certainly not in thrall to equality of opportunity practices, were beginning to show the effects. Employment of women compared to men went up; women gained access to jobs previously the preserve of men; and people from ethnic minorities enjoyed substantially better employment prospects.

By means of successive Acts, the effective power of local authorities in the labour market has been drastically reduced. Most effective was the Local Government Act 1988, which abruptly uprooted the burgeoning contract compliance culture. This was not outlawed, but the imposition of compliance criteria could be challenged by any potential contractor as an illegitimate restraint of trade. Virtually all contract compliance programmes ceased to operate once the Act came into force, with just four out of over two hundred authorities managing to sustain the practice.

The government also moved to implant a new culture—the contract culture. This has been achieved by positive moves to bring about a fundamental reduction of the power of local authorities as direct employers through the development of compulsory competitive tendering (CCT). The Local Government Planning and Land Act 1980 required authorities to tender an increasing proportion of repair, maintenance, highways and sewage work, and the Local Government Acts of 1988 and 1992 extended CCT to more manual fields, sports and leisure management, and a range of white collar services.

Compulsory competitive tendering is a particularly rich example of the way that ostensibly gender-neutral government action can have profoundly negative effects on sex equality. The policy has ideological, economic and political features. It is firmly based on the neo-liberal view of markets and the proper role of government. The high levels of local authority employment, and the prevailing practices of employment were held to be distorting the labour market. Hence the determination to break the power of authorities as large employers and providers of local services. In economic terms, the Conservative government was seeking to control public expenditure, a significant proportion of which took place at the local level. CCT offers the means of transferring expenditure from the public to the private sector in order to garner efficiency gains in a competitive environment, thus reduced spending. The political context was also important. The prime targets were the large number of urban authorities, mostly held by Labour. CCT thus promised a mix of outcomes that was very attractive.

However, as the Equal Opportunities Commission warned during the passage of the 1988 Act, unintended negative effects were foreseeable unless it contained specific provisions from the Sex Discrimination Act relating to the assessment of potential contractors' equal opportunity policies. No such changes were made, and subsequent research on the impact of CCT bears out the predictions.[5]

The main research findings demonstrate that some of the government's aims have been realised. Local authority employment dropped significantly (down 16% between 1989 and 1993), a contract culture of tendering, contracting out of services, internal markets and business units quickly developed, and the labour market is now characterised by a growing sector typified by low-wages and part-time work. The policy has played its part in creating a 'flexible', low-wage labour market, reducing the costs to employers of taking on new staff. However, the situation of women was adversely affected both in respect of their original position and in comparison to men. Female employment falls were greater, wages for women declined but rose for men (at least in the refuse collection services), greater numbers of women fell below the National Insurance lower earnings limit, and more women became temporary workers, with fewer employment rights. In sum, existing differences between permanent and casual work, between full-time and part-time jobs, and between male and female employment have been accentuated.

These findings are important, because they document an effective reversal of the improving employment prospects of women under local authorities in the 1980s. The claim that a flexible and deregulated market is an aid to equality of opportunity is not sustained on this evidence. The government's commitment to sex equality is brought into question, raising doubts about the value of a policy so clearly subordinated to the ideological, economic and political priorities outlined above. The restrictions placed on local authorities effectively force them to relinquish any practical action to promote equality of opportunity, even though that, too, is a specified responsibility under the Acts. They now operate the same policy as central government, one of words but few deeds.

Opportunity 2000

To underscore the policy orientation of central government, it is instructive to pursue the idea that government is sanctioning an effective privatisation of responsibility for sex equality. In October 1991, Opportunity 2000 was launched, with considerable fanfare, on the steps of 10 Downing Street. The location, and the presence of the Prime Minister surrounded by a (modest) phalanx of (mostly junior) female members of the government, led many to assume that a new initiative to combat sex discrimination in the workplace had been announced. At the time, the Equal Opportunities Commission had produced figures showing that the gap between women's and men's earnings was substantially wider in the UK than in other EU countries. Other comparative reports placed Britain at the bottom of the EU league in terms of public provision of childcare for children under five and showed that Britain has been subject to more legal actions for its failure to adhere to sex equality legislation than any other EU country.

A new government initiative may have seemed very timely, but Opportunity 2000 is not a government initiative at all. It is a self-financing campaign set up by an organisation called Business in the Community, operating under the Charities Act. It claims to represent a new and significant—even unique—development in the movement towards equality in Britain in the 1990s. According to Opportunity 2000, equality laws are 'little more than theoretical tools' which have 'failed miserably to achieve their intended results'.[6] This is precisely the kind of criticism that has been levelled at the legalist approach to equality measures by radical proponents of equality of opportunity for at least twenty years. By implication, Opportunity 2000 intended to address this weakness by stepping into the gap between a stated political commitment to bring about change and the necessary action to ensure that change is brought about. The new approach struck John Major as 'the boldest corporate equal opportunities initiative we have yet seen' (*The Guardian*, 27.10.92). It aimed to 'increase the quality and quantity of women's participation in the workforce and move towards a more

representative balance between women and men at all levels in organisations, but especially in management, and based on ability'.[7]

The use of the terms participation and representative balance are
rhetorical flourishes not usually associated with conservatism. They
intimated, instead, an underlying radical and liberal democratic ethos,
and served to create reasonably high expectations about the performance of the initiative. The focus on ability, however, points to a merit-
based or conservative conception of equal opportunities, while the
attention to management suggests that the interests of a relatively small
section of the working population of women are to be singled out for
special treatment compared to other women. Further claims by Opportunity 2000, however, show that participation and representation are
not fundamental arguments. Indeed, it is argued that a pragmatic
approach is required. According to its campaign director, Liz Bargh, the
campaign is 'absolutely rooted in business needs and business-driven'
(*Financial Times*, 23.10.91). The primacy of the 'needs' of business
rather than the needs and rights of women as a group means that
market considerations outweigh equality principles. It leads to the claim
that 'equality in employment will henceforth be an indispensable
element of business development'.[8] Far from being new, this is in all
important respects equivalent to the argument proposed by the equality
strategy proposed by the Equal Opportunities Commission under its
then chair, Joanna Foster, in 1988, and subsequently abandoned five
years later, a dismal failure on all the predicted criteria of success.[9] As
we have seen, the same assumptions underpin the rhetoric concerning
the benefits of 'flexible working'.

The market imperative also emerges in the conduct of Opportunity
2000. Its literature refers to three key steps for an organisation joining
the campaign: first, the preparation of a programme of organised reform
to provide a full range of equal opportunities; second, the development
of targets; and third, a public statement of commitment by the company,
followed by annual progress reports. In effect, the responsibility for
change rests with the organisation (as it always has done under the
existing legislation). Part of the attractiveness of Opportunity 2000
relies upon the impact of a public undertaking by senior management
to enhance equality for women. As a mark of that commitment, and to
have access to the benefits of membership, each organisation is required
to pay an annual fee (a minimum of £1,000). In effect, Opportunity
2000 successfully charges organisations for its range of advisory,
information and network services, most of which are provided by the
Equal Opportunities Commission free or at a tiny fraction of the
Opportunity 2000's membership charge.

Over four years have elapsed since the initiative was announced.
Since then, the number of organisations which have joined has grown
steadily. Indeed, over a quarter of the working population are now with
such employers, including the National Health Service, the largest single

employer of women in the EU. Success has been claimed by the organisers, but the latest figures on employment, equal pay, and the share of women in management all suggest that progress has been patchy or marginal. At present, there is no study available which is capable of detecting whether any advances are statistically significant, nor is there evidence which can distinguish between any general, long-term trend in improvements in the position of women and the impact of Opportunity 2000. In the face of reports that the presence of women in senior management and executive boards is still negligible, the chair of Opportunity 2000, Lady Howe, claimed that targets are designed to change the corporate and work culture of organisations to allow women to reach the very top posts (*The Times*, 4.11.93). Quick change is now regarded as an unrealistic goal. Whilst it is true that improvements for women have historically been slow, it is important to note that the original drive for targets to ensure increased participation has now been diluted somewhat, with the emphasis shifting to the important but much more nebulous notion of cultural change.

From the practitioner's point of view, this was a most unwelcome change of emphasis. Opportunity 2000 was attractive to many sceptical practitioners precisely because it legitimated positive action recruitment and promotion targets. Employers publicly committed themselves in advance to one of the most controversial but effective tools of implementation available under the current law, where the changes would be easily measurable and lack of success difficult to disguise.

The first two of 'the four key learning points' promulgated by Opportunity 2000 in its Winter 1992 Newsletter underscore the underlying philosophical impetus of the initiative. These are 'Never stop selling the business case—it's vital for winning line managers over to the argument', and 'Timing and tenacity are critical for success—wait for the right moment to launch an initiative (i.e. when it meets a business need)'. If the business case and business needs are given priority, this must contradict the claim that change in the culture is desired, since it assumes that the business culture is ungendered, undiscriminatory in its practice, and should itself remain unchanged. The implication is that the benefits for women are contingent and not even necessary. The underlying culture which is consistently reinforced by the literature is that the economic imperative is paramount. It may be argued that such an approach is appropriate for private enterprise. However, this approach is also applied to public sector organisations, for which 'the business case' is an even more dubious proposition. Accordingly, it is sometimes referred to as 'the quality case', in order to stress the Citizen's Charter requirements of public organisations. It is in this respect that the Opportunity 2000 view of equality of opportunity and the understanding of the purposes of public sector organisations coincides with the government's view of both women and public administration. The imperative of the business/quality case—a profit and loss mentality, the reduction of every proposal to economic efficiency, the introduction of market disciplines—is at the heart of the drive to reform public administration and redefine the responsibilities of the state. It is restated as 'quality' on the basis that the citizen has a claim to be served as a customer, the values and definitions of which are derived directly from a free market ideology.

Equality campaigners, equal opportunity professionals and unions have voiced criticisms of Opportunity 2000. The concentration on employees in the management and professional categories overlooks the needs of the much more numerous women in lower grades, many of whom are denied the right to benefit from childcare and career-break policies recommended for women further up the hierarchy. Moreover, Opportunity 2000 steers clear of issues relating to women's pay, raising fears that the likely benefits will be restricted to a few highly-paid women in each organisation. The focus on the enrichment of the upper reaches of the organisational hierarchy, the emphasis on training and skills, i.e. a formal notion of merit, and the lack of concern about the needs of women as a group is consistent only with a conservative approach to equality of opportunity.

Opportunity 2000 has failed to make any detectable impression on government policy in the key areas of pay, childcare and improved legislation. Indeed, Lady Howe is said not to want Opportunity 2000 to be a lobbying organisation. Yet the number of large companies, and the claimed coverage of the workforce, puts the campaign in a strong position to speak in a representative manner about women's participation and support the kind of legal provisions which would make effective change less subject to the vagaries of the market, and less dependent upon the equivocal 'change of culture' requirement. In the context of the political opportunity structure, it can be argued that Opportunity 2000 has created the potential for a new and powerful voice. The refusal to use that voice to transmit the demands of women, or to represent their interests, throws into sharp relief once more the conflict between their needs and those of business. If the strategy adopted by Opportunity 2000 is found to be inadequate except within narrow boundaries, then its critique of the law—'little real impact'— may well apply to itself.

The new politics of equality

The change from a contract compliance culture to a contract culture at local government level, and the support of the Opportunity 2000 initiative, have revealed the foundations of the Conservative government's philosophical approach and given clear indications of the public policies that are beginning to augment traditional, liberal anti-discrimination measures, suggesting that the gender analysis of these developments needs to be augmented by a class analysis. The government views equality for women as fundamentally an employment issue, yet the negation of the active role of local authorities in the labour market has been followed by the abolition of the Wages Councils. As far as the Equal Opportunities Commission is concerned, the Wages Councils were 'one of the most effective systems in the UK for maintaining and protecting the principle of equal pay'. Not only was their abolition in its opinion a breach of the EU Equal Pay Directive and the Treaty of Rome, 'the government had done so in the full knowledge that its actions were likely to have a disproportionate adverse impact upon women workers' — women workers who come from the poorest section of society.[10]

To establish the contrast between the rights, protection and opportunities afforded to part-time workers and poorly-paid women and those women in full-time employment and professional classes, it is instructive to consider the internal workings of government. Here interventionist policies, including positive action, are recognised as valid and effective means of bringing about real change. The civil service, for example, has developed relatively sophisticated policies for the implementation of equal opportunities. The Prime Minister has lent his weight by telling ministers that he would expect to see a woman on every short-list or have a good reason why there was none. The ten-year progress report on equality for women in the civil service shows that significant, if modest, changes have been achieved in some areas since 1984, and contextualises the higher promotion rates for men with the report that a benchmark (yet another euphemism for a target) has been set of 15% women (currently 6–10%) in the top three grades of the service by the year 2000.[11] The National Health Service is actively pursuing a wide range of policy initiatives on equal opportunities for women at all levels. This drive, too, has had unequivocal ministerial support. However, privatisation, contracting out and the proliferation of agencies, trusts and quangos means that the civil service population is actually decreasing. Thus the policy and the Prime Minister's own laudable intentions apply in an increasingly narrow area, and are more likely to affect well-paid women (see Helen Margetts in this volume).

Despite the equal opportunities programme in Whitehall, responsibility for change in society as a whole is not accepted by the Prime Minister, who will countenance nothing like an interventionist stance in the drive for equality. The government is merely one actor among many, its role restricted to encouraging voluntary action by employers. Confirming this minimal role, Mrs Angela Rumbold, then one of the Home Office ministers, said that she considered the legal framework is in place to provide the machinery for tackling both direct and indirect indiscrimination. In her opinion, the main responsibility for pushing forward sex equality now lay with employers (*Financial Times*, 28.11.91). More recently, former Social Security Secretary Peter Lilley claimed, when announcing the much-criticised equalisation of state pension age, that 'the difference in state pension age is the last glaring inequality in our treatment of men and women'.[12]

The government's approach is completely consistent with the conservative account of equal opportunities. It confines itself to removing barriers to achievement, and acknowledging advancement. The legislative framework which outlaws discrimination is, therefore, the most that government should do. The adoption of a formal, legalistic approach to equality within a minimal state has an important effect. It allows the government to argue that it has no role in respect of the way that people behave outside the framework of laws covering sex discrimination in the work situation. In this way, its own responsibilities for women's equality are neatly contained. It can avoid responsibility for a much wider agenda of political concerns in respect of the family, childcare, education, social welfare, poverty, health, violence in the home and in the public arena.

Reviewing the policy environment

Current developments suggest that the effective privatisation of sex equality policies has caused a significant shift of power away from women in society. Chafetz has argued that 'in gender-stratified societies women constitute a pool of labour whose members are manipulable by the powerful actors who fill roles that allow them to control dominant social institutions and organizations'.[13] Preventing local authorities from exerting a positive influence in their realm, imposing Compulsory Competitive Tendering, the abolition of Wages Councils, and political support for Opportunity 2000, are all manifestations of powerful (male) actors manipulating the labour market to the detriment of women. Privatisation of equality policy thus represents a serious threat to the kind of development of equal opportunities practice seen in Europe in the past thirty years. Apart from restricting the possibility of further development, it closes off the political opportunity structure to a majority of women in significant ways, as their capacity for organisation and voice is reduced by economic changes. Some professional women may benefit, making marginal changes to the profile of organisations. Such change is bound to be presented as evidence of improvement in the situation of women and used as evidence against further legislation. Indeed, the pressure on the welfare state — on grounds of cost or ideology — is a powerful motivation for all governments to divest themselves of any part of the apparatus which is deemed capable of sustaining itself. In other words, segments of the public sector and public sector responsibilities will always be prone to the privatisation solution because the overall apparatus is developed enough in terms of the legal base, professional and agency experience, and there is in the 1990s a sufficient basis of public awareness and voluntary commitment to ensure that a politically acceptable level of activity will continue.

Until recently, sex equality policy analysis has tended to focus on the limits of implementation within the theoretical and practical limitations of the liberal state, i.e. on prescriptions, not principles. The main concerns have been: the inadequacy of the legalistic approach; the need for new and stronger laws (relating to group entitlements, class actions and protection for women); the nature and extent of positive action and positive discrimination policies; the role of elected governments at national and local level; the role of civil administration; policy issues (moving beyond the standard public realm concerns over employment, education and poverty to private realm matters such as pornography, abortion, health, welfare, rape, violence and harassment). However, the changes in the policy environment identified here suggest that this traditional approach needs to be extended to take account of the neo-liberal conception of a minimal state. There is to some extent an emerging new agenda affecting the sex equality policy debate, which is by no means another bout in the battle between utilitarianism and radicalism. Utilitarianism has been an acceptable minimum justification, even to radicals, since it incorporated a notion of the well-being of society combining with demonstrable self-interest. In contrast, the new agenda withdraws from both the social and personal elements of this form of liberal justification. 'The business case' is an altogether different type of justification. It prioritises an economically-derived conception of just one part of society (based on the fiction of the competitive firm). That definition is used to derive the concept of the person and their motivations. In effect, support for equal opportunities becomes associated with a set of values unrelated to equality, difference, justice or diversity. These developments represent significant challenges to the equal opportunities movement, and undermine the very possibility of sex equality policy. This will continue to be the case until the ideological fixation on the 'flexible' labour market loses its hold on policy-making. Such a change is not likely to occur without a change of government. Until that time, the equal opportunities movement will constantly be on the defensive, sustained only by the possibility of favourable judgements from the European Court of Justice and (to a lesser extent) British courts and interventions by the European Union.

1   D. Perrons, 'Measuring Equal Opportunities in European Employment', *Environment and Planning A*, 1994.
2   Lord Lester of Herne Hill, 'Discrimination: What Can Lawyers Learn from History?', *Public Law*, 1994, p. 231 and pp. 234–5.
3   'Part-time and Atypical Work' (Equal Opportunities Commission, 1995).
4   J. Lovenduski, 'Implementing Equal Opportunities in the 1980s: An Overview', *Public Administration*, Spring 1989.
5   K. Escott and D. Whitfield, 'The Gender Impact of CCT in Local Government (Equal Opportunities Commission, 1995).
6   H. Collins, *The Equal Opportunities Handbook* (Macmillan, 1992), p. 88.
7   L. Bargh, 'Opportunity 2000: A Promise of Change', *Local Government Management*, Summer 1992.
8   Collins, op.cit., p. 94.
9   'From Policy to Practice: An Equal Opportunities Strategy for the 1990s' (Equal Opportunities Commission, 1988) and I. Forbes, 'Race, Gender and Inequality', in *Focus on Britain* (Philip Allan, 1994).

10 'The Equal Opportunities Commission and Equal Pay' (Equal Opportunities Commission, 1995).

11 'Equal Opportunities for Women in the Civil Service: 10-year Progress Report' (HMSO, 1995).

12 'Equality in State Pension Age' (HMSO, Cm 2420, 1994).

13 J. S. Chafetz, *Gender Equity* (Sage, 1990).

Legislative Constructions of Motherhood

BY SUSAN MILLNS

OVER THE past two decades feminist writers have increasingly turned their attention towards the interaction of feminism, politics and the law in order to investigate the treatment that women receive at the hands of the legal system. This attention has involved exploration of the way in which women are discriminated against both in the public sphere, for example in paid employment, and the private sphere, in areas such as violence in the home and sexual abuse.[1]

In the public sphere the political implications of the way in which women are treated are highly visible. The role of the state in regulating the relationship between employer and employee, for example, has overt political overtones in terms of reflecting particular aims such as market deregulation and increased competition. These aims have had knock-on effects for women in the way in which they have increased the availability of part-time and fixed-term contracts, a high proportion of which are occupied by women. Equally, in the area of welfare and social security, state manipulation of the benefits system reflects a particular view of which women and men are considered to be in need of public financial support.

In the private sphere, however, the role of the state is less immediately visible because traditionally state intervention in conflicts which are played out in the domestic arena has been more restrained. Nevertheless the slogan adopted by some feminists that 'the personal is political' has brought the realm of the domestic sphere to public attention and has brought about state action and legal intervention in that area too. One clear example of this is the decision of the House of Lords in the case of *R v. R* [1991] 4 All E.R. 481. This decision, for the first time, brought 'marital rape' within the legal definition of rape, demonstrating the state's willingness to intervene in the privacy of the home environment. This now means that abusive husbands can be convicted of rape and are no longer permitted unlimited sexual access to their partners regardless of consent.

As the state has come to play a greater role in the regulation of women's lives, both in public and private sphere activities, it has become important to understand the way in which women are viewed by one of the primary adjuncts of the state, the legal system. This has meant consideration being given to the question of how women are seen through the eyes of those who participate in the law-making process, in particular Members of Parliament involved in shaping legislation and members of the judiciary involved in applying that legislation and in making common law decisions. In examining the relationship between the state, the law and feminism, it is possible to chart the way in which the process of law-making tells the story of women and their lives and constructs a certain typology of the women to whom legislation will be applied.[2] This has led to questions being asked about the extent to which law-makers are (in)accurate in their perceptions of women when creating legislation and jurisprudence and the extent to which their perceptions are (in)consistent when, for example, different laws are made which regulate women in different spheres of activity.

Here we examine the way in which women are characterised during the law-making process in one particular, but extremely important, aspect of their lives — motherhood. This will be done by considering three examples of legislation adopted in the 1990s which touch upon the status of women as mothers in both their public and private lives: the Human Fertilisation and Embryology Act 1990, the Child Support Act 1991, and the Trade Union Reform and Employment Rights Act 1993. The first deals with reproductive matters, in particular with fertility treatment services, and abortion. The second sets up a welfare system of maintenance for children where one parent is absent. The third deals, amongst other things, with maternity rights in employment.

First, the formulation of each statute will be discussed and a brief overview of its provisions outlined. It is worth pointing out at this stage that each of the three Acts was based upon a previously existing text. The Human Fertilisation and Embryology Act 1990 was based largely upon the Warnock Report produced by the Committee of Inquiry into Human Fertilisation and Embryology;[3] the Child Support Act 1991 was based upon the government's 1990 White Paper *Children Come First*; and the sections on maternity rights contained in the Trade Union Reform and Employment Rights Act 1993 were designed to implement provisions of the 1992 European Union directive on the safety and health of pregnant workers. The passage of each piece of legislation into its current form has, therefore, passed from these initial texts, through the filter of Parliament into the final legislative form.

Second, various aspects of the law's treatment of mothers taken from the three Acts are synthesised. Consideration is given to the underlying moral principle of the legislation, notably the idea of responsible parenting. Also under consideration is the definition of the legal status of parents and the nature of the relationship between the protagonists targeted by the legislation. Within the general context of the legal regulation of parenthood, this synthesis will permit an overview of the law-maker's perception of motherhood to be established. Also it allows the motivation behind the adoption of particular strategies vis à vis the role of women as mothers to be monitored.

Three ways of regulating motherhood

REPRODUCTIVE RIGHTS: THE HUMAN FERTILISATION AND EMBRYOL-
OGY ACT 1990. The Committee of Inquiry into Human Fertilisation
and Embryology, chaired by Dame Mary Warnock, was established in
1982, its remit being to consider the effects of developments in the field
of human assisted reproduction. The relevance of the Warnock Report
as far as it affects women as mothers lies principally in its discussion of
fertility treatment services. It draws attention to the perceived undesira-
bility of certain women being allowed access to fertility treatments and
therefore to the institution of motherhood. 'To judge from the evidence
many believe that the interests of the child dictate that it should be born
into a home where there is a loving, stable, heterosexual relationship
and that, therefore the *deliberate* creation of a child for a woman who
is not a partner in such a relationship is morally wrong. . . . We believe
that as a general rule it is better for children to be born into a two-
parent family, with both father and mother, although we recognise that
it is impossible to predict with any certainty how lasting such a
relationship will be.'

The disinclination to permit certain women who do not form part of
a heterosexual relationship to have access to fertility treatments was
translated into section 13(5) of the Human Fertilisation and Embryology Act in the following terms: 'A woman shall not be provided with
treatment services unless account has been taken of the welfare of any
child who may be born as a result of the treatment (including the need
of that child for a father), and of any other child who may be affected
by the birth.'

The statutory provision does not, therefore, impose a strict legislative
ban on fertility treatments for women not involved in a heterosexual
relationship. Yet the practical effect of the provision, that individual
consultants who take the decision to treat should consider the needs of
the child for a father, creates an extra hurdle to be surmounted by
women not in a heterosexual relationship in their quest for motherhood.

The Warnock Committee was concerned with reproductive technologies and embryo research and did not deal with the law on abortion.
The Human Fertilisation and Embryology Act, however, does incorporate a section on abortion. As a politically expedient measure, this issue
was introduced by the government into parliamentary discussion of the
1990 Act in the light of dissatisfaction at the state of abortion law under
the Abortion Act 1967.[4] Section 37 of the 1990 Act amends section
1(1) of the 1967 Act to permit lawful abortions to be performed by a
registered medical practitioner where two registered medical practitioners are of the opinion, formed in good faith, that one of the
following four conditions is satisfied:
the pregnancy has not exceeded its twenty-fourth week and that the
continuance of the pregnancy would involve risk, greater than if the

pregnancy were terminated, of injury to the physical or mental health of the pregnant woman or any existing children of her family; or
the termination is necessary to prevent grave permanent injury to the physical or mental health of the pregnant woman; or
the continuance of the pregnancy would involve risk to the life of the pregnant woman, greater than if the pregnancy were terminated; or
there is a substantial risk that if the child were born it would suffer from such physical or mental abnormalities as to be seriously handicapped.

While the grounds for abortion and the time-limits have changed as a result of this amendment, it carries over the formulation from the 1967 Act that a woman, in order to have a lawful abortion, must obtain the consent of two registered medical practitioners that her circumstances place her in one of the above categories. She is not legally in a position to decide unilaterally to terminate a pregnancy. The 1990 Act can therefore be said to operate broadly against notions of autonomous motherhood and the making of reproductive choices by women themselves. The role of medical consultants is given priority in decision-making in relation both to access to the new reproductive technologies and to abortion services.

WELFARE RIGHTS: THE CHILD SUPPORT ACT 1991.   While the Human Fertilisation and Embryology Act 1990 seeks to reinforce the traditional nuclear family in the area of reproduction, in the area of welfare the Child Support Act 1991 deals with the reality of one parent families, approximately 90% of which are headed by a woman. This Act was introduced by the government at top speed (*Children Come First* was published in October 1990; Royal Assent was given on 25 July 1991), amidst a blaze of publicity, a good deal of which was adverse. It provides a framework in which child support from absent parents (the vast majority of whom are men) is regulated by an administrative procedure, with the ultimate aim of reducing the state's (or taxpayer's) financial commitment to single-parent families. This has the effect of limiting the previously wide-ranging, and more arbitrary, powers of the courts to make arrangements for financial provision upon the breakdown of the family unit.

The Act instead provides for the calculation of maintenance payments on the basis of a rigid administrative formula. The system is operated by the Child Support Agency which has the power to collect the prescribed maintenance payments and can sanction those who are unwilling to cooperate with it.[5] So the 70% of lone parents who are in receipt of income support may suffer financial penalties in the form of deductions from their benefit for refusing to cooperate with the Agency, for example in refusing to disclose the identity of the absent parent.

During parliamentary debate on the Act the issue of enforced cooperation with the Agency had been focused upon by those groups

concerned with child poverty.[6] As a result of this lobbying, an amendment was introduced so that where a parent with care of the child
believes that she or her child may suffer 'harm and undue distress' as a
result of maintenance being sought, she may request an exemption. The
concept of harm and undue distress is not given a statutory definition
and is, therefore, left to be determined at the discretion of the Agency,
with guide-lines issued by the Secretary of State in 1993 giving as
examples fear of violence, rape and sexual abuse (subject to judicial
review). Where harm and undue distress cannot be established to the
satisfaction of the Agency, however, the exemption does not apply.
Women on benefit are consequently denied the opportunity to make a
fundamental choice as to whether or not they wish their ex-partner to
support their child.

One important effect of the Child Support Act is, therefore, to
perpetuate women's economic dependency upon men with whom they
may no longer wish to have contact. As far as the perception of
motherhood is concerned, the single (female) parent is again denied
autonomy, this time in decisions involving the financial support of her
children.

EMPLOYMENT RIGHTS: THE TRADE UNION REFORM AND EMPLOY-
MENT RIGHTS ACT 1993. Although the Trade Union Reform and
Employment Rights Act 1993 might well be termed legislation dealing
with employment rights, it should be noted first of all that the European
Union directive No. 92/85 on the protection of pregnant workers
(implemented in part into UK law by the 1993 Act) was introduced at
the level of the European Union as a health and safety rather than an
employment measure. This meant that the directive fell within Article
118A of the Treaty of Rome and therefore that it required only a
qualified majority in order to be agreed. The reluctance of the UK
government to sanction this measure was evidenced in its abstention
from voting. Nevertheless, once adopted by the European Union, the
UK was under an obligation to incorporate the directive into domestic
law.

It should be borne in mind, therefore, that, unlike the Warnock
Report and the White Paper *Children Come First*, the European
directive did not receive the government's support. Indeed, it was
accused by Angela Eagle MP of being 'dragged kicking and screaming
by the European Commission into making at least some concession to
the needs of women in the work force' (Commons Debate, 16.2.93)
with the result according to Frank Dobson MP that 'the welcome
improvements in maternity rights are largely to the credit of Brussels
and Strasbourg; the weaknesses are due to the prejudices of the Tory
government' (Commons Debate, 17.11.92).

The important aspects of the 1993 Act for present purposes are that,
in accordance with the European directive, it creates a new right for

pregnant workers to fourteen weeks' maternity leave and the right to return to the same job after that period. During the period of leave, all contractual rights such as holiday and pension entitlements continue to accrue. In addition, the Act improves the protection afforded to women against dismissal for any reason connected with their pregnancy. It introduces the right to be suspended from work on full pay on grounds of maternity, where to continue in employment would be unlawful or contrary to a Code of Practice.[7]

The Act does not, however, provide for payment during the period of maternity leave, nor does it cover discriminatory treatment on grounds of pregnancy in areas other than dismissal (such as recruitment and promotion). The Act also does not make provision for paternity, as opposed to maternity, leave. An amendment to the bill was proposed by the Opposition to grant 'paternity rights' with the effect that an employee whose wife or partner had given birth would be entitled to take ten working days leave on full pay at any time from the birth until the end of three months following it. An alternative amendment was also introduced on 'parental leave' to entitle each parent to a period of leave of three months full-time or six months part-time. These clauses, which were introduced primarily for discussion purposes, were subsequently withdrawn without being voted upon.

But the new maternity rights created by the legislation and their formulation in terms of health and safety have marked a shift in the legal perception of pregnant workers.[8] Whereas under the previous employment legislation qualifying thresholds required a certain time in service and a certain number of hours worked per week before a woman could take advantage of the rights provided for, under the new Act there is no such qualifying period. Rights are therefore accorded on the basis of being a pregnant worker rather than on the basis of being a loyal employee.

Nevertheless, the new legislation is not beyond criticism. Anne Morris and Susan Nott point out that the amount of benefit to which pregnant workers are entitled is still low in comparison with their European counterparts. In addition pregnant employees receive equivalent rates of benefits to their non-pregnant colleagues who are absent through illness. The coupling of pregnancy and illness maintains the perception that pregnant women are in some way sick, a perception which is strongly resisted by many women, yet which has also been much emphasised in case law. This is despite the fact that the European directive in its opening statement expressly seeks to disconnect pregnancy and illness.

The 1993 Act is therefore to be welcomed as a preliminary step for its introduction of new rights for pregnant workers. But it needs also to be viewed cautiously for its failure to incorporate fully the needs of pregnant women into the workplace.

In the light of the outline of these three pieces of legislation affecting the status of women as mothers, it is possible to draw together some of the more prevalent themes in the legal discourse on motherhood. These themes have been grouped around two issues: first, the legislative enactment of the principle of responsible parenting and, second, the legal definition of the relationships of those covered by the legislation. These themes tend to show the manipulation of the legal formulation of motherhood and parenting where necessary to achieve certain social and economic ends. In so doing, it is equally apparent that the orientation of the legislation does not always match the everyday reality of family life.

Enacting a moral principle

THE RESPONSIBILISATION OF PARENTS.   The statutes in question can be seen to impose a certain moral perception of parenthood in general and of motherhood in particular. This perception hinges upon the theme of responsible parenting, within which a rather traditionalist idea of what parenthood means has been adopted, with all its consequent implications for the role of women as mothers. It should also be borne in mind that, from the point of view of the government, the insistence on parental responsibility for children rather than state responsibility has the added (perhaps primary) benefit of reducing the financial burdens of the state for the care of children. The coincidence of moral principle and state irresponsibility has therefore been usefully exploited in the legislation.

To begin with, the Child Support Act 1991 is expressly premised on the moral principle of responsibility. In its first section it is stated that 'each parent of a qualifying child is responsible for maintaining him' (s.1(1)) and that 'an absent parent shall be taken to have met his responsibility ... by making periodical payments of maintenance' (s.1(2)). The reinforcement of the moral and financial responsibility of parents was, however, couched by the Secretary of State for Social Security in the language of 'benefiting children' and 'protecting the interests of children' (Commons Debate, 14.6.91). Although this did not prevent accusations by Joan Lestor MP that the Act was rather more concerned with 'putting the Treasury first and children second', the broad principle of parental responsibility underlying it was not challenged by the parliamentary opposition. Rosie Barnes MP, for example, in the debate on the bill's second reading, stated that 'all reasonable people agree that absent parents should make a reasonable contribution to the upbringing of their children and should not be allowed to turn their backs on their financial responsibilities'.

Instead, the bill received its most severe criticism within parliament from the House of Lords, leaving one commentator to remark that 'the consequence of the Opposition's substantial failure to oppose the bill was to relinquish to the House of Lords the task of acting as the effective opposition to the elected government. Such a position is not one which inspires confidence in the parliamentary process'.[9] It might be added that this is particularly the case given that the Act received such vehement criticism from interest groups such as those concerned with child welfare and the rights of women whose voices were largely unrepresented in Parliament.

Under the Child Support Act, the insistence on parental responsibility might additionally be seen as an attempt to reinforce the crumbling model of the two-parent family. This attempt at maintaining an ideal of family life is increasingly unrealistic where family breakdown is more prevalent than ever before. Nevertheless, the media debate about single-parenting, fuelled by the advent of the Child Support Act, created a backlash against single mothers particularly, many of whom were portrayed as benefit-scroungers socially unfit to bring up their children.

The reinforcement of the traditional two-parent family has had unfortunate implications for second families or step-families whose financial position can be severely affected where one parent is obliged to maintain children from his or her first family. The effect may be therefore to discourage parents from leaving their first family and therefore again to help reinforce the traditional family model of a partnership for life.

Equally, the Human Fertilisation and Embryology Act can be said to demand responsible parenting in its adoption of criteria governing the selection of those deemed suitable for access to fertility treatments. Section 13(5), in requiring that account be taken of the welfare of the child to be born as a result of the use of fertility treatments (including the child's need for a father), has the effect that the ideal candidate to fulfil the responsibility of motherhood is viewed as a woman in a stable relationship with a man.

As a result, 'atypical' women who do not fulfil this requirement are less likely to find themselves selected to receive fertility treatment services. Obvious examples here are those of lesbians and single women who probably fall outside the requirements of the legislation and therefore, in the eyes of the legislators, presumably make less than adequate mothers because of their inability to provide a father-figure for their child.

It should be added, however, that the Warnock Report acknowledged that even heterosexual relationships may prove to be unstable: 'it is impossible to predict with any certainty how lasting such a relationship will be.' Nevertheless the instability of a heterosexual relationship is preferred to the absence of any relationship at all or to the presence of a same-sex relationship.

Other 'atypical' women are marginalised by section 13(5). The case of older women is particularly noticeable. It would appear that section 13(5) permits the refusal to allow older women access to the new reproductive technologies on the grounds of their age. This view has been affirmed by the failure to allow a 37 year-old woman leave to seek judicial review of a decision by Sheffield Health Authority which denied her fertility treatments. It was decided that the application of an age criterion by the Health Authority was lawful because a lack of resources meant treatments ought to be limited to those women who would most benefit from them.[10]

As far as the abortion provisions in the 1990 Act are concerned, it is possible to make a similar observation concerning responsible parenting. Here, however, the position is inverted in that the woman seeking an abortion is required to show that she would be an irresponsible mother in order to obtain the termination of her pregnancy. The closer a woman comes to proving her unsuitability for motherhood, a factor in which may be her lack of relationship with a man to support her for example, the more likely she will be to secure the assent of two registered medical practitioners to terminate her pregnancy.

In the field of employment, on the other hand, the issue of responsibility for children is regarded somewhat differently. Here the concentration upon maternity leave and the lack of provision for paternity leave in the Trade Union Reform and Employment Rights Act 1993 is striking in acknowledging the absence of the role of fathers at this level of child care. It is paradoxical that the idea of responsible parenting dictates that the need of a child for a father is crucial when fertility treatments are sought, is equally crucial when child maintenance is sought, but is unimportant when time off work is requested to fulfil the practical responsibility of child care. It appears that the day-to-day responsibility of caring for children is still perceived as a woman's responsibility.

The overall result of these pieces of legislation, when taken together, is that the child's father is still conceptualised in terms of his role as father-figure and as financial provider rather than as carer. Conversely the role of mother is dependent upon that of a father-figure except where child care, perceived as a traditionally female activity, is at issue.

ENFORCING RESPONSIBILITY. While on the one hand these three pieces of legislation seek to enforce parental responsibility (in its various guises as a moral, economic or caring responsibility), on the other hand there is present within the legislation a distinct reluctance to accord autonomy in decision-making as far as the fulfilment of that responsibility is concerned. It appears that the execution of the task of responsible parenting is not wholly to be trusted to women themselves who, it might be concluded, are viewed as insufficiently competent or trustworthy to act responsibly on their own.

For example, in the area of reproduction it is the consultant who will ultimately take the decision to place a woman on a programme of fertility treatments in the light of his or her assessment of her suitability to receive treatments. In the area of abortion a woman needs the consent of two registered medical practitioners to her termination, again showing the importance of the clinical overseer in validating her admission of unsuitability for motherhood.

In the area of child maintenance the Child Support Act sets about imposing responsible parenting upon those who are viewed as reluctant to undertake this responsibility. For single women with care of their children, this means acting responsibly in accepting the perceived wisdom of a father-figure in the lives of their children. For men who are the absent parents, it means undertaking financial responsibility. Furthermore, the obligation to face up to parenthood can be strictly enforced through the intervention of the Child Support Agency, which has the power to act regardless of previous agreements between the parties involved. Indeed, the responsibilisation of some parents may even be achieved through coercion where the parent with care of the child fears that she may lose welfare benefits because of her failure to cooperate with the Agency.

In the sphere of employment there is again a certain curtailment of female autonomy. Here, the legislation sets about ensuring responsible mothering at the stage of pregnancy by outlining the restrictions which may be imposed by an employer on the activities of the mother-to-be in the workplace. These restrictions are legitimised on the basis that pregnant women are a special risk group in need of extra protection.

The pregnant woman and her employer are therefore required to work together to protect the woman and, importantly, to protect her foetus from the hazards of the work environment (such as exposure to harmful substances like lead or radiation), or from adverse physical agents (such as extremes of temperature), or from activities involving unsuitable movement or posture. In the context of the 1993 Act this requirement may mean the suspension of pregnant women from their jobs where this is necessary to comply with laws about health and safety. Before suspending the woman, however, the employer is under an obligation to offer her any suitable alternative work. If refused, the woman will be liable to forfeit her right to pay. Nevertheless, the alternative work should not be on terms or conditions which are 'substantially less favourable' than those applying to her regular employment.

In one respect the provisions of the 1993 Act are laudable in that they make it unlawful to simply dismiss a pregnant employee on the basis that to continue her employment would be a breach of health and safety rules. On the other hand, however, the Act imposes what has been described as 'a more benevolent paternalism' towards pregnant women.[11] This paternalism is reminiscent of the protective legislation of the nineteenth century which prevented women from working in industries such as mining, and may prove dangerous if its effect is to reduce women to the sum of their biological functions.

It is interesting to note also that this marked display of concern for women's reproductive health in the workplace is not matched by similar concern for that of men, who may nevertheless also be at risk from hazards at work. The enforced responsibilisation of the mother-to-be in the employment context needs therefore to be viewed with caution where it means that women may be excluded from the workplace in order to protect the interests of their foetus, regardless of their own volition.

Defining parental relationships

The second major theme which runs through these statutes is the need to define the nature of the relationship between the various parties implicated. This is a necessary and common feature of legislation, which is often charged with the task of marking the limits of competing rights or with spelling out the status of the parties involved.

THE LEGAL STATUS OF PARENTS. The first step in making parents responsible for their children demands that mothers and fathers can actually be identified. This may sound like an obvious point. However, with the advent of new structures of family life and new ways of starting a family, the question of who is deemed the mother and father of a child is no longer as straightforward as it once was. In particular, the increase in the scope of reproductive technologies and the potential for several women and men to play a role in the creation of a child (for example through the donation of sperm and eggs or the use of another woman's uterus for gestation) has led to the need to clarify exactly who are the legal parents of a child born in this way. Once this legal definition of parents has been established, it can be used to define to whom other legislation applies which sets out the rights and obligations of 'parents'.

The Human Fertilisation and Embryology Act, therefore, defines explicitly who is to be considered the legal mother and father of the child born as a result of the use of fertility treatments. Section 27(1) states that 'the woman who is carrying or has carried a child as a result of the placing in her of an embryo or of sperm and eggs, and no other woman, is to be treated as the mother of the child'. In support of this definition of the mother, Lord Mackay, the Lord Chancellor at the time of debate on the 1990 Act, argued that any other definition would ignore 'the practical, physical and emotional realities of the post-natal situation and the fact that the only person who can be guaranteed to be present to care for the child at its birth is the carrying mother. It would take no account of the emotional attachment which arises as a result of carrying a child through to term, sometimes at significant physical cost and the bonding that occurs between the carrying mother and the child during pregnancy and at birth'(Lords Debate, 20.3.90).

Despite the insistence on biological gestation as the rationale for defining the legal mother as the carrying mother, the legal father is nevertheless defined in section 28 of the Act as the husband or partner of this woman. This is despite his obvious lack of physical connection with the child. The rationale for this definition is financial and was spelt out by Lord Mackay. First, it means that the child will benefit from the man's estate on his death. Secondly, it prevents children born to unmarried couples from being legally fatherless (and therefore potentially being a greater liability for the state). Thirdly, 'the formal recognition of the man's fatherhood may help to cement and strengthen the relationship with the informal family and reduce the risks of breakdown with its consequences for the child and, indeed, too often the taxpayer. That may well lead to a more formal enduring relationship instead of the informal one from which it started'.

For financial considerations, therefore, the Act adopts a definition of father and mother which might be described as less traditionalist in that it enforces a model of the social family (as opposed to the strictly genetic family). On a more pragmatic level, however, it prevents the sperm or egg donor from being considered a 'parent' of the child born through the use of fertility treatments. This, therefore, ensures that third parties continue to be willing to donate their gametes without fear of the imposition of responsibility for any resulting child.

The Child Support Act logically adopts this perspective of the legal parent for the purpose of pursuing maintenance claims from absent parents where a child has been conceived through use of the new reproductive technologies. Conversely, where artificial insemination has taken place outside the confines of the 1990 Act, for example where a woman has artificially inseminated herself, it is now the case that the male sperm donor may be pursued by the Child Support Agency for maintenance for the child. This may be explicitly contrary to the wishes of the woman who has deliberately chosen to have a child outside of a heterosexual partnership. The same is true for women who may have engaged in sexual intercourse simply for the purpose of achieving a conception, where their intention is to raise the child alone or with a female partner. For example, it was reported in June 1994 that a lesbian who achieved a conception after having intercourse with a male friend and subsequently became with her partner the first lesbian couple to be granted joint parental rights over the child, found that the child's biological father was being pursued by the Child Support Agency for maintenance payments. This was despite the fact that an agreement had been drawn up between the parties stating that this man was not to play a role in bringing up the child.[12]

BALANCING INTERESTS. Having defined who is legally considered to be the parent of a child, it is then necessary to identify to whom rights and obligations are accorded in decisions affecting that child. Where conflicts over decision-making are likely to occur it is important that legislation achieves an appropriate balance when setting out the limitations on the rights of the parties involved. One must consider, therefore, the way in which the interests of mothers are balanced against those of the other protagonists affected by the legislation.

First, under the Human Fertilisation and Embryology Act it has been shown that there is an implicit preference in the allocation of fertility treatments for women who are involved in a relationship with a man. The interests of the woman seeking treatment are therefore implicitly viewed alongside those of her male partner. There is, nevertheless, a presumption of consent on the part of the male partner to the treatment, and on the basis of this presumption the legal status of father is defined. Only if the presumption is rebutted can a woman's partner disclaim the role of father.

On the other hand, as far as abortion is concerned, there is no requirement made for the consent, or indeed consultation, of a male partner where a termination is sought. Not only is this not required by the 1990 Act, there is equally case law of the British courts and of the European Court of Human Rights to confirm this position.[13] Equally, at this level the fact that the parties may or may not be married makes no difference to the inability of a potential father to interfere in the decision of his partner to undergo an abortion. Therefore, although the presence of a father-figure is seen as desirable in the creation of a family using new reproductive technologies, his presence is minimised as regards the granting or denial of the request of a woman to have an abortion.

Under the Child Support Act one aim of the legislation is to maintain the tie between ex-partners through the provision of maintenance for the child by the absent parent. The effect here is to minimise the relationship between the carer and the state and to maximise that between the carer and the absent parent. While at one level it might be argued this ensures a redistribution of income from absent parents (predominantly men) to carers (predominantly women), the adverse effect of this arrangement is increased economic dependency by women upon men. Emma Knights of the Child Poverty Action Group has argued that 'it can mean that although the parent with care is carrying almost all the day-to-day responsibility for the child, she feels she no longer has full control and is now answerable to the absent parent as paymaster'.[14] Mothers may feel less threatened by a closer relationship with the state than by an enforced relationship with an absent father who may, for example, view closer contact with the child and supervision in decision-making as the counterpart of his obligation to pay maintenance.

A further development in relation to the campaign against the Child Support Act has been the solidarity of fathers in their opposition to the Act and their consequent hostility towards the mothers of their children. Notably, the incorporation of an allowance for the parent with care into the formula used to calculate the maintenance payment has caused resentment. This is particularly so where the parent with care may have formed another relationship. Thus it is not just women who feel threatened by the provisions but also their absent partners, some of whom face large increases in the level of their maintenance payments.

This challenge to the Act by large numbers of 'respectable' middle-class men, and focused around vocal groups such as Families Need Fathers, has often been perceived as more legitimate than the opposition of single mothers and feminists, whose claims have been treated with less credibility. Nevertheless, it is the case that both women and men have seen themselves as losers by the state's imposition of closer ties between them.

In the sphere of employment the balancing of rights is less concerned with the competing rights of parents (the role of the father being largely eclipsed), but rather with those of employer and employee. The concern of the government has consistently been to ensure that neither the employer nor the state suffers too great a loss from the employment of a worker who is pregnant or who may become so. Hence, in presenting the Trade Union Reform and Employment Rights Bill before the House of Commons for its second reading, the Secretary of State for Employment, Gillian Shephard, explicitly stated that the bill had 'two main objectives: first to strengthen and extend the rights of the individual . . .; secondly, to increase the competitiveness of the economy and remove obstacles to the creation of new jobs' (Commons Debate, 17.11.92).

Being based upon the European directive, the 1993 Act has to a certain extent reformulated the balance between a pregnant woman and her employer more favourably towards the pregnant woman, for example by granting an obligatory period of maternity leave. However, this new formulation is not sustained and in certain respects the primacy of the interests of the employer is still maintained. For example, although the woman worker now enjoys greater rights when actually pregnant, once she has given birth she is not protected against dismissal if she has to take time off work due to the long-term effects of her pregnancy.[15] Anne Morris and Susan Nott conclude that there is 'no guarantee that a woman's ability to combine motherhood and paid employment will be substantially improved as a consequence of the 1993 Act'.[16] In this way it can be said that the employer retains a privileged position in relation to pregnant employees, and that the cost of child-bearing and child-rearing in the employment context is still borne predominantly by women.

Conclusion

In conclusion, it is apparent that the thrust of these three pieces of legislation of the 1990s is still a marked reluctance to break away from a rather traditionalist view of family life, despite the increasing lack of realism of this view. Thus the traditional heterosexual family unit is fairly consistently privileged over any other family structures. This is manifestly evident in the areas of reproduction and child support, where the role of woman as mother is implicitly conditioned upon the presence of a father-figure who is able to support her and her children economically.

The traditionalist perspective is taken to its extreme in the sphere of employment, where the failure to legislate upon paternity leave has the effect that it is still women who are perceived as bearing the brunt of child-rearing. Would it not, however, be more logical to expect that responsible parenting, which is made to figure so heavily in relation to the creation and financial maintenance of a family, might extend also to the provision of child care by both parents, and therefore that paternity leave should be routinely granted to fathers? This may be logical, but of course it is not necessarily desirable from the perspective of the state and employers because it imposes extra financial burdens. Equally, such a solution may not be any more satisfactory from the perspective of those women who seek to control their own destiny as mothers and who, therefore, may not welcome the spectre of a father-figure haunting their reproductive choices.

It is evident in each of the areas under consideration here, reproduction, welfare and employment, that a politically expedient solution has been sought whose effect is to reduce the financial responsibilities of the state, even though this may be couched in terms of helping the taxpayer or employer. The adverse effect of this has been to construct the role of women as mothers as contingent upon the role and interests of others and has thereby reduced the scope for autonomous motherhood.

1   See C. Smart, *Feminism and the Power of Law* (Routledge, 1989); A. Bottomley and J. Conaghan (eds), *Feminist Theory and Legal Strategy* (Blackwell, 1993); J. Bridgeman and S. Millns (eds), *Law and Body Politics: Regulating the Female Body* (Dartmouth, 1995).
2   See C. Smart, 'The Woman of Legal Discourse', *Social and Legal Studies*, 1992/1.
3   M. Warnock, *A Question of Life: The Warnock Report on Human Fertilisation and Embryology* (Basil Blackwell, 1984).
4   For the background of D. Morgan and R. G. Lee, *Blackstone's Guide to the Human Fertilisation and Embryology Act 1990* (Blackstone Press, 1991).
5   See C. M. Lyon, *The Law Relating to Children* (Butterworths, 1993) pp. 111–19.
6   E. Knights, 'The Women's Point of View' in Feminist Legal Research Unit (University of Liverpool), *"For Richer or Poorer?" Feminist Perspectives on Women and the Distribution of Wealth*, Working Paper No.2, University of Liverpool, 1995.
7   See I. T. Smith and J. C. Wood, *Industrial Law* 5th ed., Butterworths, 1993, chapter 6.
8   A. Morris and S. Nott, 'The Law's Engagement With Pregnancy' in J. Bridgeman and S. Millns (eds), op.cit.
9   H. Barnett, 'Reflections on the Child Support Act 1991' (1993), *Journal of Child Law*, Vol.5, No.2.
10 *The Times* and *The Independent*, 18.10.94.
11 A. Morris and S. Nott, loc.cit.
12 *The Independent*, 30.6.94.
13 *Paton v. Pregnancy Advisory Service Trustees* [1979] Q.B. 276; *C v. S* [1987] 1 All E.R. 1230; *Paton v. United Kingdom* (1981) 3 E.H.R.R. 408.
14 E. Knights, loc.cit.
15 *Herz v. Aldi Marked K/S* [1991] I.R.L.R. 31.
16 A. Morris and S. Nott, loc.cit.

The Politics of Childcare Policy

BY VICKY RANDALL

DESPITE constantly renewed expectations that something was at last about to happen, childcare policy during John Major's premiership has continued on much the same minimalist lines as under Mrs Thatcher, and indeed as under earlier Labour governments. Although the issue has received much greater public attention since the late 1980s, with new actors and concerns coming into the frame, the basic constraints and determinants of policy appear to have altered remarkably little. The making and implementation of policy remain severely fragmented and underresourced, with little evidence of the political will to surmount such obstacles.

Here we will outline the development of childcare policy from the end of the last war up to the first Thatcher government, identifying the key constraints and influences. We then consider policy during the Thatcher years, when new government priorities coincided with new sources and forms of demand, including those from feminist-inspired organisations. Finally, we focus on the making of policy and the parameters of public debate in the 1990s and assess the extent of continuity or change. But first childcare policy must be defined. For present purposes childcare is taken to refer to all forms of provision, whether in the public, private or voluntary sector, that entail looking after children under school age during the day or some part of it. As such, it covers not only child daycare but nursery education. In practice, concern with childcare as a policy issue has mainly centred round two questions: how much there should be and how responsibility for provision should be divided between the different sectors. Arguably, and given the present domestic division of labour between women and men, childcare is also, or should be, very much a feminist issue, though in practice feminist campaigning in this area has been limited. It must further be noted that although one can infer a childcare policy from what has actually been done, or not done, it is questionable whether there has been an explicit national policy. In a sense, therefore, Britain does not have a childcare policy. A growing number of groups have been pressing for government to take the lead in formulating one but this has yet to emerge.

Childcare policy after the war

After the second world war, national government responsibility for childcare, in the broad sense defined above, was divided between the

Ministries of Education and Health. The Ministry of Education was concerned to the extent that the 1944 Education Act required local education authorities to 'have regard to the need for' nursery education. Provision of nursery education in fact remained very limited given other calls on local education budgets, and there was moreover a cumulative shift from the mid-1950s from full-time to part-time modes of attendance. The Ministry of Health, under legislation going back to 1918, was responsible, again through local authorities, for state-provided child daycare. Despite dramatic expansion of provision during the war, the Ministry made clear in 1948 that day nursery places were intended only for children in 'special need'. By 1963, 13 (out of 48) County Councils and 13 (out of 79) County Boroughs had ceased to offer any places at all.[1]

However, the number of women in paid employment was growing steadily, including increasingly mothers of young children. This was associated with a startling rise in the numbers of private nurseries and of childminders. Another relevant development was the expansion of 'child-centred' professions such as child psychologists and educationalists. A final catalyst for change was the so-called 'rediscovery of poverty' led by social scientists like Richard Titmus, combined with a renewed faith in the power of environment, and specifically of education, to shape human development, which kindled a new interest in nursery education.[2]

Against this background, three successive government reports discussed aspects of under–5s provision. Plowden (1967) advocated nursery education on demand, though on a part-time basis; Seebohm (1968) argued for some expansion of local authority day nursery places and better coordination of under–5s services; and Finer (1974) stressed the daycare needs of the growing contingent of one-parent families.[3] Partly in response to these recommendations, government embarked on a limited expansion. Most famously, a 1972 Department of Education White Paper, under the auspices of the then Minister, Mrs Thatcher, announced that nursery education would be expanded to cater for all 3–4 year olds by 1982; local authorities were also set targets for increased day nursery provision by the Department of Health and Social Security. Before these programmes could get under way, however, they were severely cut back, among the first casualties of public expenditure restraints from 1974 onwards.

How do we explain this pattern of postwar provision? On the demand side, the answer may appear fairly simple. There was no effective childcare lobby, although by the late 1970s a network of groups with some interest in the issue was beginning to emerge. The two main professional groups most directly concerned, nursery teachers and nursery nurses, both suffered from low status (not coincidentally they were overwhelmingly female). In addition, nursery teachers looked down on nursery nurses, who received less training, and between them was mutual mistrust. 'Experts' put arguments about children's educational needs but children could not be mobilised on their own behalf. Similarly, experts urged the daycare needs of children 'at risk' or from one-parent families but tended to believe that pre-school children should be at home with their mothers. This belief, whose origins went back at least to Victorian times, had received a new boost and scientific legitimation, in the 1950s from the arguments of John Bowlby and others about the dangers of 'maternal deprivation'. Indeed, all three reports cited above expressed concern about the effects on young children of separation from their mothers for more than a few hours.

Despite the growing numbers of working mothers, their demand was implicit only, lacking either the political organisation or the ideologically acceptable framework of ideas through which it could be expressed. Although second-wave feminism was emerging by the late 1960s and one of the four demands of the 'founding' Women's Liberation Conference in 1970 was for 'twenty-four hour nurseries', the issue was a divisive one, raising many ideological and practical problems. Women's groups undertook numerous local nursery campaigns but no national campaign came together until the 1980s.[4]

On the supply side, the immediate obstacle was the fragmentation of responsibility between central departments and between central and local governments. Again, one theme apparent in all three reports was the need for closer integration. This was expressed with particular force by a group of academics and researchers, emerging in the early 1970s, committed to a 'holistic' approach to childcare. The theme was taken up by the two main local authority associations, the Association of Metropolitan Authorities and the Association of County Councils. Partly in response to these concerns, beginning informally in the early 1970s, a forum for interministerial consultation was instituted and the first joint DHSS/DES circular was issued in 1976. But these developments did little in practice to reduce the fragmentation. It has been suggested that advocates of greater 'coordination' did not even agree amongst themselves what they meant by this, itself a further symptom of the problem.[5]

Underlying this fragmentation were more fundamental constraints. These concerned the kind of issue childcare is and the institutionalisation and ideological assumptions of policy-making. As a redistributive issue, childcare implied the transfer of resources broadly from 'haves' to 'have-nots' — not only in class terms but from men to women, or mothers. This meant that to have much chance, it needed to be taken up by the Labour Party and trade unions. As an issue, secondly, closely associated with the family, it touched on beliefs about the respective roles of parents as private actors and of the state. However the state was heavily 'gendered': policy-makers, both elected politicians and senior department officials, were mostly men and often patriarchal in their assumptions. This was of course true of policy-makers in a number of other countries, where public childcare provision was much more generous.[6] An important difference was that in Britain these assumptions were compounded by a 'liberal' tradition which regarded state intervention in the 'private' spheres of the family or the market as intrinsically suspect and in need of careful justification.[7]

The Thatcher years

It was a Conservative government which first undertook, in the early 1970s, the expansion, however limited, of publicly funded under–5s provision; and it was a Labour government which, from 1974, reined in that expansion. The point is not so much that a Conservative leadership championed the cause of childcare, as that Labour happily subscribed to a consensus which accorded it very low priority. As Labour politicians have more recently reproached the government for its uncaring attitude, their Conservative colleagues have not been slow to point this out.

That said, the years when Mrs Thatcher was Prime Minister were particularly unhelpful to the childcare cause. While Labour had at least presented cutbacks as temporary and regrettable, under successive Conservative governments targets for expansion in public under–5s provision were abandoned. At the same time, in the case of daycare, there was a pronounced shift in official emphasis from public to private and voluntary provision. The view was that it should be 'primarily a matter of private arrangement between parents and private and voluntary resources except where there are special needs'(John Patten, Commons Debate, 18.3.95). Though, especially in the early 1980s, there were Conservative voices questioning whether mothers should be working outside the home at all, these were generally back-benchers, and by and large Cabinet ministers refrained from such overt moralising.

It is sometimes suggested that Mrs Thatcher was herself opposed in principle to the expansion of child daycare. In this context, her warning in a radio interview in 1990, against the prospect of a 'generation of crèche children' is frequently quoted. She was not entirely consistent, and in her earlier career had expressed much greater sympathy with the plight of the home-bound mother. However it is certainly clear that there was no positive pressure for a more effective national childcare policy from the first mother to be a British Prime Minister.

During the 1980s, despite rising unemployment in the early years, participation in the labour force by mothers of young children continued to grow. From 24% in 1983, the participation rate grew to 41% by 1989, although around 70% of these were working part-time. At the same time, the number of lone mothers continued to rise. By 1989, 17% of all families with dependent children were headed by a single parent, nine-tenths of whom were women. By 1991 an estimated 2.2 million, or almost one in five children, were being brought up by lone parents. Against this background, a very diverse and loosely coordinated national childcare lobby was taking form. It included not only academics, child-centred professionals and local authority associations but feminist groups such as the National Child Care Campaign and the trade unions. Significantly, the arguments advanced no longer focused simply on the daycare needs of the socially disadvantaged or nursery education as a means of counteracting poverty but increasingly cited the needs of working mothers.

Both the Liberal Democrats and the Labour Party paid more attention to the issue of childcare. Feminists were becoming increasingly influential within the Labour Party. Locally this was evident in the blossoming of 'municipal feminism', which in many cases, most outstandingly that of the Greater London Council from 1982, resulted in a dramatic expansion of local authority childcare provision. Many such authorities became important laboratories of good practice, combining educational and care functions in innovative ways. Though not directly contributing to national policy, this helped to generate new sets of vested interests and pools of expertise that fed into national policy debate. In 1985, the Labour Party's national leadership produced its own Charter for the Under–5s.

Government was not entirely unresponsive to these developments. Not only did it generally avoid condemnation of working mothers, it continued to recognise, in theory at least, the need for an integrated approach to under–5s provision. Official statements also stressed the need to extend and share knowledge about childcare. In deference to expert opinion, the importance of the quality of provision was increasingly acknowledged. Nonetheless, national policy-making in the childcare field continued to be an essentially two-track affair. The Table summarises trends in the numbers of places provided over these years.[8] Though Mrs Thatcher had been the Minister responsible for the 1972 Education White Paper, pledging expansion of nursery education, under her government it languished. An early indicator was the provision in the 1980 Education Act making local authority responsibility for nursery education discretionary only. A 1985 White Paper envisaged that 'plans for local authority expenditure should allow provision to continue in broad terms within broadly the same total as today'. In fact, numbers of 3 and 4-year old children receiving some form of pre-school education did grow during this period but most of this was part-time; nursery schools as such became fewer and some of the children were put into 'reception' classes for infant school. School Inspectors (HMIs) in particular were concerned that the education they received in these reception classes was inappropriate to their needs.

In the face of such modest change, advocates of nursery education found new champions in the House of Commons Committee on Education, Science and Arts. While investigating primary education in the early 1980s, its members were persuaded of the importance of the

Child Care Places in England, 1980–1991

	1980	1991	% change
Nursery education	130,997	177,863	36+
Reception class	205,673	272,178	32+
Local authority day nurseries	28,437	27,039	5−
Private nurseries	22,017	79,029	259+
Playgroups	367,868	428,420	16+
Childminders	98,495	233,258	137+

pre-school experience. They were especially impressed by the evidence put forward by the HMIs. As a consequence, in 1988 the Committee undertook its own inquiry into Educational Provision for the Under–5s. Reporting in 1989, it urged resumption of the 1972 target of universal provision and recommended that the Department of Health and Social Security and Department of Education and Science, in conjunction with the Department of Employment undertake a survey of existing demand and provision for the under–5s. The government's response was for the DES to establish a committee of inquiry, under Angela Rumbold, whose focus would be the quality of educational provision for 3 and 4-year olds. Its report, in 1990, made many acute observations and stressed the need for improved coordination but signally failed to address the fundamental issue of resources.

In the meantime, policy within the DHSS reflected the new shift from state provision to reliance on the private and voluntary sectors. As the Table shows, the number of local authority daycare places actually declined between 1980 and 1991. The contribution of the private sector, notably childcare provided by private nurseries and childminders grew by contrast. In practice, the main new government departure was a series of 'Under–5s Initiatives', through which the Department, largely bypassing the local authorities, sought to work directly with a range of voluntary agencies that were one way or another engaged in providing pre-school services. The first and largest programme ran over four years, 1983–87. Fifteen agencies were enlisted, with some care taken to ensure that their projects were fairly distributed in geographic terms. However, only some of these schemes were concerned with daycare as such. Moreover, the emphasis remained on helping disadvantaged families, defined as families with single parents or where both parents had to work, families facing stress and isolation or families belonging to ethnic minorities. The schemes were generally short-term and pump-priming. When originally announced, in 1982, the overall sum mentioned was £20m but actual expenditure was closer to £7m. The first Initiative was followed by a small grants scheme running from 1987 and involving only six agencies. A second Initiative was then launched, to run from 1989 to 1992. It was allocated only £2m and, though concentrating on daycare, was targeted particularly at families living in temporary accommodation.

In addition to these initiatives, beginning with a consultation paper in 1985, the DHSS sought to update the provisions of the 1948 Nurseries and Childminders Regulation Act in order to ensure rather more systematic regulation of the expanding private sector. Under Section 19 of the Children Act, local authorities were obliged, where before it was optional only, to register and inspect childcare services. In addition, a clause included in the bill late in committee stage, with little apparent prior consultation, required local authorities to conduct a three yearly review. This amendment reflected government concern to be seen to be responding to the sense of increased urgency associated with the announcement of the 'demographic time-bomb'.

Defusing the demographic time-bomb

Hogwood and Gunn have argued that an issue is more likely to get on the political agenda if there is a crisis that makes it impossible to ignore.[9] Such a crisis briefly seemed imminent towards the end of the decade. The Department of Employment released figures in May 1988, which the National Economic Development Council (since disbanded) followed up in a report in December. It was anticipated that by 1993 the number of school-leavers would fall by nearly one third. Though numbers were predicted to rise again by the mid-1990s, it would not be to the original level. The inference drawn was that government and employers would need to persuade mothers of young children, especially those with badly needed skills, to return to paid work.

Certainly this announcement appeared to provide the childcare lobby with a tremendous opening. Pressure groups stepped up their campaigning, conferencing, networking, publishing and exploiting of unprecedented media opportunities. The Equal Opportunities Commission brought out its report on the childcare question, *The Key to Real Choice*. The TGWU organised a conference on 'Equal Opportunities and Childcare'. Employers showed new interest. Individual firms approached childcare organisations like Daycare Trust and the Workplace Nurseries Campaign in dramatically increased numbers for advice on setting up nurseries for their employees, while the CBI organised its own conference on this theme and in its report, *Workforce 2000*, urged the government to give the issue of childcare assistance its serious attention.

Interestingly, and it might seem promisingly, the government's response this time did not emanate from either of the two main ministries hitherto identified with childcare but from the interdepartmental Ministerial Group on Women's Issues which had been meeting, since 1986, under the auspices of the Home Office (in 1995 it was lodged in the Department For Education). The Group's chairman, John Patten, announced a five-point programme in March 1989. Yet, while described as 'designed to pave the way for the provision of childcare which meets the needs of the family', the programme was incremental in the extreme. It included amendments to the Children's Bill improving childcare registration and enforcement procedures; encouragement to employers and providers of childcare to adopt an accreditation scheme that would provide information about childcare facilities and guarantee their quality; support for the voluntary sector through pump-priming projects and encouraging collaboration with employers and encouragement to employers to use tax reliefs available for providing childcare. All the measures it envisaged were things either already being done or in the pipeline. One minor government concession attributable to the changed political climate was to waive the tax, imposed since 1984, on workplace nurseries.

It would be wrong, then, to suggest that there were no positive developments in the field of child daycare, during the 1980s. An embryonic childcare lobby was forming and received a special boost from the demographic scare at the end of the decade, which helped to recruit a number of employers' organisations to the cause. Its arguments increasingly included some reference to working mothers, in terms either of their rights or at least of their urgent childcare needs. The Labour Party national leadership, under Kinnock, referred more frequently to childcare in its policy statements, in part a consequence of the enhanced influence of feminists coming from the 'moderate' Left of the party. Following the 1987 general election, Hilary Armstrong was elected frontbench spokeswoman on education, and in that capacity paid particular attention to nursery education and childcare, developing an impressive command of the complex issues involved. For its part, the government was more willing, especially when faced with the prospect of a skilled labour shortage, to acknowledge in principle working mothers' needs.

While, therefore, there was growing recognition (though by no means amounting to consensus) of the need for expanded child daycare provision, this was offset by even greater aversion than under previous governments to state expenditure or intervention in what it was felt should normally be a matter for private arrangements. The government remained reluctant to shoulder responsibility for formulating a national childcare strategy and institutional fragmentation persisted. Moreover, Thatcherism succeeded in steadily altering the terms in which policy change was envisaged. Thus a group like the National Child Care Campaign, committed when it was founded in 1980 to state-funded, free, day nurseries, by 1990 accepted, if reluctantly, the need to charge fees, to use childminders and workplace nurseries. It still harboured misgivings on the question of tax relief for childcare, arguing that it would not benefit those mothers whose childcare needs were greatest. However the Working Mothers' Association, formed in the early 1980s, was happy to take this policy option on board. As these examples illustrate, by shifting the terms of policy debate about how childcare was to be delivered, the Thatcher government also managed to sow further seeds of discord within the childcare lobby already afflicted by the divisions of interest and perspective that mirrored the way in which childcare provision had been institutionalised.

Trends post-Thatcher

We come now to what is in some ways the most difficult part of this analysis, assessing the extent of any policy shift since Mrs Thatcher's fall from power in November 1990. Events are still too close for trends to be confirmed. Still, if we are looking for immediate, tangible policy change, we can report very little on the child daycare front. By the mid-1990s, rather more significant policy changes did appear imminent on the nursery education front, but it was still unclear how they would be implemented and with what consequences. John Major early sought to identify himself with the consumer, which could have included parents as consumers of childcare provision. Sensitive to earlier criticism of his failure to promote women in his party, and in contrast to Mrs Thatcher, he appointed two women to Cabinet posts following the April 1992 general election. He also gave his public support to Opportunity 2000, an employers' initiative to boost women's employment opportunities. But these mildly auspicious signs heralded no big breakthrough for childcare.

However, the issue of childcare did not go away and government had to engage with it. Although recession soon muted the labour shortage argument, the loose coalition of interests it had helped to mobilise survived. At the same time a series of developments in related fields ensured that the issue of childcare, meaning also nursery education, remained on the public agenda. In response, the government seemed if anything even more averse to state intervention in the provision of child daycare but was increasingly prepared to consider ways of subsidising demand. It also began more seriously to consider ways of expanding the provision of nursery education. But there was still government reluctance to take responsibility for a nationally coordinated and integrated childcare strategy.

By 1992 the demographic time-bomb was defused but arguments about the needs of working mothers persisted. A number of employers who had shown interest in setting up workplace nurseries and collaborating in local schemes now withdrew. However, others drew the conclusion from the straitened circumstances of recession that while they could make a contribution, proper childcare provision by its nature required that government take a strong lead. This was the contention of the pressure group, Employers for Childcare, formed in June 1993 with the support of the CBI and including representatives of Midland Bank, Shell, TSB and British Gas. It complained that without such leadership 'isolated examples of good practice in childcare provision are swamped in a patchwork of inconsistent and badly coordinated services'.[10]

The childcare needs of working mothers were also explored in an inquiry by the House of Commons Employment Committee, launched in 1992 and resulting in a report, *Mothers in Employment*, published in February 1995. Though raising, without overtly resolving, the question whether mothers of young children should go out to work, the tone of the report was extremely sympathetic. While not insisting that additional child daycare should be publicly provided or funded, it did emphasise the need for quality and affordability. Finally, it urged 'the formation and implementation of a national strategy for childcare'. Response to this report came from the Department of Employment. Indeed beginning with concerns about the labour market at the end of the 1980s and especially with the appointment of Gillian Shephard as Secretary of State for Employment in 1992, that department had increasingly developed its own agenda in the area of childcare. Most concretely it had introduced a new scheme providing limited funding for after school provision for children aged five and over, to be administered through the Training and Enterprise Councils (TECs). But the recommendations of the Employment Committee received short shrift from the new Secretary of State for Employment, Michael Portillo, in the formal reply published in May 1995.

The issue of childcare also featured, now more now less explicitly, in the mounting government concern about 'lone mothers'. This category was proportionately larger in Britain than in any other EC country. While their numbers were rising, the proportion of lone women with dependent children who were in paid employment actually declined from 45% in 1981 to 39% in 1993–94. Alarm at the growing cost to the Exchequer was already apparent in the later Thatcher years. One government response was to set up the Child Support Agency to try to make absent fathers pay for child maintenance. In 1993 two much publicised 'home alone' cases appeared to highlight the issue of lone mothers: in February we heard about Yasmin Gibson who left her eleven year-old daughter at home while she went on holiday to Spain and in July Heidi Colwell was jailed for leaving her three year old daughter at home while she went to work. Other cases followed. Though these stories, especially Yasmin Gibson's, might be taken as confirmation of the irresponsibility of lone mothers, they inevitably also pointed up the childcare problems such women faced. Cabinet concern became clear when a briefing paper on the question was 'leaked' in the autumn of 1993.

One modest policy development, that can be seen as a response to both kinds of concern, the needs of working mothers and the growing number of single mothers, was the provision in the November 1993 Budget for a childcare tax allowance. This was targeted primarily at those already receiving family credit. The actual suggestion was said to have emanated from the Department of Employment but it was of especial benefit to lone mothers since they were disproportionately represented amongst family credit recipients. The measure was generally welcomed by the childcare lobby, although it was pointed out that it would only help a limited number of families (the actual number was disputed) and that it did not directly deal with the problem of restricted supply.

The question of childcare also persisted, in the form of a revived national debate around issues related to nursery education. As we have seen, the 1990 Rumbold Report steered clear of resource considerations. It was published with little fanfare and in 1991 Kenneth Clarke, as Secretary of State for Education, was reported as describing Mrs Thatcher's 1972 commitment to eventual universal nursery education provision as a 'mistake'. Nonetheless, public interest in this objective could not be ignored for long. During the 1992 general election campaign, both the Labour and the Liberal Democratic Parties committed themselves to universal provision. The Labour Party pledged to achieve this by the year 2000, though the time limit was later removed. The Liberal Democrats made it a central plank of their electoral manifesto, famously promising to fund it if necessary through an extra 1p on income tax. The government had to decide whether it could afford to neglect a policy issue to which rival parties were paying so much attention.

The Home Office began to show new interest in nursery education. Alarmed by an apparent increase in juvenile crime, as dramatised in the 1991 Tyneside riots and most horrifically when James Bolger was murdered by two boys not yet in their teens in February 1993, they were impressed in particular by evidence of the long-term effects of a nursery education project in the United States, commonly referred to as High/Scope. This project monitored the development of over 120 children from 'disadvantaged' black American families, comparing the progress of those who had been through a high quality pre-school programme with that of a control group which had not. Although at age 11 the first group's comparative advantage appeared to diminish, it clearly re-emerged, when the groups were monitored at ages 19 and 27. The project's director was able to make a strong cost-benefit case for the programme, including its effects in reducing crime.

In 1993, also, the National Commission on Education, a prestigious independent advisory body established in 1991, produced its report, *Learning to Succeed*, in which it devoted a chapter to pre-school education. It concluded that 'high-quality publicly-funded education provision should be available for all three and four year-olds'. A similar case was made in a report under the auspices of the Royal Society of Arts, *Start Right*, in March the following year, though this is unlikely to have carried so much weight with government. In sum, the government was faced with the apparent growth of a informed consensus on the need for expanded nursery education provision, increased media concentration on the issue, evidence from a number of surveys that parents wanted more education for the under-fives and the associated possibility, though no certainty, that this could be a significant electoral issue. It appears, finally, that this was an area in which the Prime Minister himself now took a particular interest. At any rate, suddenly on 23 December 1993, he announced that the government did after all intend to move towards the goal of universal nursery education for three and four year-olds. This came only a month after the Secretary of State for Education, John Patten, was quoted as ruling this possibility out because of the prohibitive cost.

Officials in the Department for Education now had to put together a feasible proposal. However, it appeared to meet with considerable resistance, not least from the Treasury but also from Education ministers, notably Lady Blatch. Accordingly objectives were steadily modified. By October 1994, John Major confirmed that the focus was to be on four year-olds and that nursery education was to be provided not only by nursery schools or classes but by reception classes and playgroups. Even this would involve additional government funding, and there were indications of further differences within the government about what form this would take, with increasing interest shown in some kind of voucher system. Finally, in July 1995, the government announced its intention to introduce a voucher scheme, beginning with a pilot run in 1996 and coming fully on stream the following year. Under the scheme, parents of four year-olds would receive a £1,100 voucher which they could spend on local authority provision, private nurseries or playgroups. The announcement met a guarded response, with fears expressed about the adequacy of provision, and especially the likely impact on existing local authority nursery places.

Under John Major, then, the issue of childcare kept coming back, but it did so within at least three different kinds of agenda: the needs of working mothers, which at times extended to questions of equal opportunities; the 'problem' of lone mothers and the burden they placed on the Exchequer; and the need for more nursery education. The government enacted the childcare tax allowance and took steps towards ensuring some form of nursery education for all four year-olds. But these measures were not part of any integrated plan for childcare: government seemed no nearer accepting a responsibility for devising and leading a national strategy.

There were further subtle but noteworthy changes in the politics of childcare over these years. First, it should be stressed that the tendency under Mrs Thatcher for government to avoid moral judgements about 'working mothers' continued and, if anything, became more pronounced. This is so despite the publicity surrounding John Major's 'Back to Basics' initiative in October 1993 and despite the best efforts of the Conservative Family Campaign, founded in 1986, whose manifesto, *Families in Danger*, sought an end to state subsidy of workplace nurseries and wanted measures to encourage mothers to stay at home. Thus when Labour frontbench spokeswoman, Harriet Harman, initiated a debate on childcare (on amendments to the 1994 Finance Bill), nobody suggested that mothers of young children should not go out to work. Indeed, both Stephen Dorrell, the minister concerned, and another young Conservative MP, Matthew Carrington, declared that they had recently become fathers and that their wives intended to continue working. Matthew Carrington stated, 'The importance of childcare is not in dispute in the House. We all accept that we must ensure a diversity of available child care which will become more important as our society develops' (Commons Debate, 19.4.94).

Under Mrs Thatcher, government had shown much interest in ways of transferring responsibility for child daycare provision from the state to private agencies. Under her successor, attention shifted further towards questions less of the supply of childcare than of subsidising demand. One approach considered was through taxation, or the benefits system. A Conservative campaign for Tax Relief on Child Care (TRAC) was set up in June 1990 whose long-term goal was to secure tax relief on all forms of registered childcare. This drew criticism from the Left because it could not help those whose level of income fell below the taxation threshold. Within government, it was criticised by those who argued childcare assistance had to be targeted to the most needy, a similar point though from a very different ideological standpoint. However, primarily with reference to nursery education, interest also grew in the use of vouchers. Emanating from the Adam Smith Institute and the Centre for Policy Studies, this approach was taken increasingly seriously by government, though it seems not all ministers were happy about it. Amongst those accepting the general principle, there were further disagreements about how vouchers were to be funded and how generous they were to be.

Government policies, too, including those begun under Mrs Thatcher, had an impact on the pattern and interaction of childcare lobbying groups. Two particular instances can be given. The number of private nurseries had been steadily growing and they were represented by two bodies, the Childcare Association and the National Private Day Nurseries Association. Between the passing of the Children's Act and the drawing up of Guidelines in 1991, and again between the appearance of the guidelines and a government memorandum on their implementation in January 1993, requirements for registration of day nurseries were weakened and the necessary staff-child ratio was reduced. The private nursery associations were prominent amongst the groups pressing for these changes. As a second example, the Pre-School Playgroups Association had been founded in the early 1960s but now in the 1990s it found itself regarded with especial favour by government and its subsidy increased. Emboldened by its good fortune, the Association began to argue that playgroups could provide the answer to the shortage of child daycare. In 1994 it produced a booklet, *The Way Forward*, which claimed that playgroups could offer the means of fulfilling the government's new nursery education target. This enraged some of the other lobbying groups. Thus government policies continued to generate new divisions within the childcare lobby. The lobby did not, however, just sit back and let this happen. Observing the way that government was able to exploit its divisions during consideration of the 1992 Education Bill, which failed to make any mention of nursery education, childcare protagonists agreed to set up an Early Children Education Forum to bring these groups together, so that they could speak with a more united voice.

Conclusion

The EC Council Recommendation on Child Care, which the British government rather grudgingly ratified in 1992, amongst its other prescriptions, urges member states to 'promote and encourage increased participation by men, in order to achieve a more equal sharing of parental responsibilities between men and women'. That proposal, however, seems light years away from what is currently on the agenda of any of the main political parties in Britain, apart, of course, from having little relevance for single mothers. In the meantime, it would seem that an effective childcare policy must involve substantial redistribution of public resources, to improve supply or even to subsidise demand. Such a policy was not in prospect in 1979, and is no nearer today; if anything, it is further away, although it is likely that a Labour victory at the next general election would produce some modest improvement. Nor has there been significant progress towards the development of a national childcare strategy.

The underlying picture, though, has by no means been static. The range of interests and arguments supporting childcare has widened considerably. The link between childcare and women's equal opportunities is now more firmly grasped not only by feminists but by trade unions and many employers. There has been a growth, too, in expertise amongst childcare specialists. Good British child daycare provision, where caring and educational elements are properly integrated and related as closely as possible to the needs of both children and working parents, is amongst the best in the world.

Still, the lack of progress is in some ways baffling. One factor has been fragmentation of the policy process. It is unlikely that this will be significantly remedied by the merger, announced in July 1995, of the Department for Education and the Department of Employment. Presently it seems that momentum for change is concentrated on the nursery education front, but where will this leave child daycare? When the momentum was building, during the demographic scare, for a more effective childcare policy, nursery education, which unquestionably needs to be integrated with childcare, was largely out of the picture. As far as child daycare is concerned, one main catalyst for change has been the simple fact of increasing numbers of working mothers. But they, and the feminists who might represent them, have not exerted strong, direct political pressure. The pressures have come more indirectly, through social workers, child experts or trade unions encountering the negative consequences of the present lack of provision. An underlying constraint has been the combination of patriarchal and liberal (anti-state) traditions in Britain's political institutions and culture. Liberal assumptions have been reinforced with a vengeance since 1979. Patriarchal values are more muted in public life but by no means routed. Even today, when most politicians are careful not overtly to question mothers' right to work outside the home, is there not still some lingering disapproval and resentment, a feeling that they have brought these childcare problems on themselves?

1 For the postwar period, up to the early 1980s, see D. Riley, *War in the Nursery* (Virago, 1983); J. Tizard et al, *All Our Children* (Temple Smith, 1976); M. Ruggie, *The State and Working Women* (Princeton University Press, 1984).
2 K. Banting, *Poverty, Politics and Policy* (Macmillan, 1979).
3 Central Advisory Council for Education (England). *Children and Their Primary Schools* (HMSO, 1967); Committee on Local Authority and Allied Social Services, *Report of the Committee* (HMSO, 1968); Committee on One-Parent Families *Report of the Committee* (HMSO, 1974).
4 See J. Lovenduski and V. Randall, *Contemporary Feminist Politics* (Oxford University Press, 1993), ch. 8; V. Randall, 'Feminism and Child Day Care', *Journal of Social Policy* July 1996.
5 G. Pugh, *Services for Under Fives* (National Children's Bureau, 1988).
6 See V. Randall, 'The Politics of Child Daycare: Some European Comparisons', *Swiss Yearbook of Political Science 1994*, (Editions Paul Haupt, 1994).
7 The argument is developed in V. Randall, 'The Irresponsible State? The Politics of Child Daycare Provision in Britain', *British Journal of Political Science*, July 1995.
8 Source: National Commission on Education, *Learning to Succeed* (Heinemann, 1993).
9 B. W. Hogwood and L. Gunn, *Policy Analysis for the Real World* (Oxford University Press, 1984).
10 See D. Summers, 'Employers Seek Political Lead on Childcare', *Financial Times*, 2.6.93.

Feminist intervention and local domestic violence policy

BY STEFANIA ABRAR

DOMESTIC violence here means mental, physical, sexual, emotional or economic abuse of one partner by another. It is largely perpetrated by men over women. We examine the ways in which feminists have operated to influence the uptake of policy on domestic violence by the local state. Policy promotion at this level has been crucial since it is here that women experiencing domestic violence have direct contact with public officials. Three localities are compared to investigate the factors leading to the adoption of policies. The process surrounding their institutionalisation illustrates the nature of local feminist intervention.

Commentators in the USA and Canada have noted the importance of local feminist advocacy groups in setting local agendas on domestic violence. However, there is a recognition that these groups need allies to achieve success. Andrew's detailed account of the establishment of the Centre Against Violence (Ottawa-Carleton, Canada) stresses the interrelations between community mobilisation and the local state. The establishment of this centre was the result of a coalition forged by a female local councillor with an interest in domestic violence. Institutional structures and local political agendas played an important part in legitimising the coalition.[1] Brownhill and Halford's critique of the distinction often made between women's 'formal' and 'informal' political organising is reflected in Andrew's analysis. They argue that there are significant similarities and interconnections between feminist action both inside and outside the state. Indeed, on a practical level 'people are constantly meeting, consulting or working jointly and resources may change hands'. For them, unravelling this process is central. 'We need to challenge and transform such categories as the informal and the formal to tease out the political processes which underlie them. These processes included gender, differing access to executive power and differing agendas for change.'[2] Therefore, to understand how local policy on domestic violence is made it is necessary to consider the nature of local institutions, women's mobilisation and the dynamics of the relationship between them. We must also consider how political agendas of the various camps coincide to produce policy which works in the interests of women.

Other useful public policy perspectives focus more explicitly on interest group analysis. Some point to the significance of particular configurations of policy networks[3] and coalitions[4], others, most notably

Dowding,[5] focus on the bargaining capacity of interest groups and their differential access to power resources. The latter, informed by a rational choice perspective, identifies a number of resources used by groups to further their interests: legitimate authority, information and expertise, reputation, conditional/unconditional incentives (such as money). The distribution of these resources among actors in a policy network can be assessed to predict the policy influence of any one group. Change is the result of a change in the resources available to groups, often brought about by an exogenous event.

These approaches may complement each other. Dowding suggests that systematic inequalities in power depend upon resources which themselves may depend upon social location. Thus the institutionalisation of male interests in society together with what Schattschneider has called 'the mobilisation of bias' against new interest groups may explain the consistent exclusion of women's interests from the policy process.[6] In addition, ingrained cultural hostility towards both female presence and feminist intervention has made change even more complex, leading feminist political action to occur at the margins and incrementally. Thus the policy networks approach, though useful in mapping resources, must be complemented by the consideration of contextual factors which shape the distribution and use of these resources.

Accordingly, we detail the policy history of domestic violence in each local authority to examine the exogenous factors shifting the distribution of resources and then describe the ways in which these opportunities have been managed by feminists to achieve woman centred policy. First, a brief summary of the wider national context which forms the backdrop against which local policy-making on domestic violence has occurred.

Domestic violence: the rise of a woman's issue in public policy

Women's issues have traditionally been classified as private issues and outside the public policy domain. Where public policy has focused on women it has been to reinforce their domestic and familial roles. A functionalist and professionalised ethos in public service agencies together with male-dominated hierarchies have tended to obscure and exclude women's interests. The 1977 Homeless Persons Act which imposes a statutory duty upon local authorities to rehouse women with children, and women subject to domestic violence is the only piece of legislation securing the rights of women to service delivery. To this day, there is no other statutory duty preventing local authorities from discriminating against women in terms of service provision. (The 1975 Sex Discrimination Act placed obligations on local authorities as employers rather than as service providers and, with the exception of education departments, local government services were exempt from the effects of the Act.)

Despite the 1977 Act, domestic violence is a relatively new issue on the public policy agenda. Its location in the private sphere, more insidiously than many other women's issues, has meant that historically it has been regarded as a legitimate feature of interpersonal relations. As late as 1975, the Association of Chief Police Officers, in its submission to the Commons select committee, maintained that in a domestic violence case 'every effort should be made to reunite the family'.[7] Moreover, research on the incidence of the crime suggests that it is severely under-reported to statutory agencies and in national crime surveys. The North London Domestic Violence Survey, for example, found that violence was not reported to any agency in 78% of cases.[8]

The rise of domestic violence to national public agenda status since the 1970s has had a profound impact on its uptake at a local level. Its origins lie in the feminist movement, in particular the women's refuge movement which emerged in 1974 as the Women's Aid Federation. By 1987 the English branch of the federation included 200 refuges. Although primarily engaged in providing shelter to women fleeing violence, it was committed from the beginning to educating the public. One of its five aims is to: 'educate and inform the public, the police, the courts, the social services and other authorities with respect to the battering of women, mindful of the fact that this is the result of the general position of women in our society'. It had significant input into legislation in the 1970s.

However, despite the passing of the Domestic Violence and Matrimonial Proceedings Act (1976), the Magistrates Courts Act (1978) and the Housing (Homeless Persons) Act in 1977, both the police and local authorities remained unwilling to use the law to protect domestic violence victims until well into the 1980s. Change came about principally as the result of the legitimation crisis faced by the police in the early 1980s. This created the opportunity for a combination of women's agitation, increased service provision for women, critical feminist research and media attention to sexual violence, to bring the issue to the attention of the national criminal justice community. During the 1980s a number of agencies produced reports on domestic violence.[9] In 1986 a Home Office circular prompted the Metropolitan Police to set up a working party which led to a Force Order in 1987. By the late 1980s and early 1990s, domestic violence units started to appear in police forces across the country. Interest extended to other agencies in recognition of the fact domestic violence crossed many institutional boundaries. In 1989/90 a senior Home Office researcher produced a report incorporating a feminist critique of statutory agencies and recommended a coordinated multi-agency response to the problem. This was followed by moves to encourage local crime prevention projects sponsored by the Home Office via the Safer Cities Programme to take up initiatives around domestic violence. Finally in the 1990s various national level agencies began to take the issue seriously.[10]

Even so, contradictory proposals made in 1995 indicate a lack of coordination at central government level. For example, the proposed Family Homes and Domestic Violence Bill improves legal remedies for removing violent persons from the home. It sits uncomfortably with another more recent government proposal to amend housing legislation which will remove the duty established by the 1985 Housing Act to house permanently those in priority need. Domestic violence victims, the third largest category of people accepted as homeless by local authorities, will find even greater difficulties in securing permanent accommodation. Moreover, continuing reductions in social security and housing provision impede the ability of women to leave violent men.[11]

Progressive moves at the national level throughout the 1980s and early 1990s masked what is still a piecemeal, fragmented response to domestic violence. This is complicated by the fact that responsibility for domestic violence is shared by a wide range of agencies such as the police, the courts, probation, social services, health, housing, education. Until recently, each operated in a discrete policy community. Smith stated in 1989, 'it almost seems as if each agency defines the problem in such a way that it is someone else's responsibility . . . the end result is that the victim can be left virtually helpless'.[12] The most significant incentive provided by central government to encourage the adoption of domestic violence policy at the local level has been funding through what are known as Safer Cities projects. This development results from the coincidence of the new 'crime prevention' orthodoxy in the Home Office[13] and the rise of domestic violence on the national agenda. Since its launch in 1988, 52 cities have been chosen, on the basis of indicators of inner-city deprivation and high crime rates, to receive funding for crime prevention initiatives. To date there have been 111 small-scale initiatives on domestic violence funded by Safer Cities at the local level. Safer Cities initiatives are short-term injections of funds designed merely to stimulate the uptake of crime prevention projects by local agencies. No permanent funding has been made available.

At the local level, where the agencies dealing with women experiencing violence are situated, response is patchy and underfunded. A survey by the London Housing Unit found that local authorities vary in their definitions of domestic violence as well as how they interpret the notoriously unclear statutory duty to rehouse women experiencing violence.[14] Some housing departments have adopted the feminist approach of taking a woman's word as proof of violence and follow the Department of Environment's Code of Guidance (a progressive interpretation of the 1985 Housing Act), whereas others require legal action as evidence of abuse. Social services department practice also varies widely. Some local authorities lead a coherent multi-agency response, others deny that domestic violence is a problem in their communities. A few have developed good practice guidelines at the corporate level, together with information/education campaigns and training of their front-line service deliverers. Most will at least have produced a leaflet on accessing help. A commitment to employing paid officers is key: as one domestic violence expert put it, 'a lot depends on the particular officers in post. Where there are officers in post, they do all this outreach work, they have lots of conferences. Other local authorities are either not spending the money or are not putting the same energy in. You don't expect Tory authorities to do this stuff.'

The uptake of domestic violence projects by local authorities has had a distinctive dynamic. A key role has been played by women's committees and/or established posts with special responsibility for women's issues in local authorities. These are mainly to be found in progressive Labour local authorities which, responding to changes in party membership and feminist involvement after 1979, altered local policies on women and women's issues. This has not been a uniform development across the country and is largely dependent on particular local social relations and the locality's overall economic and political profile.[15] In 1991 less than 12% of local authorities in mainland Britain had set up women's committees.[16] No country-wide surveys have been carried out on the extent of local authority-led domestic violence policies at the local level but anecdotal evidence suggests their comparative rarity.

Development of domestic violence policy in three local authorities

The three localities studied (interviews with key policy-makers) have been anonymised to protect the identities of individuals working in the field. One is a Metropolitan District and the two others are London boroughs. For the present purposes they have been renamed Radicalton, Progressiveham and Conservativeville. Each has different political and cultural characteristics and each has experienced different levels of feminist involvement. Radicalton is a traditional Labour-controlled Northern city where a women's committee was set up in 1982 following significant local feminist activism in the 1970s and early 1980s. Progressiveham was one of the flag-bearers of the new urban left in the 1980s. A women's committee was set up there in 1981 but, unlike Radicalton, the council has not been directly influenced by a local autonomous women's movement. Lastly, Conservativeville, as its name suggests, is a Conservative council. It has never had a women's committee, despite the presence of a significant number of influential female councillors. Feminist activism in the area in the 1970s and 1980s stayed firmly outside the local state machinery.

RADICALTON. Radicalton in the late 1970s and early 1980s, was characterised by active feminist mobilisation around issues of male sexual violence which was strengthened by the psychological landmark created by the Radicalton sex murders (13 killings and 7 attempted murders 1975–80). The significant role played by women's groups in lobbying for the establishment of the women's committee in 1982 led to their strong input into committee decisions through a system of community representatives. The interest in sexual violence in the community was thus reflected in the work of the committee and the single local government women's officer from an early stage. Radicalton City Council became the first council in the country to sponsor conferences on sexual violence and succeeded in raising the profile of the issue in the wider arena. In addition, access to the police through the county council police committee, enabled the women's committee to pursue legitimately a critical part of the domestic violence problem: it's 'no crime' status with the police. Senior police officers' attitudes to this involvement were initially hostile. 'The man in the street,' the women's committee representatives were told at their first meeting with the police, 'is simply not interested in prosecutions for domestic violence'. Determined to change this attitude, the women's committee continued to meet with the police throughout the early 1980s to discuss women's policing needs. Meanwhile, a wider legitimacy crisis was occurring in the district police: race issues, the miners' strike and media exposés of police treatment of rape victims undermined the force's credibility. In 1985 media coverage of the case of a local victim of a domestic killing brought police practice once more under intense scrutiny. Bowing to public pressure, the police allowed feminist activist researchers, funded by the county council, to investigate the force's response to domestic violence. The recommendations of the subsequent report were strongly endorsed by the Chief Constable, thereby symbolising a new commitment by the police to multi-agency cooperation and a formal recognition of the crime status of domestic violence. The women's committee, led by its chair, a former community representative, was able to capitalise on the publicity generated by the Chief Constable's statement by organising an inter-agency working party on domestic violence which she chaired. This included a core of representatives from local authority departments and the voluntary sector.

As a networking device it proved useful. Initially comprising committed individuals rather than influential policy makers, members of the inter-agency working group were able to lobby inside their own agencies. In the housing department, for example, this resulted in the employment of a woman's officer with special responsibility for domestic violence. However, the need for a full-time worker to develop the multi-agency work became apparent and the chair was able to secure funding from the three council committees most directly implicated in domestic violence work: Housing, Social Services and Equal Opportunities committees. A coordinator with extensive experience of sexual violence work at Rape Crisis was appointed. Her background and the close working relationship that the women's committee had built up with women's organisations over a number of years ensured close links with the voluntary sector.

The Radicalton InterAgency Project, as it became known, is one of the most comprehensive and successful projects of its kind in the country. Its unusual structure, part-voluntary sector, part-local authority, has enabled it to secure funding from a variety of sources and has allowed it autonomy with political backing from the local authority. Funding was secured for eleven workers, with the Home Office providing the leading contribution of 25% of the project's total funding. Some of the posts are funded by the local authority, others through central government section 11 money (available specifically for the employment of black workers) and other posts receive funding as short-term 'action research projects'. Its resources and expertise have meant that, according to its coordinator, '[Radicalton] InterAgency project is extremely well-respected and we are seen as a very professional organisation, we deliver very good quality training, we go in and negotiate . . . we are seen as being quite powerful locally . . . we do have political support, we have the support of a huge number of agencies.'

There are three elements to its work: an inter-agency forum, a comprehensive domestic violence training scheme, the development of good practice guidelines and policies with agencies, and most notably the Good Practice Pilot project which has been launched in one area of the city. This has entailed the training of all relevant workers in the locality and the establishment of special education, health and court based projects in the area.

Political change has occurred in a range of agencies both inside and outside the local authority: housing, social services, health, Crown Prosecution Service (CPS), police, probation, education. Local authority policy is a model of woman-centred practice on the issue, but more dramatic changes are starting to occur in other local agencies. The project coordinator is beginning to see the results of five years work. 'Just the other day there was a criminal prosecution that was taken forward and the CPS prosecutor was absolutely brilliant. Apparently the magistrate who was there gave this man 80 hours of community service, which is, I think, unheard of in domestic violence cases and a fine. We think he is one of the magistrates that has been brought through our training programme. The different agencies are actually starting to support each other. It's wonderful.'

Although the main avenue for policy change has been the InterAgency Forum, where high level decision-makers from agencies meet once every three months, policy change has been most apparent when there are institutionalised gateways into organisations such as women's officer posts, where sympathetic individuals are in positions of authority, and where the project coordinator has been able to build upon external events such as national level interagency agreements.

PROGRESSIVEHAM. Women's safety issues had been a concern of the Progressiveham women's committee since its inception in 1981. Unlike in Radicalton, there was no active women's movement forcing the council to take the lead on domestic violence policy and coordination. Rather, progress in the borough was the by-product of increasing pressure on the Metropolitan Police by feminists (both in the Greater London Council and in London-wide pressure groups) and the media to offer more effective policing of domestic violence. This led most notably to the Metropolitan Police's Force Order in 1987 and a commitment to the establishment of Domestic Violence Units across the city. By the 1990s multi-agency working was also coming into vogue having been pioneered by cities such as Radicalton. Thus in 1990 a local female police officer encouraged the women's unit to revive a domestic violence working party that had existed in the early 1980s.

In the light of growing awareness of domestic violence in the borough and at a national level, the women's committee produced a report detailing inconsistency in council provision for domestic violence victims. However, the Director of Housing and Social Services, whose department was targeted by the report, was unsympathetic and was able to ignore its recommendations for the appointment of staff with responsibility for the issue. Fortunately, the establishment of one of the Home Office Safer Cities projects in Progressiveham in 1991 provided a second forum for the report and the head of the women's unit was successful in securing temporary funding for a Domestic Violence Coordinator post based inside the women's unit.

Full funding of the post was taken over by the council two years later. This came about due to a number of factors. The rising profile of domestic violence nationally and the presence of a high prestige Home Office action research project for policing domestic violence and offering crisis intervention work in one of Progressiveham's police divisions (itself the result of collaboration by London-based feminist academics with ties to the Home Office, Progressiveham Police and the Safer Cities Coordinator for the borough) gave the issue a particularly strong legitimacy with decision makers. The results of a domestic violence survey commissioned by the council shocked councillors. Its findings that a high percentage of women in the area experience domestic violence made a strong case for the importance of the issue in the locality. These factors combined with the ability of the coordinator to produce guidelines and develop networks over the preceding two years, convinced leading members of the council to support the application for permanent funding for the post. As was the case in Radicalton, the decision by the head of the women's unit and the women's committee to employ a worker with a background in Women's Aid tapped directly into voluntary sector expertise.

Located inside the council's women's unit, the coordinator develops good practice and policy, training, and facilitates the borough-wide domestic violence working party established by the council in 1990. The location of the women's unit at a corporate level has given the domestic violence coordinator direct access to powerful and supportive senior officials. The downside of her location inside the bureaucracy is that the coordinator has had to work hard to neutralise the negative reputation that being a member of the women's unit entails. A number of strategies help her to do this. Within the authority, she seeks to foster personal relationships in order to establish informal avenues for her work. In her dealings with external agencies, she seeks to influence policy through training and guidelines to front-line service deliverers at the forum. The women's unit did secure representation on what is known as the Safer Progressiveham Strategy Group, a multi-agency group of senior decision makers but policy change has not occurred here. In any case links with the criminal justice community have been considerably less important than in the case of Radicalton. This is a direct result of the presence of a unique Home Office crisis intervention project in the borough which concentrates on fostering these links. That project is also staffed by feminists and although policy networks rarely overlap, relationships between the two foci for domestic violence policy are cooperative.

CONSERVATIVEVILLE. Despite the rise of domestic violence on the national and London-wide agenda, Conservativeville council has done little about domestic violence policy beyond disbursing funding to the local refuge and fixing a limited number of alarms in women's homes. In 1983–84 a Conservativeville 'Women speak out survey', sponsored by the Conservativeville Policing Campaign and funded by the Greater London Council's police and women's support committees, had little impact on the locality in terms of public policy (though the council may have dismissed the GLC report for political reasons). In the 1990s, initiatives at a borough-wide level did occur due to the establishment of a Safer Cities initiative in the area which, unusually, had an all female staff. In 1991, the feminist assistant coordinator, inspired by Home Office conferences and her period of study with a prominent domestic violence activist and academic, set up the multi-agency Conservativeville Domestic Violence Forum. Drawing on her extensive links with the voluntary sector and initial support from the police due to her previous crime prevention work in the borough, links were made relatively easily. However, she was unable to secure high level political or officer support from Conservativeville council. Persistent hostility by the council, which perceived the autonomy of the Safer Cities project itself as a threat, scuppered both its chances of policy influence and the sustainability of its initiatives: 'they saw us as being radical and as far as they were concerned. Safer Cities was there to give them money to supplement the poll tax, they were flooding us with applications to mend roads and fences. They felt they owned Safer Cities.' Resistance to council domination led to 'the most terrible antagonism that continued from start to finish'. This meant that a crucial part of the domestic violence policy network was closed off. 'Trying to get domestic violence policy incorporated as general council policy was impossible, so we had to settle for what we could do as individuals who were committed to working together setting up projects that we could do.' Relations with the council were so antagonistic, by contrast to Radicalton and Progressiveham, that no funding bid was submitted to the council for a coordinator to continue with the Safer Cities work. Instead, the domestic violence forum became reliant on the intermittent patronage of the police and the probation service for support.

By mid 1995, the forum was without influence and funds and had no coordinator. It relied on the goodwill of the front-line service-delivery agencies to sustain it. With the end of Safer Cities funding, outstanding work was 'sneaked through typing pools'. Its continued existence was viewed by participants primarily as an 'elaborate statement of our good will'. By comparison to Radicalton and Progressiveham, its achievements over the past four years are minor, limited to small-scale promotion of awareness of domestic violence in the community and a networking device.

Feminist intervention at the local level

In keeping with the framework set out at the start, the policy histories reveal a two-stage process. The first stage is a series of events which enable feminists to establish the need for specific posts to coorindate local approaches to domestic violence. These events are exploited by a variety of feminists located both inside and outside the state, confirming Brownhill and Halford's hypothesis that formal and informal distinctions collapse in the arena of feminist political action. The second stage is the deployment of resources by feminist lobbyists to push for domestic violence policy. This occurs in a series of bargaining situations with sections of the local bureaucracy or other agencies.

All three localities experienced varying types of feminist intervention. In Radicalton, feminist activists, academics and politicians coordinated their efforts to create structures that were feminist led but partially autonomous from the council. In Progressiveham, the intervention was largely bureaucratic, with the head of the women's unit securing funds initially from external sources to create a feminist post within the council. In Conservativeville such activity that there was, was driven temporarily by a feminist located in the Home Office's Safer Cities project. The initiatives in these arenas built upon the activities of a wider feminist movement active in a variety of ways since the 1970s. Radicalton was the only area to experience direct impact by the local feminist movement. In London, a more indirect effect was apparent as feminist ideas trickled down to the local level after surfacing first at the metropolitan and national levels (many London activists in fact doubled as national activists). In all three localities, those in London in particular, the legitimacy of local authority-sponsored posts to promote domestic violence policy was partly dependent on wider cultural and political changes occurring in other professions and agencies,[17] particularly the police. Indeed, police participation in local government domestic violence networks accorded feminists with prestige which enhanced their reputation in the local authority setting.

The case studies suggest that the issue of domestic violence receives the most adequate local attention when feminists are established in the relevant local institutions and when the support of local politicians is available. It can be seen that even though the Radicalton and Progressiveham women's committees benefited from what Dowding would term legitimate authority or what Brownhill and Halford would call high levels of executive access, both committees sought to develop their legitimacy in the issue area and take on new personnel to work on domestic violence. However, women's committees seeking to establish their legitimacy and to increase their staffing faced two obstacles: their marginalised status in male-dominated local authorities and funding constraints operating on local authorities in the 1980s, which made local councils resistant to the growth of innovative posts.

Local government women's committees are marginal and largely deprived of the most powerful resources for influencing outcomes: statutorily defined responsibility, money and, in many cases, 'reputation' among other bureaucrats. Instead, their bureaucrats and politicians have had to take advantage of externally created opportunities to launch their initiatives. As a result, policy influence has been incremental but patchy, characterised by a long preparation of the ground, followed by a ruthless seizing of opportunities presented by external events. 'It is a process of talking to people, seizing opportunities. It is an intensely personal process which uses political machinery as a way of developing that into actual action. You talk to them within the confines of the Labour group, you talk to them at the Labour party, you raise issues where you think they are pertinent and you might be able to draw connections between one issue and another. Occasionally you jump up and down and have a real go at them, but largely you don't do that, or you will get side-lined into a corner somewhere. Politics is a male arena and you are likely to be told "well, this is political reality; you either play by the rules or you do not play at all".'

The wider institutional context is important in establishing legitimacy. Most crucially in Radicalton, the women's committee, had access to police governing structures which enabled them to force a relationship with the police. This made them the natural custodians of the inter-agency domestic violence initiative recommended in the feminist academics' report. The women's committee in Progressiveham had the support of politicians but lacked guaranteed access to the Metropolitan police, and were thus without the same opportunities to benefit from the reputation gained by such a liaison. They had to wait until the establishment of the Safer Cities project before they were able claim a legitimate role.

In Conservativeville, feminists had neither political support nor institutional resources. The absence of a women's committee or any other suitable conduit into the local authority, combined with a political ideology hostile to feminism (one prominent female councillor remarked: 'I do not feel as a local authority it is [our] job to change society and the role of women') meant that the Safer Cities coordinator never found high-level support for a policy intervention. In the minds of council officials, domestic violence, women's committees and Labour Party politics all merged into one political demon. One consequence was that Conservativeville alone out of the 32 London boroughs did not participate in the 1993 London Zero Tolerance campaign. The Assistant Coordinator to Safer Cities was discredited by her advocacy of domestic violence initiatives: 'I was seen as this radical feminist, leftie, every label that could get attached got attached and therefore not to be touched with a large barge pole.'

Woman-centred policy change rests on the ability of feminists to control and construct an influential policy network. Initially all the local authorities lacked coordinated, coherent policy on domestic violence. Agencies failed to cooperate with each other and essentially operated in a series of closed policy communities. In Radicalton and Progressiveham well-placed feminists were able to change this. By securing funding for initiatives and placing feminist officers at the centre of inter-agency networks, feminists within the local state created a base from which to push for the acceptance of woman-centred policy. However, there are substantial differences in the policy change achieved by the two feminist networks. This can be ascribed principally to the differing levels of resources, primarily money, that the initiatives have been able to secure.

The greater success of the Radicalton project in attracting resources is the result of at least six factors. These included, first, the high level of political support from its inception; second, the successful mobilisation of support by the founder members of the inter-agency group from within their own agencies; third, the existence of women's officers in agencies who provided a channel for joint working; fourth, the part-voluntary sector, part-local authority status of the project, enabling it to bid for a variety of funding; fifth, the strong emphasis on race inequality, enabling the project to bid for section 11 funding; sixth, and most importantly, the 'pilot' orientation of the project, (one of the coordinator's original ideas), enabling the project to become eligible for one-off action-research funding popular with the Programme Development Unit of the Home Office in the early 1990s. This amalgam of resources and expertise enabled the inter-agency project to extend its network. Such resources meant that it was able to employ specialised workers attached to particular sections of a wide-ranging network, such as the health sector, which had proved impenetrable in the past.

By contrast, in Progressiveham, the incorporation of the officer into the bureaucracy meant that her role was centred on influencing the local authority staff. The inter-agency working group and her training initiatives did give her access to a wide range of front-line service deliverers. However, securing significant policy change in other agencies was less feasible since she had less scope as a single worker than the eleven workers in Radicalton. Nonetheless, she was able to promote good practice policy and used the authority of her position in the council as well as her considerable personal reputation for expertise to do so. The absence of women's officers in other agencies and departments of the authority made informal networking important: 'I take the time to remember what is happening in people's lives and meet up with them every so often.' Unlike in Radicalton, the coordinator could not benefit from important resources available from the criminal justice community as the separate network created by the Home Office Action research project at Progressiveham Police station won the funding available for such work. The combined policy outreach of the two initiatives was significant even though it did not enhance the resources base of the officer in the local authority.

Conservativeille illustrates the consequences of failure to create a feminist-led policy network. The council's refusal to participate constructively imposed a block on policy activity. The other potential ally, the police, proved unreliable and unwilling to provide financial support beyond funding its own domestic violence units.

Reconciling different agendas for change has been a significant problem for all three networks. In Radicalton, the principles of the Radicalton InterAgency Project which promotes a challenging analysis of domestic violence through its training and projects, comes under intermittent criticism for privileging women's perspectives. Project workers endeavour to overcome hostility by establishing relationships that benefit those dealing with domestic violence victims. Problems of this kind have occurred most often when reorganisation has occurred in partnership institutions, necessitating a long process of renegotiating relationships with new decision makers. In Progressiveham, the post-holder has also sought to promote a feminist interpretation of domestic violence. In the format of training sessions and paper guidelines, this has proved relatively unthreatening to the institution. Where the contradictions in political agendas become apparent is in situations of resource conflict. For example, where radical definitions of domestic violence extend expenditure to marginal groups, these definitions have been challenged. In the case of housing allocation policy, the coordinator and the women's committee had to accept a wording change to the proposed policy in order to win the bulk of their demands. In Conservativeville, the lack of strong feminist leadership of the forum together with political conflicts have meant that agendas have differed to the degree that the local Women's Aid is a rare participant at the forum. However, it would be wrong to imply that institutional political agendas are monolithic and uniform. Within a given institution a range of sympathies exist. Where feminists have been able to access most corners of the network, blockages have been offset by the discovery of other influential actors. This has not happened in Conservativeville due to the absence of a legitimate base from which to cultivate such networks.

Lastly, not all policy change is dependent on the network itself. Political will and resource scarcity also proved to be important variables. Success in changing policy beyond the employment of a domestic violence officer has been easiest in situations where resources are plentiful. Housing is a case in point. Levels of conflict faced by feminists trying to shift housing policy to prioritise women who had experienced domestic violence were directly related to resource scarcity. In Radicalton, where council housing resources were under less stress than in Progressiveham and Conservativeville, a change in housing policy encountered no resistance. Inner London authorities, by contrast, have traditionally faced greater housing demands and have thus felt the effects of central government legislation prohibiting the construction of public sector housing more acutely. Indeed, financial constraints led some London authorities in the early 1990s to reverse provisions for women experiencing domestic violence. In Progressiveham the women's committee had to wage a three and a half year battle to change housing policy. The situation was particularly acute in Conservativeville, where an aggressive 'right-to-buy' policy was promoted. This led to sections of housing stock being ring-fenced for sale, forcing the housing department to be increasingly ruthless in its allocation of properties. It was said to be operating a 'how desperate are you?' policy, designed to put people off applying for accommodation rather than encouraging it. Individual women's groups felt that lobbying for policy change was useless in such an environment.

Conclusion

In the three case studies, feminist bureaucratic and political structures have provided crucial avenues for the introduction of domestic violence policy at the local level. In Conservativeville, where there was no women's committee, the local authority was resistant to policy change on this issue, content instead to define it as the responsibility of the voluntary sector. However, the mere presence of feminist political and bureaucratic structures has not been the cause of change. The exogenous events leading to domestic violence initiatives are the culmination of years of feminist pressure group activities in a number of sites. What women's committees provided was a vehicle for change generated outside the local authority by local level feminist political action, the rising influence of the feminist activism and expertise at a national level, changing professional orientations and the opening up of policy communities in previously closed professions such as the police and social workers.

The skill with which feminists have manipulated the resources at their disposal is a testimony to the expertise of feminists situated both inside and outside the state. Almost fifteen years of experience of women's committees has equipped feminists with a range of strategies to manipulate state resources. Nonetheless, domestic violence coordinators have certainly been an island of growth in an era which has otherwise been characterised by the disestablishment of women's officer posts.

Finally, employing feminists directly from voluntary sector sexual violence projects has meant that state feminists have reinforced links with feminist activists. With backgrounds in the feminist sexual violence networks, many of those appointed identify with radical feminist perspectives and maintain close ties with radical feminist activists and workers in the voluntary sector. Thus on a day-to-day basis women's political organising on domestic violence issues is a joint effort and continues to operate across formal and informal boundaries.

1 C. Andrew, 'Getting Women's Issues on the Municipal Agenda: Violence Against Women', *Urban Affairs Special Issue*, 1995.
2 S. Brownhill and S. Halford, 'Understanding Women's Involvement in Local Politics: How Useful is the Formal/Informal Dichotomy?' *Political Geography Quarterly*, October 1990.
3 D. Marsh and R. Rhodes (eds), *Policy Networks in British Local Government* (Oxford University Press, 1992).
4 P. Sabatier, 'Policy Change Over a Decade or More' in Sabatier and Jenkins-Smith (eds), *Policy Change and Learning: an Advocacy Coalition Approach* (Westview Press, 1993).
5 K. Dowding, 'Model or Metaphor? A Critical Review of the Policy Network Approach,' *Political Studies*, March 1995.
6 J. Gelb and M. L. Paley, *Women and Public Policies* (Princeton University Press, 1982).
7 J. Hanmer, *Women, Policing and Male Violence* (Routledge, 1989).
8 Cf. J. Mooney, *Researching Domestic Violence: The North London Domestic Violence Survey*, 1993.
9 Home Office circulars in 1983 and 1986 advocated a police policy on domestic violence; the Women's National Commission produced a Cabinet Office report in 1985; the GLC Strategic Policy Unit's police monitoring group issued a report in 1986.
10 The Department of the Environment released a Code of Guidance on Housing recommending emergency provision for women escaping violence; the Law Commission issued a working paper on 'Domestic violence and the occupation of the matrimonial home'.
11 J. Lovenduski and V. Randall, *Contemporary Feminist Politics* (Oxford University Press, 1994).
12 L. Smith, 'Domestic Violence: A Review of the Literature' (Home Office Research Study 107, 1989).
13 N. Tiley, 'Crime Prevention and the Safer Cities Story', *The Howard Journal*, February 1993.
14 London Housing Unit briefing report, March 1995.
15 S. Halford, 'Women's Initiatives in Local Government: Where Do They Come From and Where Are They Going?', *Policy and Politics*, 1988/4.
16 S. Edwards, *Local Government Women's Committees* (Avebury Press, 1995).
17 R. Dobash and R. Dobash, *Women, Violence and Social Change* (Routledge, 1992).

The Zero Tolerance Campaign: Setting the Agenda

BY FIONA MACKAY

THE Zero Tolerance campaign, a groundbreaking public awareness initiative to challenge social attitudes and myths surrounding violence against women and children, originated with Edinburgh District Council's women's committee in 1992. A crime prevention strategy, inspired by a Canadian initiative and informed by the long-term drink-driving campaign, it was launched with broad political, civic and church backing. Since then, the Zero Tolerance campaign has been taken up by an increasing number of councils in Britain. More than 25 countries have made inquiries about the campaign and it was launched in South Australia in 1995. Success has been marked in terms of public response, uptake from other authorities and public bodies, widespread support from the statutory sector, including the police, and the voluntary sector including Women's Aid and Rape Crisis groups. As a campaign, it has won awards for design and has succeeded both in generating high levels of public and political debate and in progressing the issue of violence higher up the political agenda. It is widely regarded as a radical but genuinely popular initiative.

The Zero Tolerance case study is a useful site to examine key questions about women and power and women's access, presence and agency within the local state. Whereas the focus of much work has been upon the recruitment of women into political channels, less work has addressed the issue of what difference women are likely to make as women once they are present.[1] It also highlights the ambiguous relationship between autonomous women's groups and the local state.

Feminism suggests that the entry of women into decision-making channels will have an impact, although different models suggest different degrees of outcome in terms of success in implementing social change. In Britain the dominant school of feminist thought in the 1970s viewed the state as a functional tool of capitalism and patriarchy and concentrated its energies on building a culture of opposition; however, the position has become more pragmatic and now involves cautious engagement with the state. Therein lies the dilemma: the state is seen as playing a crucial role in the perpetuation of gender inequality but is the only site in which many of feminism's demands can be met, for example childcare provision, action on violence against women and the implementation of equal opportunities employment practices.[2] Since the 1980s there has been a small but increasing feminist penetration of the state through political parties, trade unions and the state bureaucracy, particularly through local government women's and/or equal opportunities committees.[3] Similarly other groups have increasingly become involved with the state for funding for feminist service provision.

Feminist policy research has suggested that the formulation and promotion of policies which challenge existing social and political power relations are most likely to meet with resistance and backlash. Thus radical policies in general and feminist politics in particular encounter both general and gendered resistance. Feminists engaging with the state from within and outside have found that issues have been distorted or diluted resulting in what Joyce Outshoorn has described as the creeping process of issue modification. Joni Lovenduski and Vicky Randall point out, as do others, that feminists have tended to lose control of definitions because policy-makers and administrators inevitably muted the impact of radically conceived reforms. This has resulted in limited outcomes in terms of social change.[4] However, whereas feminists and other 'outsider' or 'thresholder' groups have in general found that involvement with the state, or the policy-making community, has resulted in the dilution or modification of their concerns, in the instance of Zero Tolerance the local state has proactively promoted a radical definition of the issue of violence against women which has been formulated by the women's movement itself.

Here we suggest that feminists may be gaining some leverage from their intervention in the state through women's committees and women's units to control and define certain issues. The view is that there has been a gradual convergence between women's movement activists and the agenda of women working in local authorities as elected members and as officers. We examine the importance of women's committees as proactive agents of feminist change, the role of both 'official feminists' and unofficial feminists in pursuing social and political change for women; and the diffusion of feminist ideas within the wider community. Before describing and analysing the Zero Tolerance campaign in detail, it is useful to explain some of the issues and terms within the article; and secondly to outline the specifically Scottish context of the campaign.

The issue of violence

The true scale of violence against women and children is unknown, however, rape, sexual assault and domestic violence are believed to be massively under-reported. There are several key features to the issue: men are predominantly the perpetrators of violence and sexual violence; women and children are predominantly its victims; statistically, they are more at risk in their homes from men they know than out of doors from strangers. A useful survey of domestic violence studies suggests that violence against women in the home occurs in between 10 and 25% of all relationships.[5]

The issue of violence against women has been the focus of social and political campaigning by feminists in the second wave of the 20th century women's movement from the 1970s onwards.[6] The seventh and final demand of the Women's Liberation Movement was: 'Freedom for all women from violence, or the threat of violence, and sexual coercion, regardless of marital status, and an end to all laws, assumptions and institutions that perpetuate male dominance and men's aggression towards women.' Feminists have also been instrumental in raising the issue of child sexual abuse from the mid-1980s and in linking differing forms of violence against women and children. Feminist anti-violence campaigns have involved political mobilisation around issues of protection and prevention; and feminist groups such as Women's Aid and Rape Crisis have been at the forefront of provision of practical help in the form of refuges for women escaping violence, crisis help-lines and long-term support and counselling for survivors of violence and sexual assault.

Explanations of violence are varied but have traditionally fallen within two headings: those which concentrate on the individual pathology of the victim or perpetrator (that is that either the victim or the perpetrator- or both — are 'mad' or 'bad') and those in terms of reaction to social structural factors, for example stress caused by poor housing or unemployment. The major distinctive feature of a feminist analysis of violence is that it explains it as an issue of power and the result of the unequal status of women and men in society. Thus violence is framed within a political context rather than as a private problem or a social welfare issue. Feminist service delivery is also distinctive. A key part of feminist service provision is the emphasis upon the empowerment of women. Women seeking help are seen as survivors rather than victims and practical help is underpinned by the belief that women can be agents of change in their own lives. This philosophy of self-help results in tension between organisations such as Women's Aid and welfare professionals who intervene as 'experts'. The Zero Tolerance campaign was, therefore, based upon and informed by twenty years of groundwork by the women's movement.

Violence against women is an issue on the political agenda for all the parties in Scotland and Britain. Within the Scottish Labour Party it is discussed in terms of both feminism and social welfare debates; within Conservative circles it is seen as part of the wider law and order debate; the Scottish National Party (SNP) and the Scottish Liberal Democrats frame violence against women against broader policies of equality of opportunity.

Political contexts

The Zero Tolerance campaign has also taken place within a specific Scottish political context which differs from the overall British picture. Electoral support for the Conservatives in Scotland has declined sharply since the mid-1950s when they polled more than 50% of the popular vote. By the 1992 general election, the Conservative share of the vote fell to 26% and just 11 MPs were returned to the House of Commons. At the local government elections held for the shadow local authorities in April 1995 the vote fell to a fraction above 11%. The governments of Margaret Thatcher and John Major have been markedly unpopular in Scotland and the most recent campaign for electoral reform has grown in strength through the 1980s and 1990s. A situation where a party with a minority of support from the electorate can implement policies against the wishes of the majority of the Scottish people has given rise to a mobilisation of political and civic groupings to combat what is seen as a democratic deficit.

In contrast, Labour is the strongest party both at Westminster, where in 1992 49 out of the 72 Scottish MPs were Labour, and at local government level. Almost three-quarters of the Scottish population live in Regions that have always been, or almost always been, controlled by Labour. Political culture varies from the stereotyped white, male workerist, 'wee hard man' macho culture, which prevails especially in the West of Scotland, to more reformist and progressive cultures in the central east and east coast.[7] Alice Brown and others have charted the rise of activism amongst women in the Scottish Labour party around the issue of women's representation, which in part mirrors feminist activity in the Labour Party in the rest of Britain, and in part is distinctive to the Scottish context and the idea that women suffer from a double democratic deficit: firstly on a general level because of the political system; and specifically as women because they are grossly underrepresented within the power structures of political parties and as elected members of local and national decision-making assemblies (see Alice Brown in this volume). Catriona Burness has argued that gender equality has become an intrinsic part of the broader debates of democracy, accountability and representation in Scotland.[8]

Similarly, there has been an active women's movement in Scotland since the early 1970s which paralleled concerns of the women's movement in the rest of Britain. Esther Breitenbach argues that the movement has become more distinctively Scottish in the 1980s and 1990s, partly in reaction to the perceived adverse affects of Thatcherism for women, but more specifically as a result of mobilisation around the issue of constitutional reform in Scotland.[9] The Zero Tolerance campaign also happened within a specific context of local government in Edinburgh which has been led by a youngish, progressive Labour Left administration since 1984. Women are visible as both councillors and officers. Edinburgh District Council has had a women's committee, with specialist staff, in place since 1985, and the administration remains committed to an equality agenda.

The Zero Tolerance campaign is distinctive for several reasons: it is radical in that it seeks to challenge existing power relations and effect far-reaching social change; it is feminist in the way it links sexual violence, domestic violence and child sexual abuse as part of the 'continuum of violence'; it names emotional and psychological abuse as forms of violence. The campaign uses a feminist analysis of violence as a male abuse of power and it challenges men to take responsibility for their violence. In addition, it specifically uses empowering images of women — rather than victim imagery. Feminists have challenged the public-private divide with the slogan that 'the personal is political' and have been active in highlighting the politics of issues of the body, such as reproductive health and reproductive rights, sexuality, violence and harassment. Feminism places gender as a central analytical category in political and social analysis and highlights unequal gender power relations at institutional, ideological and personal levels. Zero Tolerance can thus be seen as a part of a feminist tradition of radical politics.

We draw upon research in four participating Scottish local authorities to examine the genesis of the Zero Tolerance campaign in terms of the process by which this campaign reached the agenda, how consensus and legitimation were constructed and other factors accounting for its success. The campaign has, in contrast with many previous case studies, been characterised by a lack of sustained or organised backlash. The reasons for the limited backlash are complex but essentially mirror the factors for its general success which relate to the political management of the issue: the specific Scottish and Edinburgh contexts; the ground-work of feminist anti-violence groups; the salience of the issue with women generally and the diffusion of feminist ideas within the larger community; and the penetration of the local state by official and unofficial feminists. Zero Tolerance has been a successful campaign in both conventional terms and feminist terms and has demonstrated women's politics in action.

The Zero Tolerance Campaign

'It was a bit like I'd died and gone to heaven. There above all the shoppers in Edinburgh's Princes Street ran the bold message, "There is never an excuse." There on the grassy bank halfway up the Mound sat a white Z of flowers. There at Hibernian a huge 'Z' symbol was emblazoned across the nets. Men on the terracing were eating their pies out of cartons and boxes overprinted with Zero Tolerance statistics. In doctor's surgeries patients sat beside posters proclaiming, "No Man has the Right". In swimming pools school galas splashed off beside the happy image of three young women, and the message, "When They Say No, they mean no". The campaign for zero tolerance of violence against women is really HAPPENING all over Edinburgh.' Broadcaster and journalist Lesley Riddoch, writing in the Scottish feminist magazine *Harpies and Quines*, voiced the sense of pleased astonishment and empowerment felt by many women in Scotland since December 1992 when Edinburgh District Council Women's Committe launched its campaign.[10] Its long-term objectives are to generate public debate and focus on strategies to prevent crimes of violence against women; to highlight the need for adequate support services; to highlight the need for appropriate legal protection for women and children survivors of violence. In the shorter term the campaign sought to highlight the prevalence of various crimes of violence against women and children linking these crimes as part of a continuum of male abuse of power; to promote a clear message that these forms of violence are crimes and should not be tolerated; and to debunk some of the myths around these crimes. In particular, the campaign challenges commonplace perceptions that violence is solely a working-class problem, that women and children are most at risk from strangers, and that sexual violence only happens to certain women because of their age, appearance, dress or behaviour.[11]

The campaign was developed in response to two pieces of research commissioned by the Edinburgh District Council's women's committee. Local women involved in a major consultation exercise in 1990 identified violence against women and women's safety as one of their main issues of concern. Secondly, a survey of secondary school pupils examined adolescents' attitudes which revealed disturbingly high levels of acceptance of, and misconceptions about, domestic violence. A six-month public awareness campaign was produced in-house by women's officers and a local freelance photographer, in consultation with local women's groups. It consisted of posters challenging stereotypical views, displayed throughout the city as well as indoor sites. An evaluation of the first phase by the University of Glasgow Media Group indicated that Zero Tolerance was extremely successful in attracting attention, raising people's knowledge of, and discontent about, the shortfall in provision of services, providing people with new perspectives, and has been thought provoking.

The Edinburgh campaign has had significant effects on awareness and reporting of violence. It also sparked great interest from other local authorities. More than twelve took up the idea within a year, including the Association of London Authorities. It now covers most of Scotland. In 1994 it was launched by Tayside Regional Council with support from Dundee, Strathclyde Regional Council with Glasgow, and Central Region. It was also taken up by the City of Aberdeen. Strathclyde, the largest local authority in Britain until its abolition in 1996, and Central both worked in partnership with their district councils, including Conservative-run authorities, health boards, voluntary sector groups and other agencies. Edinburgh continued to innovate, with a 'No Excuses' bus advertising and poster campaign in 1994 which challenged excuses commonly given for violence. It also launched a football initiative with star players from the city's two football clubs pledging their support and Zero Tolerance publicity prominently displayed at the club grounds. Parallel to the public face of Zero Tolerance, the District Council has also developed a 'within council' strategy including a domestic violence policy for its own staff, drawn up with the help of the public sector union UNISON and believed to be the first of its kind in Britain. The campaign has resulted in a marked increase of women seeking help.

There is growing evidence in participating authorities to suggest that the campaign enables women to come forward in greater numbers to seek support. There is also some evidence that women seeking help are more informed about the nature and the interlinking of differing forms of male violence. In addition Women's Aid and Rape Crisis groups report a massive increase in calls from other agencies, for example social work departments requesting information. There is also initial evidence of increased and sustained interest by the media in issues of violence and a greater acceptance of women's groups such as Women's Aid and Rape Crisis, together with Zero Tolerance campaigners, as 'experts'.

Following the success of the Edinburgh campaign, and a remarkable speech by sexual assault survivor, 'Judy', at the Scottish Conservative Party Conference in May 1993, the Scottish Office developed its own anti-violence initiative. 'Judy', a prominent party activist, put violence against women firmly on the political agenda when she spoke of her ordeal after being attacked by a bogus priest in her Edinburgh home and her horror later when she discovered that her attacker's life sentence had been reduced to six years on appeal. The Scottish Office Crime Prevention Council launched a £300,000 advertising campaign in June 1994, targeted at male offenders, which was launched on television to coincide with World Cup matches. The 40-second commercial with graphic flashback images of the battered face of a woman aimed to highlight the hidden nature of domestic violence and the message that it is a crime.

A poster campaign showed a man's clenched fists with 'LOVE' and 'HATE' tattooed on his knuckles and the question 'Which One Will You Give Her Tonight?' The Scottish Office stated that the campaign was seen as the first stage in a long-term public awareness campaign. However, this campaign has been criticised for its graphic depiction of victims and for its failure to challenge stereotypes.

Zero Tolerance was high risk in its radical approach. The women's unit had expected political and public backlash, especially from men. This was based upon previous experience as well as its challenging nature. Yet the campaign has been characterised by high levels of support. There has been some criticism from politicians from all parties, both men and women, the most serious when the SNP Lord Provost of Edinburgh complained to the *Sunday Times Scotland* that he did not support the 'extreme' campaign, but was powerless to act because 'any word of criticism is seen as male chauvinism'. He later withdrew his comments. There were some angry phone-calls and letters to the local press accusing the campaign of the message that 'all men are rapists'.

There have also been sporadic instances of the defacement of posters. However, these have been wobbles rather than storms. In comparison with the reaction provoked by the work of women's committees in the 1980s, criticism has been surprisingly muted. Support for the Zero Tolerance campaign has been cross-party. For example, in Edinburgh, one of the key supporters was a Conservative woman councillor and former Conservative Group leader.

The campaign was able to tap into parallel debates within women's circles in the Conservative Party around violence against women, in particular erratic sentencing policies. Several Conservative councillors from Edinburgh were involved in the back-stage manoeuvrings which brought 'Judy's' story to the Scottish Conservative Party Conference, using the District Council women's unit briefings and Zero Tolerance statistics to prepare their cases.

The fact that Zero Tolerance was a strong, innovative and well-conducted campaign was no guarantee of success. However, there were several key factors which reduced the possibility of conflict and failure: the relative strength of Scottish initiatives in general and the Edinburgh women's committee in particular; Scottish women's networking; the highly effective political management of the campaign; the presence of sufficient women in the local state; and the social, political and personal salience of the issue of violence.

Women in the machine

The feminist project has always faced the dilemma of how to seize and use power to transform society without sacrificing feminist principles and processes. Feminist values of non-hierarchical, collective and democratic processes are antithetical to the workings of state bureaucracies. However many of the demands of the contemporary women's movement can only be met through the state. The women's movement in Britain, in contrast to the US and Australia, for instance, has been markedly reluctant to engage with the state. This reflects both the New Left anti-state roots of the movement; and also the closed nature of British state bureaucracy. However, the 1980s saw a growing feminist engagement, particularly at local level, in a number of ways: autonomous women's groups, particularly the refuge and rape crisis movements, increasingly relied upon the state to fund their service provision; feminists entered trades union and elective politics; and feminists are present in the local state as professional feminists or 'femocrats', servicing women's committees.

Women's committees and similar initiatives have been a feature of local government since the early 1980s. Two main types of initiative exist: those with the explicit aim of promoting the interests and welfare of women, and those which promote the related issue of equality of opportunity for women and other disadvantaged groups, particularly in terms of employment. The first full standing women's committee and women's unit was in Greater London Council in 1982. It was abolished in 1986, but in its short life distributed £30 million to various projects, almost half of that money for childcare provision. The first Women's Committee in Scotland was set up by Stirling District Council in 1984. By 1995 there were eleven full women's and/or equal opportunities committees and four sub-committee/advisory group structures; 11 Scottish authorities have one or more specialist staff in post. More than half of all British local authorities have now devised policies which fall within the broad remit of equal opportunities; however, a far smaller proportion have specific structures. In 1994 there were 32 full women's/ equal opportunities committees, which means that Scotland, with around 9% of the UK population, has around a third of all such initiatives. As elsewhere in Britain, women's/equal opportunities committees in Scotland have had a turbulent history marked by press campaigns of derision, hostility from other parties, notably the Conservatives, and entrenched resistance to change from politicians within their own ruling parties and from council officers.[12] Few women's committees and units are adequately staffed or resourced, and most have had to struggle in marginalised positions. Several have not survived. In addition the structures have to operate within a deeply macho culture. Many officers appointed to women's initiatives in the early days were 'outsiders' and found themselves floundering in the unfamiliar and unfriendly structures of local authority bureaucracy.

Positive change for women is a possible but by no means certain outcome of feminist interventions in the state, where the objectives and values of feminism can be co-opted and distorted. Presence is not the same as influence, and women's initiatives — or 'municipal feminism' — has sometimes failed to deliver for women's groups and women in the community. This has resulted in a difficult and sometimes painful relationship between insider 'femocrats' and feminists outside the state. However, despite real difficulties, there has been a steady growth of women's and equal opportunities initiatives in Scotland which may be contrasted with the position in England and Wales where development has been more uneven.[13] In Scotland there is cautious optimism, women's committees are seen as having had a limited but marked impact as agents of change and, in the case of Edinburgh, as succeeding in challenging and changing the ethos of the authority.[14] In the rest of Britain, pessimism about their viability has been expressed. Labour MP Margaret Hodge, former leader of the London Borough of Islington, said of women's committees in January 1995, 'They were brave but maybe they were not right'. Similarly Joni Lovenduski and Vicky Randall, whilst noting their importance in creating a new class of professional feminists, comment that there are signs that the immediate potential of women's committees has been exhausted and that they can expect their future to consist of 'straightforward equal opportunities work for local councils and in servicing local women's groups'. They do however acknowledge that the situation in Scotland appears to be different.

This underlines the importance of political context to feminist interventions in the state. The Scottish context has created space for feminists to create and implement initiatives. The networking of feminist groups promoting change for women is a marked feature of the Scottish political landscape. Several key activists in the women's refuge and rape crisis movement are now Labour councillors. In other cases, councillors from all parties have subsequently become involved in anti-violence work or campaigning. Membership tends to overlap, for example, *Engender* the Scottish feminist research and campaigning group, draws members from political parties, trades unions, women's organisations, the women's movement, academia and the public and voluntary sectors. Informal and formal networking between women's groups is facilitated by geographical size, but also by the mobilisation of a wide cross-section of women, partisan and non-partisan, feminist and non-feminist, around the issue of women's representation in the proposed Scottish parliament.[15]

In addition, there is the Edinburgh context. Edinburgh District Council women's committee, which was set up in 1985, is one of several proactive or radical model committees in Scotland, and is commonly recognised as one of its most innovative. It has learned lessons from the GLC, in particular it has become skilled at producing alternative information/publicity about its work to counter media attacks and has maintained good communications with women's groups and community groups. By the time the women's unit launched Zero Tolerance it had developed strategies of popular consultation and had strong, well-rooted links with women in the community. In addition, unlike the experience of some other women's units, especially in the 1980s, it was well-established (although still vulnerable) within the political and organisational structures of the authority; its agenda was seen as largely legitimate and in keeping with corporate policies; and it was staffed by officers experienced both in local government and in campaign work.

Evidence from Scandinavia and elsewhere suggests that once women are found in sufficient numbers, or 'critical mass', within politics they begin to make a difference of style, agenda and promoting positive change for women.[16] The level of women's representation in Scotland at national level is poor compared to other European countries, although it is higher at local government level. In 1995 women were 17% of Regional and Islands councillors and 22% of District councillors. Although they do not generally identify themselves as feminists many are 'pro-equality' and do act as agents or supporters of change. For example, in a recent cross-party survey (the Scottish Women Councillors Study) female politicians showed high levels of awareness of women's groups and women's issues, some 83% had aims which they perceived as relevant to women, and 49% saw themselves as representing women. In 1989 Lieberman reported that the position of Conservative councillors in Scotland could generally be described as one of 'overwhelming hostility to the concept and existence of Women's Committees'.[17] However, evidence from more recent research is mixed. Initial findings from the Scottish Women Councillors Study indicates high levels of support for equal opportunities work among women councillors across party; there is also support, although in some cases highly qualified, for the work of women's committees and other equalities structures, with 53% giving general support, and a further 28% giving support for a limited remit—more usually for equal opportunities work in a women's committee. This would seem to indicate a greater sense of the acceptance of gender/equalities structures as legitimate across parties within local government than has generally been argued.

Work in Scotland suggests that successful agenda setting and effective implementation of equalities initiatives in local authorities need a combination of not only sufficient numbers of senior female politicians but also adequate numbers of senior female officers. Ellen Kelly notes that local authorities where these conditions exist almost invariably also have women's/equal opportunities structures in place and specialist officers in post.[18] All the participating authorities running Zero Tolerance have such structures in place. In addition, they have at least one specialist officer who has liaised through an informal Zero Tolerance officers' network. A majority also have what can be argued to be a threshold, albeit at lower levels than is generally understood, of female councillors (20%). This indicates a more complex picture than the 'critical mass' literature would suggest. Initial findings from Zero Tolerance indicate that women can achieve 'critical mass' at lower levels than is generally predicted where there is a presence of women not only as elected members but also as middle-ranking officers. The case study also suggests that other factors come into play, such as the existence of networks. In addition, where women have less presence (between 13 and 19%), there is evidence that motivated individuals or small groups of women—elected members and officers—have been able to use leverage of various kinds as agents or supporters of change. Similarly, in America, Ellen Boneparth and Emily Soper have argued that the presence of elected women office-holders, whether feminists or not, is one of the factors in the successful promotion of women's issues at local and state level.[19]

Political management

A crucial factor in the success of Zero Tolerance was the skilful political management of the campaign and the construction of durable rafts of legitimacy and consensus. The campaign was legitimised by popular consultation and targeted research. The expertise of specialist women's groups was recognised and they were consulted about the material. In addition, six months was spent pre-launch in lobbying to build up a broad consensus of support for the issue from key political, religious and community groups. The campaign secured advance support, 'sight unseen', from various key groups, including Lothian and Borders Police, all the main churches and, crucially, the local media. The city's evening paper the *Edinburgh Evening News* adopted the issue and ran its own parallel 'Free Us From Fear' campaign. Cross-party support was secured, but again the detailed content of the campaign was not discussed. Apart from the convenor of the Women's Committee, no other politicians saw the material prior to the launch. This was a deliberate strategy by the officers who were clear that they needed to keep the campaign under wraps till then to prevent the radical message being diluted.

Despite the careful building of planks of support whilst retaining control of the agenda, the Zero Tolerance campaign with its uncomfortable message was still a high-risk strategy. However the scale of public support far beyond the expectations of the campaign team, bolstered any 'wobbles' in the maintenance of political consensus. This highlights the salience of the issue for women in particular. Research used by the campaign estimates that two in every five women have been raped or sexually assaulted at some point in their lives. Domestic violence accounts for a quarter of all reported violent crime in Scotland. The issue tapped a well-spring of recognition from women in the community, and also women in the local authority: officers, workers and councillors. In the first few months the unit received hundreds of letters and phone calls.

Similarly there is tentative evidence of an emerging common agenda for women politicians and the women's movement. Possibly the most crucial political support for Zero Tolerance has come from women councillors. Some women councillors, mostly feminist Labour, share the analysis of violence against women. However, political support was broader than that. Others who did not share, and sometimes objected to, the feminist analysis nevertheless gave support. This was given in a number of ways. Councillors worked with officers and with activists within their own parties (in the main Labour) to push the campaign in their areas. In one local authority, resistance to the proposed campaign within the Labour group evaporated when a councillor disclosed her experience of sexual abuse as a child. Several councillors in participating authorities have publicly spoken about their own experience of violence and there is some evidence that male politicians, who were generally sceptical, have changed their minds as a result. Personal testimony has been a characteristic feature of feminist strategy, especially in issues of the body (for instance abortion campaigning). They have also worked to lobby for support amongst male councillors. A number of Labour women interviewed believed that Conservative women in participating authorities had 'kept the men in line' in their party groups. Initial findings indicate that high levels of legitimacy are given to the campaign by women councillors across party. Interviewees were asked whether they thought Zero Tolerance and similar campaigns were a legitimate function of local government, to allow them to express opposition to the campaign without being identified as 'pro-violence'. All but a few agreed that it was indeed the legitimate function.

As noted earlier, the issue of violence against women was put on the social and political agenda by the women's liberation movement in the 1970s and has been kept there through the work of the women's refuge movement, the rape crisis movement and feminist legal campaign groups such as Rights of Women and the Women's Legal Defence Fund. Hague and Malos comment that the government in the 1990s is open in its condemnation of domestic violence in a way that would have been unthinkable when the issue began to enter the public arena in the 1970s, as a result of the activities of the women's movement of the time. However, feminist groups have had less success in promoting their analysis of violence as a male abuse of power and therefore a political, rather than a social welfare, problem.[20]

Feminist groups have been successful, to a large degree, in being recognised by sections of the policy community as expert service providers. However, they have not succeeded in securing a national government strategy on violence and adequate funding for refuge spaces. There is a built-in shortfall in funding to women's aid and rape crisis groups at both national and local government level which has siphoned off much of their energy into fund-raising and keeping services afloat.

Conclusions: Zero Tolerance pulls it off

Evidence from the case study suggests that feminists may be gaining and maintaining leverage from their intervention in the state through women's committees and women's units. It emphasises the importance of maintenance of such spaces and structures within the state. The Zero Tolerance campaign reflects the shared values of feminists within the state and the women's movement. The definition of the issues by the various groups involved was shared by the women with power—the femocrats—within the policy community. It was not given to the politicians or senior managers for definition: the existence of a full-time campaigns officer in the women's unit meant that, in this instance, the policy community was the women's unit and women's movement groups were 'insiders'. This was in marked contrast to the experience of women's groups in the run-up to the Scottish Office campaign where, although they were included in the policy process, they were unable to shape the agenda. Indeed, the Scottish Office was able to flag their involvement in the working party as evidence of cooperation, despite their substantive reservations about that campaign.

The Zero Tolerance Campaign also took an aspect of the work of women's groups which is least understood, especially by welfare professionals—that of empowerment. It was a 'no bruises' campaign which showed positive images of women and children as survivors. Despite increased workloads and as yet little pay-off in the shape of increased resources, women's groups have taken a long-term view that the campaign will provide them with leverage to press for adequate funding and has shifted the focus of public perception about the issue from one of social welfare to one of political concern.

The case study supports the view that there has been a gradual convergence between the agenda of women's movement activists and the agenda of women working in local authorities as elected members and as officers. It provides evidence that women's committees which are adequately supported, which are seen as legitimate and which have developed 'insider' strategies, can act as proactive agents of feminist change. There is evidence that the presence of women in politics and in middle and senior positions in local government, and their shared concerns as women, has resulted in an emerging common agenda. Women councillors themselves are becoming increasingly convinced that their presence makes a difference in terms of the promotion of women's interests.

The evaluation exercises show that there is a gender gap with men, especially older men who are less enthusiastic about the campaign. Many, including politicians and officers feel threatened by the messages of Zero Tolerance. However, backlash has been minimised by a range of factors: political management of the campaign; and the construction of rafts of supports by women's officers and politicians using a range of devices from securing prior political and media support to the use of personal testimony. The high levels of public support, and the changed social and political context in which violence against women is discussed, makes it difficult for male politicians and other opinion-formers to oppose campaigns without appearing 'pro violence'. In addition, the kudos of a successful campaign has served to dampen potential sources of opposition in participating authorities. Some women identify the desire of males to be associated with a successful campaign as a lever for getting it approved within their ruling groups.

Although not all women agree with the feminist analysis of violence as an abuse of power, many from all backgrounds have experience or personal knowledge of violence. The case study suggests that violence is an issue around which women, political and non-political, feminist and non feminist can work together. It also suggests an emerging 'women's politics', where women as women are successfully intervening in the local state and making a difference.

---

1   For the literature on recruitment see P. Norris and J. Lovenduski, *Political Recruitment: Gender, Race and Class in the British Parliament* (Cambridge University Press, 1995) and J. Lovenduski and P. Norris (eds), *Gender and Party Politics* (Sage, 1993).

2 For feminist theories of the state see S. Franzway, D. Court and R. Connell, *Staking a Claim: Feminism, Bureaucracy and the State* (Polity Press, 1989); for Britain, see S. Halford, 'Feminist Change in a Patriarchal Organisation: The Experience of Women's Initiatives in Local Government and Implications for Feminist Perspectives on State Institutions' in M. Savage and A. Witz (eds), *Gender and Bureaucracy* (Blackwell, 1992); for the differences between Australia and Britain see S. Watson, 'Femocratic Feminisms', ibid; for comparison of US, Britain and Sweden see J. Gelb, 'Feminism and Political Action', in R. J. Dalton and M. Kuechler (eds), *Challenging the Political Order* (Polity Press, 1990).

3 P. Seyd, *The Rise and Fall of the Labour Left* (Macmillan, 1987); H. Wainwright; *Labour: A Tale of Two Parties* (The Hogarth Press, 1987); S. Rowbotham, et al, *Beyond the Fragments* (Merlin Press, 1979).

4 See J. Outshoorn, 'Is This What We Wanted? Positive Action as Issue Peversion' in E. Meehan and S. Sevenhuijsen (eds), *Equality Politics and Gender* (Sage, 1991); J. Lovenduski and V. Randall, *Contemporary Feminist Politics: Women and Power in Britain* (Oxford University Press, 1993); G. Stedward, 'Entry into the System: A Case Study of Women in Scotland' in J. Richardson and G. Jordan (eds), *Government and Pressure Groups in Britain* (Clarendon Press, 1987); E. Boneparth and E. Soper (eds), *Women, Policy and Power: Toward the Year 2000* (Pergamon, 1988).

5 M. McWilliams and J. McKiernan, *Bringing it Out in the Open: Domestic Violence in Northern Ireland* (HMSO, 1993).

6 For campaigns in the 19th Century see L. Smith, *Domestic Violence* (Home Office Research Study, 107, HMSO, 1989).

7 For cultural identities see Lindsay Paterson, 'Editorial: Scottish', *Scottish Affairs 1993/4*.

8 C. Burness, in *Parliamentary Brief*, March 1995.

9 E. Breitenbach, 'Sisters Are Doing It For Themselves: The Womens Movement in Scotland' in A. Brown and R. Parry (eds) *The Scottish Government Yearbook 1990*(The Unit for the Study of Government in Scotland, University of Edinburgh).

10 L. Riddoch 'Zero Tolerance: The Second Wave' in *Harpies and Quines*, no. 12 March 1994.

11 F. Mackay, *The Case of Zero Tolerance: Women's Politics in Action?* (Waverley Papers, Department of Politics, University of Edinburgh, 1995).

12 For an account of the 'Loony Left' media campaigns on the GLC and other women's committees, and more general discussion of the difficulties of women's initiatives within the bureaucratic structures of the local state see, for example: S. Goss, 'Women's initiatives in Local Government' in M. Boddy and C. Fudge (eds) *Local Socialism?* (Macmillan, 1984); S. Halford 'Women's initiatives in Local Government', *Policy and Politics*, 1988/4.

13 J. Lovenduski and V. Randall, op.cit.

14 E. Breitenbach, *Quality Through Equality* (Equal Opportunities Commission, Scotland, 1995).

15 For a detailed discussion of the mobilisation of women around the issue of women's representation in the Scottish parliament, see A. Brown, op.cit.

16 D. Dahlerup, 'From a Small to a Large Minority: Women in Scandinavian Politics, *Scandinavian Political Studies*, vol. 11, no. 4, 1988. See also E. Haavio-Mannila et al, *Unfinished Democracy: Women in Nordic Politics* (Pergammon Press, 1985).

17 S. Lieberman, 'Women's Committees in Scotland' in A. Brown and D. McCrone (eds). *The Scottish Government Yearbook 1989*.

18 Kelly, op.cit.

19 Boneparth and Soper, op.cit, p. 14.

20 Gill Hague and Ellen Malos, 'Domestic violence, social policy and housing', *Critical Social Policy*, Winter 1994/95, p. 113. For the refuge movement and groupings around violence more generally see Lovenduski and Randall, op.cit., ch. 9.

Women, the European Union and Britain

BY ELIZABETH MEEHAN AND EVELYN COLLINS

MOST literature on the sex equality policies of the European Community (EC)[1] is critical on two main grounds. First, the Commission has little to do with substantive equality but is restricted to providing a legal and regulatory framework within limits determined by the Council of Ministers.[2] Secondly, that framework is directed at men and women as workers, not sex equality in society at large.[3] Such accounts often concede, however, that the existence of Community sex equality policies has profoundly benefited the women of some countries; usually it is Ireland and Greece that are cited but the EC has also had a significant impact upon British women's rights at work and in social security schemes. These improvements often arise from the use made by the Equal Opportunities Commissions of Northern Ireland (EOCNI)[4] and Great Britain (EOCGB) of the European Court of Justice (ECJ), in the context of a domestic political climate that is inhospitable to reform. In making our argument about improvements in the legal status of women in Britain, we do so without ignoring the criticisms of EC policies; that is, we also highlight the difficulties in securing material equality by means which pay inadequate attention to the different social situations of women and men. Part 2 outlines the main legal developments and their underlying legal concepts. Since the scope of rights, as they have developed through the interplay between UK courts and the ECJ, has been covered elsewhere,[5] we concentrate on material aspects of sex (in)equality where there has been a significant EC influence, then consider EC influence on the enforcement of rights and the impact of legislation, leading to our conclusion which stresses the importance of a pluralist political realm for the realisation of both legal and social equality.

Legal developments and the underlying concepts

The main legal developments in respect of British women's rights in employment are the Sex Discrimination Act 1975 and its amendments[6] and the Equal Pay Act 1970 and its amendments.[7] The former applies the principle of equal treatment to non-contractual employment matters, such as recruitment, promotion, training and working conditions (and, in addition, to education and the provision of housing, goods, facilities and services). Direct and indirect discrimination on grounds of sex are prohibited and, in the employment aspects only of the legislation, direct and indirect discrimination on grounds of marital status are also unlawful. Victimization, too, is prohibited. The Act applies equally to women and men, although it is aimed primarily at providing rights for women, who were considered 'more likely to be the victims of unfair treatment on grounds of sex'.[8] The Equal Pay Act applies to contractual terms and conditions, including pay.

The sex discrimination legislation brought into being the EOCGB and EOCNI which were charged with working towards the elimination of discrimination, promoting equality of opportunity generally between men and women, keeping under review the working of the Equal Pay and Sex Discrimination Act and, when thought necessary by the Commissions themselves or the Secretary of State, submitting to the Secretary of State proposals for amendment to the legislation.

In addition to domestic legislation, the EC has played a critical role in shaping the development of the nature and standards of rights available in the United Kingdom. It has done so through its substantive law and the jurisprudence of the ECJ. Article 119 of the Treaty of Rome 1957 required member states to implement the principle of equal pay for equal work and the Equal Pay Directive of 1975 expanded this by obliging member states to bring about equal pay for work of equal value;[9] that is, the standard of the International Labour Organisation. In 1976, the Equal Treatment Directive was adopted, guaranteeing the principle of equal treatment in access to employment, vocational training, promotion, and working conditions. In this Directive, equal treatment entails the absence of direct or indirect discrimination on grounds of sex and in connection with marital or family status.

Three other equality directives have also been adopted by the Council of the EC: in 1979, one concerning the progressive implementation of the principle of equal treatment in statutory social security schemes; in 1986, one on the implementation of the principle of equal treatment in occupational social security schemes; and, again in 1986, one about equal treatment for women and men in self-employed occupations including agriculture. Also relevant to women's rights but agreed to under the health and safety framework, the Council adopted in 1992 a Directive about the protection of pregnant women from exposure to hazardous substances at work and about their rights of leave and return to work during and after pregnancy. In addition, there are exhortatory Community policies which seek to promote equality of opportunity; for example, recommendations and resolutions on such issues as sexual harassment, child care, positive action, and funds for vocational (re-) training under the auspices of NOW (New Opportunities for Women) and the European Social Fund.

These developments have taken place in a context where there is considerable legal and political controversy over the meanings of discrimination and the proper scope of action against it.[10] One dominant approach defends the view that the proper aim of the law is to establish fair processes or the elimination of harmful consequences of decisions based on prejudice. This concentrates on securing fairness for individuals by removing arbitrary obstacles which lead to less favourable treatment of one person compared to another. Such an approach presupposes that people start out as equals, with the same freedom to make choices about their destinies, or would be so if arbitrary barriers were removed. Thus it requires the equal treatment of women and men in similar situations and expects that this will bring about similar chances of success.

A second approach is more concerned with the effect of decisions and practices on groups. Here, it is thought that the proper aim of the law is to ensure an improvement in the social and economic position of disadvantaged groups, or a redistribution of benefits and opportunities from advantaged groups to disadvantaged ones. The presupposition of this approach is the outcomes, even of processes that are individually fair, will be affected by differences between groups in terms of their social and historical circumstances. Although the two approaches can clash in particular instances, the view that distributive justice is a legitimate reason for intervention also has liberal origins. And, like the first approach, the second entails comparisons between women and men as individuals, as well as members of groups.

The sex discrimination legislation of the 1970s combines elements of both these liberal approaches. The individual approach may be seen in the provisions on direct discrimination and equal pay for like work, which are premised on comparing directly the treatment of similarly situated women and men. The distributive justice approach informs provisions relating to indirect discrimination, positive action (a voluntary provision) and, to an extent, equal pay for work of equal value, all of which allow for the possibility of taking into account the consequences of group membership. It has been argued that EC concepts of equality are more strongly rooted than those of the UK in the idea of distributive justice than in the principle of equal treatment.[11]

Feminist critiques of liberal legal and political theory, even the group-oriented version, are well-known. For our purposes, it is necessary to note their focus on two issues: first, the implicit assumption that the male model of individual behaviour is the normal or 'natural' one; and, second, the reality that women are seldom in similar circumstances to men because of their historical experience, reproductive capacity, the domestic division of labour and comparable forms of occupational segregation. Particular criticism has been made of the thoughtlessness of liberal theory about biological differences and the blindness of its exponents to the implications of how they think about the public/private division. The limitations of liberal legal tools in dismantling institutionalized discrimination have been compounded by a sometimes unsympathetic judiciary, or, at least, one which adapts only slowly to new legal norms.[12]

Material areas where there has been an EC impact

Changes connected with membership of the EC have not just occurred at the level of legal developments. They can be seen in two material areas of everyday life: first, matters relating to the economic circumstances of women; and, second, questions of reproduction, sexuality and stereotypical assumptions about female labour.

ECONOMIC CIRCUMSTANCES.   Here, the effects of the EC are evident mainly in retirement, pay and pensions and, to some extent, in income taxation.

In the Sex Discrimination Act 1975, there was an exception for provisions relating to death and retirement and subsequent domestic case law confirmed that different normal retirement ages for men and women were excluded from the Act. The ECJ, however, ruled that the Equal Treatment Directive prohibited this exception.[13] While different statutory pensionable ages could be maintained, the connection between these and different retirement ages was contingent, not necessary. Being made by an employer to retire was a form of dismissal and dismissal was covered by the Directive.

Ms Marshall (the protagonist in the lead case in this area) and, at the time, other women in satisfying occupations welcomed the ruling as an increase in opportunities. However, reflecting the fact that many people—neither women nor men—do not enjoy fulfilling work, public opinion indicated a greater preference for both sexes to be able to retire when they wished between the ages of 60 and 65 than for equality at the upper age. The British government amended the law to ensure equal treatment for women and men on retirement age in the public and private sectors, including the right for women to continue working until the age of 65. It also made consequential alterations to provisions for voluntary redundancy and early retirement schemes.

The related question of state and occupational pensions has proved complicated and is not yet fully resolved. Part of the problem stems from whether an occupational pension is part of pay (that is, subject to the equal treatment principle of Article 119) or whether, if a 'contracted-out scheme', it is a substitute for the statutory pension (thus exempt, as allowed in the Directives, from equal treatment requirements). And part of the problem stems from the practical effect on occupational pensions of hitherto different pensionable ages for men and women under the state scheme.

With regard to the first part of the problem, the ECJ ruled in 1990 that contracted-out pension schemes are part of pay and, like other occupational schemes, covered by Article 119 on equal pay. Such claims have often arisen when men have sought access to an occupational pension at the same (younger) age as women—a difference based on the convention of matching occupational pensionable ages with those of the statutory scheme. The 1990 decision raised a whole series of other related questions on pensions—such as its retrospective effect; the use of actuarial assumptions; the raising of the female pensionable age to that of men; and access to occupational pension schemes by part-time workers. These questions have been addressed by the ECJ in a number of decisions issued in 1994[14] which, while providing clarity on some issues and confirming rights for part-time workers, have raised further concerns.

The fear that women would be made worse off has been confirmed by the government's recent decision (heralded at the 1992 General Election) to equalise the state pensionable age at the age of 65, not 60— on the ground that 'the 60 option' would cost the country £7b. According to the EOCGB[15] this will cost every woman now under the age of 30, £15,000. Contrary to the governments' view, the Trades Union Congress calculates that equalising upwards is not cheaper than equalising downwards—because subsequent retirements at 60 would make way for the unemployed, many of whom have children, and remove them from other, expensive benefit rolls.

The income taxation system was also excluded from the scope of British legislation, though some changes to bring about more privacy for married women were introduced in 1990. In addition to being affected by vociferous domestic criticism of the previous rules, the government may have been influenced by the EC. Although member states retain competence over taxation, the European Commission has taken an interest in how taxation rules affect women. In 1984, it presented a Memorandum on this subject to the Council of Ministers. This recommended a system of totally independent taxation for all and at least the option of independent taxation for married couples. Though the British reforms fell short of completely independent taxation, the changes were at least partially positive and the reported possible threat to them is regrettable.[16]

REPRODUCTION, SEXUALITY AND STEREOTYPES. The three main areas of EC influence in this field are pregnancy and maternity rights, sexual harassment and protective legislation.

Pregnancy discrimination and maternity rights form one of the most difficult issues under British law. Some statutory rights for pregnant workers—such as protection against unfair dismissal, maternity leave and maternity pay, time off for ante-natal care, and the right to return to work—are protected by an exception in the Sex Discrimination Act 1975. The Equal Treatment Directive also contains an exception from the principle of equal treatment in respect of pregnancy and maternity.

However, the 'equal treatment' basis of sex discrimination law has caused difficulties in the courts. At first, tribunals in Great Britain held that, since a man could not become pregnant and, therefore, that there was no possibility of comparison, the dismissal of a pregnant woman worker could not amount to direct discrimination. This approach was superseded by one which looked to the possibility of pregnancy being compared with 'analogous circumstances', such as sickness, experienced by men.[17] While an improvement on earlier rulings, this approach was still inappropriate—since pregnancy is not an illness and it is unhelpful, in terms of women's access to the labour market, for it to be considered as such.

The Northern Irish tribunals adopted an approach similar to that which was to come in the European Court. One NI tribunal held that the correct approach was to compare 'mothers-to-be' with 'fathers-to-be' and another that discrimination against motherhood is the same as sex discrimination. The matter was clarified in 1990 in the ECJ in two cases which established that it is directly discriminatory for an employer to refuse to hire or to dismiss pregnant women, though not necessarily so to dismiss a woman because of extended sick leave (even if the illness is related to pregnancy)—if men are dismissed in situations of comparable periods of sick leave.[18]

In 1992, the Council adopted Directive 92/85/EEC, referred to earlier, on the protection of pregnant women workers. It provides for 14 weeks' continuous maternity leave and the maintenance of contractual rights, other than pay, during this time. Payment during this period must be at least equivalent to what would have been received by someone on sick leave, though it is permitted to make this dependent upon employment for the previous twelve months. Although the Directive is important because it explicitly protects women against dismissal, it received only a lukewarm welcome from national equality agencies—since its provisions were considerably weakened as a result of controversies during its adoption as a health and safety issue requiring a majority vote rather than an employment measure requiring unanimity. The way it is being implemented in the United Kingdom is likely to confuse further an already confused situation which should have been resolved by the Directive.[19]

A second issue in this area where there has been EC intervention is that of sexual harassment. As the problem of unwanted sexual attention at work began to be recognised, some efforts were made to deal with it through general employment law. In the 1980s, it began to be addressed as an issue of sex discrimination. In 1983, the Trades Union Congress[20] defined it in terms of unequal power relations between men and women in the workplace and a number of cases began to surface. National courts accepted that a degrading and uncomfortable work environment caused by sexual harassment could constitute a detriment under the Sex Discrimination Act.

The growing number of sexual harassment cases has been accompanied by significant action at the EC level. A European-wide study and extensive lobbying for a Directive have led to statements by the Commission and Council that the Equal Treatment Directive already outlaws sexual harassment in certain circumstances. A Council

Resolution[21] stated that conduct of a sexual nature was 'an intolerable violation of the dignity of workers'. Such conduct was to be regarded as unacceptable if it was unwanted or offensive and adversely affected a person's access to employment, training or dismissal and/or if it created a hostile, intimidating or uncomfortable working environment. This has been followed-up with a Commission Recommendation and Code of Practice about the appropriate steps to be taken. There appears to be a growing reliance on the Recommendation and Code of Practice in national tribunals. This provides guidance on good practice, though the precise legal status of the Code of Practice has still to be clarified.

Thirdly in this area is the question of protective legislation. In 1975, the Sex Discrimination Act left intact, as an exception to the principle of equal treatment, laws which excluded women from certain types of work or patterns of work. This was controversial at the time, some people believing their repeal would lead to exploitation and others that outdated laws gave employers an alibi for excluding women from work that commanded higher salaries or wages. The Equal Treatment Directive of 1976 obliged member states to review all protective measures and make changes in situations where 'the concern for protection which originally inspired them is no longer well founded'.

In carrying out the review on behalf of the government, the EOCGB accepted the argument that legislation barring women from working at night was being used as a pretext for denying sex equality and higher earnings. Its 1979 recommendation that these regulations be abolished was severely criticised but its view was corroborated in a European Commission report of 1987 that many provisions still in place across the Community had a negative influence on women's employment prospects.[22] Since then, some British restrictions have been abolished outright; for example, the ban on the employment of women in mines and on cleaning machinery. Secondly, other protective measures have to give way to the principle of equal treatment except where protection relates to pregnancy, maternity and risks specially affecting women — or where the Secretary of State uses his or her power to modify the scope of the override.

The override is most likely to be used where there is a reproductive or foetal risk. Yet such risks do not affect only women and men ought to be protected against them too, as the European Commission pointed out in its 1987 Communication. Focusing on the risks transmitted through women could lead to a continuation of 'blanket bans' on female employment, without necessarily securing the objective of protecting reproduction and foetuses.

EC influence on enforcement, remedies and voluntary compliance

The EC has affected the enforcement of equality legislation both for individuals and at the level of general policy, both of which provide another avenue for the clarification of rights in an inhospitable legislative climate.

Notably, infringement proceedings by the Commission alleging inadequate compliance have caused amendments to British laws. The powers of the two Commissions to assist individuals have also had general consequences, particularly in their financial support for complaints which involve strategic questions about the application of the law. Such cases often go on up through the legal system and may involve requests to the ECJ for a preliminary ruling on the meaning of EC law and its relevance to the case in hand. Because of the precedent principle, these interpretations are relevant to subsequent cases.

Nevertheless, the precedent principle cannot be expected to get at generally discriminatory practices and structures and, for this reason, the Commissions were given the power of conducting formal investigations. For various reasons, the use of this power proved problematic and the Commissions have turned latterly to judicial review of related legislation. In doing so, they were able to make use of the European context. For example, in seeking review of the Employment Protection (Consolidation) Act, which excluded claims for unfair dismissal or redundancy pay from people who worked fewer than 16 hours a week, they were able to refer to the ECJ's ruling that treating part-timers differently for the purpose of sickness schemes amounted to indirect discrimination.[23]

The remedies available to a successful claimant in a sex discrimination case can include a declaration of the rights of the parties, compensation and damages. In equal pay cases, there is no absolute upper limit but back-pay is restricted to a period of up to two years prior to the date on which proceedings were implemented. In the former case, the low upper limit in the United Kingdom was challenged successfully in the ECJ. Further action was taken by Ms Marshall against Southampton Health Authority. At the time of the initial domestic hearing, the upper limit was £6,250. As a result of the referral of her case to the ECJ, there is now no upper limit of compensation which can be awarded in sex discrimination cases. The consequences are perhaps best known to the public because of recent cases involving the Ministry of Defence. Apparently, the Ministry had chosen to ignore the impact of various European rulings when it continued to summarily dismiss female personnel on their becoming pregnant. In recent months, this has resulted some very large settlements in cases supported by the EOCGB.[24]

Voluntary compliance through the use of 'positive action' is another method of reducing discrimination and promoting equality—and is encouraged by a Recommendation from the European Commission. There has been a growth in the number of organisations developing equal opportunities programmes and in the 'professionalization' of equal opportunities officers. These programmes are sometimes criticised for internal defects[25] and measures which could give them 'teeth', such as 'contract compliance'—once employed by the now defunct Greater London Council—have been outlawed (in terms of sex equality issues) by the Local Government Act of 1988. However, in Northern Ireland, women's employment in major organisations is monitored (as is required by law in legislation outlawing religious discrimination) and Queen's University, for example, has an equal opportunities programme which is more rigorous, in terms of scope and content, than that which pertains in universities in Great Britain.

Impact of the legislation

It is difficult to establish causal connections between legal reform and material change. There is a perennial debate about whether the law promotes or follows change which has taken place because of wider socio-economic factors. Perhaps it is possible, at most, only to establish correlations, or their absence, between the existence of legal rights and the scope of opportunities in the labour market. It is easy to identify evidence on the domestic front for thinking that the legislation has had only a small impact; it is more difficult to say the same about the EC.

In the United Kingdom, women's pay as a ratio of men's has remained at about 75% since the late 1970s (having risen initially from 50 or 60%); the number of equal pay applications to industrial tribunals has dropped, reflecting the likelihood that 'like work' provisions have outlived their usefulness; various factors have caused a low take-up of the alternative—'equal value'; and that, even if 'equal value' steps are taken, differentials continue to exist because of differences in productivity systems and the like—or because, perhaps, of defective job evaluation schemes.

One test of the effectiveness of the Sex Discrimination Act would have been a decrease in occupational segregation; that is, if it had become normal to find a more equal proportion of both sexes working in occupations or at levels of seniority where one sex had predominated previously, it could have been inferred that employers had made their recruitment or promotion practices more open. But the statistics show only a few signs that the labour market may be becoming more undifferentiated by sex. At the same time, the legal tool of indirect discrimination—a potentially powerful lever against systemic patterns of inequality because of its focus on the proportions of men and women who may or may not be able to comply with conditions of employment—has not been used purposively by the courts. Instead, it has become bogged-down in technicalities and procedural issues.

Moreover, UK governments have been ungenerous in the way in which they comply with new requirements stemming from the EC; for example, responding slowly to some key rulings (or ignoring them until forced to do otherwise), being cautious about income taxation, making it more difficult to claim disability allowances, fighting the idea of a

Directive for pregnant women workers, and equalising retirement and pensionable ages upwards instead of downwards.

The evidence of the EC's impact is more ambiguous. The positive interpretation by Edwards and MacKie of the EC conception of equality could be reinforced by reference to ECJ definitions of key aspects of the issue; for example, its narrowing of exceptions, the broadening of the concept of pay, and retirement construed as dismissal. Other support could be found in European Commission views about sexual harassment, income taxation, positive action and so on.

On the other hand, others could argue that European policies embody a 'fiction' of sex equality—along the lines of Pateman's accounts of domestic polities.[26] They could cite the watering-down of policies to meet the willingness of the slowest partners, or the thoughtless adoption of concepts such as 'breadwinner', which, while eliminating direct discrimination, may reinforce indirect discrimination. Another illustration might be found in the statements of the ECJ that the two Directives on social security were intended to address only the situations of men and women as workers and not the general question of sex equality; and that, even so, this objective might be subordinated to others such as the relief of poverty.[27]

Also ambiguous is the special significance the Court initially attached to the bonding between mother and child in cases where it permitted the continuation of sex differences in rules about leave for adopting parents and allowances for single mothers,[28] which could be taken to indicate its traditionalism. Yet, in a further twist to possible analyses, most of the ECJ's rulings on pregnancy could be construed, not as reinforcing outdated values, but as corroborating the 'difference feminist' position that situations specific to women should have a normal place in public policy.

The fact that it is possible to have competing views argued out in more arenas than have been available in the past contributes to our conclusion—which sees some hope in the capacity of the EC to put a brake on the marginalisation of equality issues in the United Kingdom.

Conclusion—the promise of pluralism

The United Kingdom was not a member of the EC when it introduced its Equal Pay Act and the possibility of the Sex Discrimination Act existed before membership was confirmed. Thus it could be said that the United Kingdom was a pioneer in this field. On the other hand, there had been warnings during earlier applications for membership that the UK would fail the test of Article 119 (equal pay for equal work) and that this would matter. Also, by the time of discussion of a potential sex discrimination law, EC membership was certain and it was known that the EC was contemplating something like the eventual Equal Treatment Directive. So, conversely, it could be argued that it was Community membership that forced the United Kingdom to be a pioneer. Moreover, as noted throughout this paper, the government has experienced infringement proceedings in the ECJ and many of the path-breaking individual cases in the Court have arisen from allegations by British women that domestic policy did not conform with European requirements.

It has, perhaps, not been a British tradition to use litigation to enforce either individual rights or collective public policies. At a general level, many advocates of constitutional reform in the United Kingdom applaud the fact that at least in certain respects Community membership gives British citizens a kind of written constitution for the first time for over three hundred years. More particularly, in the case of the right to sex equality, it must be noted that the introduction of equal pay and anti-discrimination legislation was almost immediately followed by the advent of a series of Conservative governments noted for their deregulatory philosophy. The sea change away from mixed economies and welfare states has occurred all over Europe but in more muted forms than in the United Kingdom. In an era in which British governments have tried to minimise rights and the roles of regulatory and collective bodies, resort to European law has provided virtually the only enforceable ways of securing improvements to and filling lacunae in domestic legislation. Though further European developments on sex equality, including many of those discussed in the EC's Green and White Papers on Social Policy,[29] may take place under the auspices of the Social Agreement from which the British government has secured exemption, European standards can still be of benefit to women in Britain. This is because the platform of rights discussed in this article predates the Maastricht Treaty and continues to be applicable in the United Kingdom. One example of the continuing relevance of existing EC legislation is the current campaign to use it to mitigate the domestic decision to abolish wage councils, the absence of which is thought to be particularly damaging to low-paid women.[30]

At a more general level, it can be argued that politics is not only about competition over the distribution of material resources but is also a conflict over meanings and about the distribution of opportunities for people and groups to be able to voice their interests and for their voices to be taken seriously. Siim and Hart[31] have shown that women can succeed in inscribing their meanings into policy and practice in Scandinavia and the United States. The EC may be an arena where British and other women can do this too.

For reasons which, admittedly, are not motivated by the idea of sexual justice, European institutions are hospitable to women lobbying for their definitions of what they think they need. The Commission is more open than many national civil services and is also accessible through its numerous advisory and monitoring groups and its support for networks and groups. The extensive consultation of 1993–94 initiated by the Green Paper on Social Policy is an example of the opportunities it provides. The European Parliament is also more serious about women's rights than most national parliaments. Without wishing to overstate the significance of European policies and practices, it is clear that their existence has prevented the remarginalisation of sex equality from the political agenda in the United Kingdom. And the existence of Community institutions and transnational networks means that women have allies elsewhere and other arenas in which to stake claims that are thwarted at home.

1 Strictly speaking it is the EC, not the EU, that is responsible for sex equality; the EU includes common (EC) institutions and policies and those which are intergovernmental in character.
2 S. Mazey, 'The Development of EC Equal Opportunities Policies: Bureaucratic Expansion on Behalf of Women', *Public Administration*, forthcoming.
3 A range of the literature is reviewed in E. Meehan, 'European Community Policy on Sex Equality: A Bibliographic Essay', *Women's Studies International Forum*, 15(1), 1992. Discussions are going on in the Commission and European Parliament about whether the Intergovernmental Conference of 1996 could introduce the possibility of a European constitution which would entrench the general right of sex equality.
4 Great Britain and Northern Ireland are components of a single member state, the United Kingdom, and cases referred to the ECJ from NI in this volume are relevant to women in GB and throughout the EU.
5 E. Collins and E. Meehan, 'Women's Rights in Employment and Related Areas' in C. McCrudden and G. Chambers (eds), *Individual Rights and the Law in Britain* (Clarendon Press/Law Society, 1994). It should be noted that the SDA was amended to narrow exceptions and the EPA was amended to include 'equal value', as a result of infringement proceedings brought by the Commission against the government in the ECJ. Other ECJ rulings have, for example, broadened the definition of earnings, made retirement subject to discrimination law, and enabled married women to be eligible for the Invalid Care Allowance. The connection between retirement and pensions is complicated and dealt with in the main text (Part 3).
6 Amendments to legislation in GB include the Sex Discrimination Act 1986, the Sex Discrimination (Amendment) Order 1988 (SI 1988, No. 249), and the Employment Act 1989. In NI the comparable legislation is the Sex Discrimination (Northern Ireland) Order 1976, the Sex Discrimination (Amendment) Order 1987, the Sex Discrimination (Amendment) (Northern Ireland) Order 1988 and the Employment Act 1989.
7 Amended in GB by the Equal Pay (Amendment) Regulations 1983; Industrial Tribunal Regulations 1983, SI 1983/1794. Amended in NI by the Equal Pay (Amendment) Regulations (Northern Ireland) 1984.
8 *Equality for Women* (Cmnd. 5724, HMSO, 1974), para. 1.
9 The official, numerical references to measures mentioned in this paragraph and the next are as follows: Equal pay, 75/117/EEC.10.2.75; ILO Convention 100 of 1951, entering into force on 23.5.53; Equal treatment, 76/207/EEC, 9.2.76; Equal treatment in statutory social security, 79/EEC, 19.12.78; Equal treatment in occupational social security, 86/378/EEC, 12.8.86; Equal treatment in self-employed occupations, including agriculture, 86/613/EEC, 11.12.86; Protection of pregnant women workers, 92/85/EEC, 19.10.92.
10 The main sources for these debates are referred to in E. Collins and E. Meehan, 'Women's Rights in Employment and Related Areas' in C. McCrudden and G. Chambers (eds), *Individual Rights and the Law in Britain* (Clarendon Press/Law Society, 1994).
11 J. Edwards and L. McKie, 'Equal Opportunities and Public Policy: An Agenda for Change', *Public Policy and Administration,* 8(2) 54–67, 1993.
12 Major critiques of liberal theory include: C. Pateman, *The Sexual Contract* Basil Blackwell/Polity Press, 1988) and C. Pateman, *The Disorder of Women* Basil Blackwell/Polity Press, 1989); C. Bacchi, 'Pregnancy, the Law and the Meaning of Equality' in E. Meehan and S. Sevenhuijsen (eds), *Equality Politics and Gender* (Sage, 1991); S. Sevenhuijsen, 'Justice and Moral Reasoning and the Politics of Child Custody' in E. Meehan, and S. Sevenhuijsen (eds) *Equality Politics and Gender* (Sage, 1991). The point about the judiciary is made by P. Byrne and J. Lovenduski, 'Sex Equality and the Law in Britain', *British Journal of Law and Society*, No. 2, 1978.
13 *Marshall* v. *Southampton and South West Hampshire Health Authority,* Case No. 152/84 [1986] QB

401; [1986] IRLR 140 (ECJ) and *Beets-Proper* v. *F van Lanschott Bankiers NV,* Case No. 262/84 [1097 2 CMLR] 616.

14 The ruling that occupational pensions are subject to the law on equal pay was: *Barber* v. *Guardian Royal Exchange Assurance Group,* Case No. 262/88 [1990] IRLR 240 (ECJ). The subsequent, relevant British cases include: *Neath* v. *Hugh Steeper Ltd* [1994] IRLR 91 ECJ; *Coloroll Pension Trustees Ltd.* v. *Russell and others* [1994] IRLR 586 ECJ; *Smith and others* v. *Avdel Systems Ltd* [1994] IRLR 602 ECJ.

15 Equal Opportunities Commission (GB), *What Price Equality?* 1994.

16 European Commission, *Memorandum to Council on Taxation and Equal Treatment for Men and Women,* COM (84) 695 Final, 14 December 1984. It was reported in the *Independent* on 12.7.95 that, in view of its beliefs about family breakdown, the government was considering a paper about the retraction of these reforms.

17 The first cases were: *Reaney* v. *Kanda Jean Products* [1978] IRLR 427; *Turley* v. *Alders Dept. Stores Ltd* [1980] ICR 66 (EAT). The improvement came in *Hayes* v. *Malleable Working Men's Club* [1985] ICR 703. The case was heard by the EAT with *Maughan* v. *NE London Magistrates Court Committee* which, when reheard by the IT, resulted in a finding that dismissal for pregnancy was contrary to the SDA 1975.

18 *Donley* v. *Gallaher,* Case No. 66/86 SD. Decision 6.11.87; *McQuade* v. *Dabering,* DCLD 1, Case No. 427/89 SD. Decision 31.8.89. *Dekker* v. *Stichting Vormingscentrum voor Jonge Volwassen (VJV-Centrum) Plus,* Case No. 177/88 [1991] IRLR 27 (ECJ); *Hertz* v. *Aldi Marked K/S,* Case No. 179/88 [1991] IRLR 31 (ECJ). See also *Webb* v. *EMO Air Cargo UK Ltd* [1994] IRLR 482—ECJ, which reaffirmed that dismissal of a woman because of her pregnancy constituted direct sex discrimination. The ECJ also confirmed that financial consequences for the firm could not be considered a justification for direct sex discrimination.

19 The most public controversy was UK opposition to the legal basis on which the Directive was brought forward—that is, on the basis of health and safety (where majority decisions could be taken) instead of workers' rights (requiring unanimity). While it was accepted that part of the Directive, on exposure to dangerous hazards, etc., was a legitimate health and safety concern, it was thought that bringing all aspects together was a means of circumventing the British 'veto'. There were also general disagreements about the period of leave and level of entitlement to pay. For an overview and comments on implementation in the UK, see Equal Opportunities Commission (GB), *Formal Response to the Trade Union Reform and Employment Rights Bill 1993,* and Equal Opportunities Commission (NI),*EOC NI Comments on the Trade Union Reform and Employment Rights Bill 1993.*

20 Trades Union Congress, *TUC Guide; Sexual Harassment at Work.* TUC, 1991.

21 *Council Resolution of 29 May on the protection of the dignity of women and men at work,* OJ C157/3, 27 June 1990 and, following-up, *Recommendation on the protection of the dignity of women and men at work* of 27 November 1991, OJ L49/1, 24 February 1992.

22 The UK recommendations are in: Equal Opportunities Commission (GB), *Health and Safety Legislation: Should we Distinguish between Men and Women?,* see J. Jarman, 'Equality or Marginalisation: The Repeal of Protective Legislation', in E. Meehan and S. Sevenhuijsen (eds), *Equality Politics and Gender* Sage, 1991) and in European Commission, *Communication on Protective Legislation for Women in the Member States of the European Community,* COM (87) 105 Final, 20 March 1987.

23 *Rinner-Kuhn* v. *FWW Spezial-Gebaudereinigung GmbH and Co.,* Case No. 171/88, [1989] IRLR 493 (ECJ) dealt with sickness schemes. The judicial review case was *R.* v. *Secretary of State for Employment ex parte EOC,* [1993] 1 All ER 1022.

24 Ms Marshall's further action was in *Marshall* v. *Southampton and South-West Hampshire Area Health Authority (No. 2),* Case C–271/91, [IRLR] 1990 481-CA. Commentaries on the MOD controversies include those by E. Grice, 'Mutiny over the Bounty', the *Daily Telegraph,* 3 June 1994 and in *The Times,* 'A Tribunal Rules' (no by-line), 3 June 1994.

25 C. Cockburn, *In the Way of Women: Men's Resistance to Sex Equality in Organisations* (Macmillan, 1991). Simple quota schemes are not unlawful, see *Kalenke* v. *Freie Hansestadt Bremen,* C-450/93 ECJ 17.10.95.

26 C. Pateman, *The Sexual Contract* (Basil Blackwell/Polity Press, 1988) and C. Pateman, *The Disorder of Women* (Basil Blackwell/Polity Press, 1989).

27 R. Nielsen and E. Szyszczak, (2nd ed), *The Social Policy of the European Community* (Handelshojskolens Forlag, Copenhagen, 1993).

28 Adoption; *Commission* v. *Italy,* Case No. 163/82, [1983] ECR 3273. Allowance; *Hofman* v. *Barmer Ersatzkasse,* Case No. 184/83, [1984] ECR 3042.

29 European Commission, *European Social Policy. Options for the Future.* Consultative Document COM(93) 17 November 1993; and European Commission, *European Social Policy: A Way Forward for the Union.* White Paper. This White Paper was also influenced by another: European Commission, *Growth, Competitiveness and Employment.* White Paper COM(93) 700 final 5 December 1993.

30 V. Hart, 'Constitutional Politics: European Claims and Strategies in Britain', Paper prepared for Conference on Redesigning the State at Australian National University, 1994.
31 B. Siim, 'Welfare State, Gender Politics and Equality Policies: Women's Citizenship in the Scandinavian States' in E. Meehan and S. Sevenhuijsen (eds), *Equality Politics and Gender* (Sage, 1991) and V. Hart, 'The Right to a Fair Wage: American Experience and the European Social Charter' in V. Hart and S. Stimpson (eds), *Writing a National Identity: Political, Economic and Cultural Perspectives on the Written Constitution* (Manchester University Press/Fulbright Commission, 1993).

INDEX